Captive Victors

Captive Victors

Shakespeare's Narrative Poems and Sonnets

HEATHER DUBROW

Cornell University Press

ITHACA AND LONDON

Cornell University Press gratefully acknowledges
a grant from the Andrew W. Mellon Foundation
that aided in bringing this book to publication.

First published 1987 by Cornell University Press.

International Standard Book Number 0-8014-1975-1
Library of Congress Catalog Card Number 86-19627
Printed in the United States of America
*Librarians: Library of Congress cataloging information
appears on the last page of the book.*

*The paper in this book is acid-free and meets the guidelines for
permanence and durability of the Committee on Production Guidelines
for Book Longevity of the Council on Library Resources.*

To S.H.F.

Contents

Acknowledgments

Carleton College generously defrayed secretarial and other expenses connected with this project, and the Bush Foundation provided the grant that enabled me to complete the manuscript. The staff of the Houghton Library was very helpful throughout, as was that of the Carleton Computer Center. To thank Barbara Jenkins for typing the book and assisting with the index would be to misrepresent the extent of her obstetrical abilities: she also battled the software, edited the prose, and consoled the author. Mary Thomas Crane, Randall Findlay, and Jacqueline Walcome skillfully helped with research and translation. I wrote the manuscript while living in Harvard University's Adams House, and I am delighted to have the opportunity to thank the Master and Co-Master, Robert and Jana Kiely, for their hospitality; I am also grateful to the Adams House staff for many types of assistance that made my stay more comfortable. Bernhard Kendler of Cornell University Press has been a singularly efficient and kindly editor. I first became interested in Shakespeare's sonnets as an undergraduate, when I studied them with the late David Kalstone and Neil Rudenstine; it is a pleasure to acknowledge my debt to those teachers—and to the honors tutorial program that enabled me to work closely with such fine critics at a very early stage in my career. Many people generously have read sections of the book and have answered queries about it; in particular, I thank Stephen Booth, Jane Donawerth, Margaret Morganroth Gullette, John Hildebidle, Clark Hulse, John Klause, Frank Morral, Gordon Teskey, and James Wilkinson. My deepest debts, however, are to Barbara Bono and Gwynne Blakemore Evans, who read the entire manuscript; their painstaking editorial work and stimulating suggestions were invaluable.

[9]

Acknowledgments

Sections of this book appeared in earlier form in *English Literary Renaissance* (1986), *Harvard English Studies* (1986), and *Shakespeare Quarterly* (1981); I thank those publications for permission to make use of my essays. Quotations from scholarly editions have been reprinted by permission of the publishers as follows: Basil Blackwell (*The Works of Michael Drayton*, ed. J. William Hebel, 1931–1941); Cambridge University Press (*The Complete Works of Christopher Marlowe*, ed. Fredson Bowers, 1973); The Johns Hopkins University Press (The Variorum Spenser, ed. Edwin Greenlaw et al., 1943–1957); Harvard University Press (*Petrarch's Lyric Poems*, ed. and trans. Robert M. Durling, copyright © 1976 by Robert Durling); Methuen & Co. (William Shakespeare, *The Poems*, ed. F. T. Prince, 1960); Oxford University Press (*The Poems of Sir Philip Sidney*, ed. W. A. Ringler, 1962); Penguin Books (William Shakespeare, *The Complete Works*, ed. Alfred Harbage, 1969); and University of Wisconsin Press (*The Poems of John Collop*, ed. Conrad Hilberry, 1962).

HEATHER DUBROW

Northfield, Minnesota

Abbreviations

A & C	*Antony and Cleopatra*
AWEW	*All's Well That Ends Well*
CE	*College English*
CJ	*Classical Journal*
CP	*Classical Philology*
EETS	Early English Text Society
EIC	*Essays in Criticism*
ELH	*English Literary History*
ELR	*English Literary Renaissance*
ES	*English Studies*
Expl.	*Explicator*
FQ	*The Faerie Queene*
JEGP	*Journal of English and Germanic Philology*
MLN	*Modern Language Notes*
MLQ	*Modern Language Quarterly*
MLR	*Modern Language Review*
MP	*Modern Philology*
NQ	*Notes and Queries*
PMLA	*Publications of the Modern Language Association*
SEL	*Studies in English Literature*
SP	*Studies in Philology*
SQ	*Shakespeare Quarterly*
TA	*Titus Andronicus*
WT	*The Winter's Tale*

Captive Victors

Ev'n in this thought through the dark night he stealeth,
A captive victor that hath lost in gain.
                    The Rape of Lucrece, 729–730

So thy great gift, upon misprision growing,
Comes home again, on better judgement making.
                    Sonnet 87, 11–12

Love is all truth, lust full of forged lies.
                    Venus and Adonis, 804

For much imaginary work was there,—
Conceit deceitful, so compact, so kind.
                    The Rape of Lucrece, 1422–1423

Introduction

Winter and summer till old age began
My circus animals were all on show.
William Butler Yeats

Venus and Adonis and *The Rape of Lucrece* are often misread—and are
even more often left unread. These reactions are surprising when we
consider that such admittedly minor works as *Titus Andronicus* have
recently benefited from careful reappraisals.[1] And the situation is
even more surprising when we recall the enthusiastic reception of
these poems during the English Renaissance itself; *Venus and Adonis*
had gone through sixteen editions by 1640 and *The Rape of Lucrece*
eight.[2] Today, in contrast, the relevant question for many Shake-
speareans is less whether we should study and teach them than
whether we should regret our failure to do so.

The habits of not reading them sensitively and of not reading them
at all both stem from the same preconception: these poems are a mere
"gorgeous gallery of gallant inventions." We are prone, in other
words, to consider them literary samplers: we assume that their author is principally involved in displaying the tropes and other formal
devices that he, like his contemporaries, had so thoroughly learned in
grammar school. This assumption shapes what critics find—and,
more to the point, fail to find—in the poems. Regarding them as

[1]See, e.g., Ronald Broude, "Four Forms of Vengeance in *Titus Andronicus*," *JEGP*, 78
(1979), 494–507; Albert H. Tricomi, "The Aesthetics of Mutilation in 'Titus Andronicus,'" *Shakespeare Survey*, 27 (1974), 11–19; David Willbern, "Rape and Revenge
in *Titus Andronicus*," *ELR*, 8 (1978), 159–182.

[2]On the reputation of the poems, see A. C. Hamilton, *The Early Shakespeare* (San
Marino: Huntington Library, 1967), pp. 143–145, 167–169; Hallett Smith, "The Nondramatic Poems," in *Shakespeare: Aspects of Influence*, Harvard English Studies 7,
ed. G. B. Evans (Cambridge, Mass.: Harvard Univ. Press, 1976).

juvenile experiments, we do not look to them for much sophistication, aesthetic or ethical; scholars typically maintain that Shakespeare regularly sacrifices coherence and even common sense to cram in yet more tropes and schemes. And many assert that the interest in character that informs even early plays such as *Richard III* is subsumed and subverted in these narrative poems: rhetorical figures upstage human ones. As one typical commentary puts it, "no depth or intelligible development can be found in the characters or relationship of Venus and Adonis. . . . Character in *Lucrece* is shallow, fixed, yet inconsistent, as in *Venus and Adonis*, and for the same reason: it is brilliance of the surface which has priority."[3]

One reason scholars approach *Venus and Adonis* and *The Rape of Lucrece* in these ways is chronological: having appeared respectively in 1593 and 1594, the works are early and hence possibly immature.[4] They are also probably contemporaneous with such plays as *Love's Labour's Lost* and *Titus Andronicus*.[5] The former testifies to its author's delight in the rhetorical, the latter to some of the perils of that delight.

But our readings of the narrative poems typically reflect beliefs not only about Shakespeare's own career but also about the very nature of literature. A distrust of elaborate rhetorical devices (manifest above all in reactions against the pun) leads many modern readers to devalue works that delight in wordplay. And even those who respect such works are prone to misunderstand their aims and effects. We sometimes assume an absolute split between the rhetorical and the mimetic, maintaining that a "high" style—or, indeed, any style that could provide exempla for handbooks such as Henry Peacham's *The Garden of Eloquence*—is inimical to a concern for the subtleties of human behavior. In so doing we posit a distinction that would have been very foreign to many Elizabethans, whether they were rhetoricians, writers, or their readers.[6] These conceptions of the artistic act reflect

---

[3]Richard Wilbur, "Introduction," *William Shakespeare: The Narrative Poems and Poems of Doubtful Authenticity*, Pelican Shakespeare, rev. ed. (Harmondsworth, Eng.: Penguin, 1974), pp. 10, 18.

[4]On the dating of Shakespeare's narrative poems, see esp. Hyder Edward Rollins, ed., *A New Variorum Edition of Shakespeare: The Poems* (Philadelphia: J. B. Lippincott, 1938), pp. 384–390, 413–415.

[5]The dating of *Titus Andronicus* remains problematical. For a useful summary of the issues, see J. C. Maxwell, ed., *Titus Andronicus* (London: Methuen, 1953), "Introduction," pp. xxiv–xxxiv.

[6]One of the most influential statements of the relationship between style and various forms of realism is Erich Auerbach, *Mimesis: The Representation of Reality in Western Literature*, trans. Willard R. Trask (Princeton: Princeton Univ. Press, 1953). A. D. Nuttall has recently argued cogently for a return to a mimetic reading of literature, demon-

an equally common and potentially equally misleading interpretation of the critical act: we are prone to distinguish "intrinsic" from "extrinsic" criticism and, in particular, to divide the study of the formal characteristics of literature from the analysis of the social and psychological experiences it explores. If traditional critics approach *Venus and Adonis* and *The Rape of Lucrece* with these presuppositions, several schools of contemporary theorists would also be likely to misunderstand the achievement of these poems. Engaged in studying the riots that they see raging in the prison-house of language and in questioning the referentiality of literature, many now consider the study of character irrelevant. Indeed, character has virtually become a dirty word, quite as taboo in many circles as frank glosses on Shakespeare's sexual wordplay were to an earlier generation of editors.[7]

Yet another reason we have been prone to emphasize the rhetorical extravagances of *Venus and Adonis* and *The Rape of Lucrece* at the expense of the psychological subtleties is that there is a grain of truth embedded in these misreadings. Critics are prone to overvalue the currency in which they trade, and the author of a book that essentially comes to praise *Venus and Adonis* and *The Rape of Lucrece*, not to bury them, needs to acknowledge that these poems have their limitations. However interested in characterization Shakespeare may be, he does not employ in them one of the devices that he elsewhere uses to such effect: varying meter to show nuances of emotion and personality. Nor could the most sympathetic reader of these poems claim that their rhetorical devices are invariably used skillfully. Rented from the zoo of tropes that Puttenham and his colleagues display, Shakespeare's circus animals do trample their way through a few lines. And

---

strating the ways even conventional literary formulas may serve mimesis (*A New Mimesis: Shakespeare and the Representation of Reality* [London: Methuen, 1983]). Though his study does not encompass the nondramatic poetry, his arguments are very germane to those propounded in this book. Also compare Robert Y. Turner's argument that early in his career Shakespeare shifts from a didactic mode, in which speeches are very schematic and lack personal characteristics, to a mimetic one (*Shakespeare's Apprenticeship* [Chicago: Univ. of Chicago Press, 1974]). My study implicitly challenges his distinction between the didactic and the mimetic, demonstrating that certain speeches that would at first seem to fit neatly into the former category in fact subtly manifest the temperaments of their speakers.

[7]For a brief but useful summary of the contemporary debate about character, see Karen Newman, *Shakespeare's Rhetoric of Comic Character: Dramatic Convention in Classical and Renaissance Comedy* (London: Methuen, 1985), pp. 1–2. This study, which traces the ways the soliloquies in Shakespearean comedy reveal the temperaments of their speakers, complements my own work, and I regret that it appeared after I had completed the manuscript.

their noisy presence renders many otherwise successful passages un-
even. Thus when Tarquin approaches Lucrece's room we read:

> So from himself impiety hath wrought,
>   That for his prey to pray he doth begin,
>   As if the heavens should countenance his sin.
>
> But in the midst of his unfruitful prayer,
> Having solicited th' eternal power
> That his foul thoughts might compass his fair fair.
>
> (341–346)[8]

The pun on "prey" and "pray" (342) in fact functions quite effectively, as I will suggest in more detail in the chapter on the poem. The
contrast between the phonic similarity of the words and the semantic
dissimilarity points to the tension within Tarquin himself: he does not
recognize the incongruity to which this wordplay alerts us. But the
epizeuxis "fair fair" (346) is obvious and unoriginal, and the antithesis
between "foul" and "fair" in that same line is merely trite.

Nonetheless, the trenchant wordplay in this passage is in fact far
more revealing—and far more characteristic of the poem in which it
appears—than are the mistakes. Whether or not Shakespeare unlocks
his own heart in the sonnets, he unlocks, anatomizes, and variously
condemns and admires the hearts of the protagonists in *Venus and
Adonis* and *The Rape of Lucrece*. This study maintains that we find in
those narratives a subtle exploration of human emotion, a coherent
analysis of human character. And these achievements are in fact produced, not precluded, by the formal strategies of the poems, especially by their interpretation of genre and mode and by their use of
tropes. Embedded in the apparently conventional topoi of Lucrece's
complaints, for example, are the patterns of her distinctive temperament, as well as responses typical of rape victims. Rosalie L. Colie has
shown us how literary "forms" assist characterization in Shakespeare's
plays;[9] the same is no less true of his narrative poems. Hence one of
the most central questions explored in this book is, how do styles of
literature reflect styles of personality?

In discussing such problems, this study alludes at several points to

---

[8]All citations from *Venus and Adonis* and *The Rape of Lucrece* are to *The Poems*,
ed. F. T. Prince (London: Methuen, 1960). I have, however, added or omitted quotation marks for the sake of clarity in a number of instances.

[9]See *Shakespeare's Living Art* (Princeton: Princeton Univ. Press, 1974), esp. chap. 1.

certain issues that have recently become very popular, such as the workings of power, especially in the realm of sexual relationships, and the nature of language. The argument that these issues are present in texts normally seen as intellectually and ethically shallow may perhaps suggest that I am attempting to overvalue these poems by reading in modern preoccupations. Admittedly, to paraphrase Lillian Hellman, it is all too tempting to cut Shakespeare's conscience to fit contemporary fashions, Parisian or otherwise. One fears, indeed, that it is only a matter of time until someone interprets *Oedipus Rex* as a polemic in favor of unsealing adoption records. Nonetheless, one of the many reasons the three works we are examining deserve more attention is that they are indeed deeply involved with the uses and abuses of power and of language as well as with a number of other contemporary questions. The fact that the issues in question surface in so many places—in *Venus and Adonis* alone, for example, power is variously relevant to the physical and linguistic behavior of the heroine, the description of the horses, and the subject matter of many figures of speech—may reassure us that they are not only present in but also central to the texts.

A study predicated on the assertion that Shakespeare adopts the most conventional generic and rhetorical motifs to elucidate the most idiosyncratic psychological patterns also immediately invites another question. How can one prove that, say, the length of Lucrece's lamentations is a significant measure of her character when such complaints were customarily long? Some replies can emerge only from my readings of particular passages, but others lend themselves to generalization. The types of sophistication and coherence that I attribute to these poems (*The Rape of Lucrece*, for instance, is structured around the implications of a single figure, syneciosis) make it less surprising that they also include sophisticated and coherent characters. And analyses based on those characters' use of literary and other linguistic conventions are supported by more traditional evidence as well; thus Venus' predilection for conditionals reflects the other ways in which she attempts to reshape and manipulate experience. Moreover, Shakespeare's plays, including the comparatively early ones, offer analogues; even Egeus is characterized in part through linguistic patterns.[10]

The final section of this book explores the sonnets, focusing on the

---

[10]On Egeus, see David P. Young, *Something of Great Constancy: The Art of "A Midsummer Night's Dream"* (New Haven: Yale Univ. Press, 1966), p. 65.

same questions about character and the formal patterns that reveal it which inform my discussions of the narrative poems. Scholarship is itself freighted with conventions, and one of them is the necessity of justifying the existence of yet another analysis of Shakespeare's sonnets. In fact, however, the perspectives that shape this study preclude the suggestion that it is merely "dressing old words new" (Sonnet 76.11)[11] in examining those poems. Many students of the sonnets still focus on biographical questions at the expense of the rhetorical issues that this volume addresses. Thus, for example, Renaissance scholars have devoted far more attention to the putative identity of the Dark Lady than to the intriguing literary convention behind her darkness, the "ugly beauty" conceit. An additional rationale also lies behind my examination of the sonnets. Contexts ranging from the psychoanalytical to the Neo-Platonic are frequently adduced for these poems, and they have been less frequently, though no less usefully, examined in relation to their author's plays. Yet one context remains virtually ignored: we have seldom read these lyrics in connection with *Venus and Adonis* and *The Rape of Lucrece*.

Doing so illuminates some of the most familiar questions posed by Shakespeare's sequence—and invites us to raise others as well. Maintaining that the sonnets are less dramatic in some regards than we usually claim, this study asks how their mode compares to that of the narrative poems. And how does Shakespeare's approach to the sonnet genre relate to his ways of shaping the epyllion in *Venus and Adonis* and the complaint in *The Rape of Lucrece*? Moreover, all three poems form a type of triptych, raising as they do strikingly similar questions about human behavior and human experience. In particular, this book compares the angles from which each work investigates the issues implied by my title: is the skilled rhetorician a victor over language and his listeners, a captive of his own words, or both? who triumphs in the war games of love, and how, and at what price? and so on.

The formal questions raised by juxtaposing the three poems finally prove inseparable from the psychological ones: twinned and twined, the dancer cannot be told from the dance. Thus closure, for example, emerges as at once an aesthetic problem and a psychological one, and patterns of repetition come to reflect patterns of character. For Shakespeare never forgets, and never allows us to forget, the multiple and indissoluble links between the art of rhetoric and the art of living.

---

[11]Throughout this book I quote the sonnets from *Shakespeare's Sonnets*, ed. Stephen Booth (New Haven: Yale Univ. Press, 1977).

[1]

"Upon misprision growing":
Venus and Adonis

Reality is a cliché from which we
attempt to escape by metaphor.
                    Wallace Stevens

I

Sometime her arms infold him like a band:
She would, he will not in her arms be bound.
   And when from thence he struggles to be gone,
   She locks her lily fingers one in one.

"Fondling," she saith, "Since I have hemm'd thee here
Within the circuit of this ivory pale,
I'll be a park, and thou shalt be my deer:
Feed where thou wilt, on mountain or in dale;
   Graze on my lips, and if those hills be dry,
   Stray lower, where the pleasant fountains lie.

"Within this limit is relief enough,
Sweet bottom grass and high delightful plain,
Round rising hillocks, brakes obscure and rough,
To shelter thee from tempest and from rain:
   Then be my deer, since I am such a park,
   No dog shall rouse thee, though a thousand bark."
                    (Venus and Adonis, 225–240)

Leander's lengthy appeals to Hero show us little more about his
temperament than what the narrator has already announced: he can

[21]

act like a "bold sharp sophister" (I.197).[1] And the nymphs' complaints in the Ovidian mythological poems composed by Marlowe's contemporaries reveal virtually nothing about the individual sensibilities of those importunate and unfortunate maidens; we would hardly notice the difference if we interchanged a speech by, say, Salmacis in Beaumont's *Salmacis and Hermaphroditus* with one by Oenone in Heywood's *Oenone and Paris*. In contrast, the passage I have just quoted could have come from none of the English epyllia save *Venus and Adonis* and could have been spoken by no character within that tradition save Venus herself.

One sense in which this speech is characteristic is that the goddess of love is manipulating language to her own ends. Attempting to entrap Adonis verbally no less than physically, she is recasting the Petrarchan image of the hunt into a more enticing form.[2] She claims that she is not in fact a hunter at all, not a predator whom the deer should evade but rather a park it should enjoy. Hunters kill, parks nourish; hunters are by definition aggressive, while parks are as unmistakably passive. Elsewhere in the poem Venus twice uses the revealing phrase "call it" ("And trembling in her passion, calls it balm" [27], "And calls it heavenly moisture" [64]); here she is once again renaming things, even trying to change her own identity in order to change how Adonis responds to her. But if she is twisting Petrarchism in the hope of seducing Adonis, she is also typically becoming carried away by her own language; "I'll be a park" (231) shifts to "since I am such a park" (239). Like so many other passages in this poem—and in the rest of its author's canon—these lines raise the possibility that deceitful rhetoricians are their own principal victims, hoist with their own linguistic petards.

Equally characteristic of the speaker is her confounding of the maternal and the sexual.[3] The eroticism of the passage is obvious enough to bring a blush to a Petrarchan maiden's cheek. Yet the lines also suggest a nutritive role. The tension between these two responses to Adonis crystallizes in the word "Feed" (232), which is charged

[1]I quote Marlowe from *The Complete Works of Christopher Marlowe*, ed. Fredson Bowers, 2 vols. (Cambridge, Eng.: Cambridge Univ. Press, 1973).

[2]On hunting in the poem, cf. Robert J. Griffin's analysis of the juxtaposition of the military and pastoral worlds ("'These Contraries Such Unity Do Hold': Patterned Imagery in Shakespeare's Narrative Poems," *SEL*, 4 [1964], 43–55).

[3]On the maternal elements in the passage, cf. Wayne A. Rebhorn, "Mother Venus: Temptation in Shakespeare's *Venus and Adonis*," *Shakespeare Studies*, 11 (1978), esp. 2–4.

with connotations of both a lover's sex play and a mother's care.

Another way in which this passage is typical of Venus is that it bodies forth her delight in asserting power, an urge at once fuelled and frustrated by Adonis. The peculiar status of the imperative in English—it can express a humble plea, an imperious command, or any shade of authority along the spectrum bounded by those two modes of address—aptly reflects the peculiar status of Venus' relationship to Adonis. In some sense she is in command—and hence in a position to give commands. Yet "Feed where thou wilt" (232) emphasizes Adonis' freedom and mastery, and we surely detect a note of wheedling, even pleading, in "Then be my deer" (239). These lines testify, then, not only to the link between sex play and power plays in Venus' sensibility but also to the difficulty of determining who really has the most power in the liaisons dangereuses of sexual politics. The captive may in fact be the victor, and vice versa. Here, as in the sonnets, Shakespeare is more interested in the ambiguous and shifting thresholds between power and impotence than in the distinctions between those two states.

But this sober analysis of Venus' manipulations neglects the appealing aspects of the spells she is attempting to cast. On one level, after all, the passage is a charming rendition of the playful sexual fantasies in which lovers indulge. If Adonis finds Venus' allusions to "the pleasant fountains" (234) and "Round rising hillocks" (237) alarming, more sophisticated listeners are likely instead to find them delightful; her energy is attractive, as is her unabashed sensuality. One need only compare these lines with the coy, even adolescent, allusions to sex in other epyllia—take, for example, Marston's "Could he abstaine mid'st such a wanton sporting/From doing that, which is not fit reporting?" (209–210)[4]—to understand why one may respond positively to the openness of Venus' eroticism.

Hence the lines in question serve not only to characterize Venus but also to evoke in the reader a whole range of complex responses to her: our reactions shift back and forth between admiration and distrust, but we never totally lose our sense of involvement with the goddess of love. We may, for example, admire the frank sexuality when we read about those hillocks and respect her solicitude when we encounter the allusion to "shelter" (238). And when we read the proleptic final line, "No dog shall rouse thee, though a thousand bark" (240), it reminds

[4]Marston is quoted from *The Poems of John Marston*, ed. Arnold Davenport (Liverpool: Liverpool Univ. Press, 1961).

[23]

us that neither her physical charms nor her verbal ones will protect Adonis from death and hence stirs pity for both of them. At the same time, however, we recall that the passage is concerned with the imprisonment of an unwilling victim, a response that subverts both our respect and our pity for his jailer.

Though the stanzas we have been studying are among the most skillful in the poem, they are not atypical of it: throughout *Venus and Adonis*, Shakespeare subtly evokes the nuances of his heroine's temperament. Yet the complexities of characterization exemplified by this passage and demonstrated throughout the poem have been virtually neglected by critics; when they have commented on Venus at all, they have concentrated on elucidating allegorical resonances.[5] One explanation for this neglect is the distrust of elaborate rhetoric to which I alluded in the Introduction. Perhaps, too, the negative judgments on *Venus and Adonis* delivered by those two deans of Renaissance studies, Douglas Bush and C. S. Lewis, have discouraged many readers from devoting much attention to the subtleties of a poem that the author of *Mythology and the Renaissance Tradition in English Poetry* dismisses as "not . . . a living thing."[6]

If, however, we examine *Venus and Adonis* with more care and fewer presuppositions, we discover in the evocation of its heroine (and, to a lesser extent, in that of Adonis as well) the type of psychological acuteness we normally associate with Shakespeare. This chapter will focus on his portrait of Venus, first filling in the contours sketched on the basis of the deer park passage and then examining the formal strategies through which Shakespeare bodies forth the goddess of love. The most significant (and most surprising) ones are generic. When we play his Ovidian mythological narrative against those composed by his contemporaries, we recognize to what extent his approach to the epyllion is distinctive—and to what extent that distinctiveness is related to his concern for characterization. Working in a challengingly amorphous literary form, Shakespeare shapes the Ovidian mythological poem into a genre that is in many ways conducive to the creation of complex characters and to the evocation of complex responses to them.

[5]See, e.g., Heather Asals, "*Venus and Adonis*: The Education of a Goddess," *SEL*, 13 (1973), 31–51; David N. Beauregard, "*Venus and Adonis*: Shakespeare's Representation of the Passions," *Shakespeare Studies*, 8 (1975), 83–98.

[6]Bush, *Mythology and the Renaissance Tradition in English Poetry* (1932; rpt. New York: Pageant Books, 1957), p. 139. Also see C. S. Lewis, "Hero and Leander," in *Proceedings of the British Academy, 1952* (London: Oxford Univ. Press, n.d.), esp. pp. 24–26.

II

Readers have long acknowledged certain similarities between Venus and some of Shakespeare's dramatic characters: she shares, we are told, the earthiness of Falstaff, the sensuality of Cleopatra, and the determination of comedic heroines like Rosalind.[7] Yet we have been slow to admit that the sophisticated techniques through which she is characterized represent yet another link between Venus and her counterparts in the plays. And we have been equally slow to admit the many regards in which her behavior mimes that of actual people.

I do not mean that Shakespeare's portrait of Venus is mimetic in every sense of that term. Few women could literally tuck a young man, however slim and "hairless" (487) he might be, under their arms, fewer yet react to the death of their beloved by flying into the air. And the characterization of Venus does lack one type of complexity that we encounter even in Shakespeare's earliest plays, as well as in *The Rape of Lucrece*: the poem does not explore the relationship between a temperament and a social milieu. Moreover, we never wholly forget her symbolic significance: she is not only a lover acting in very human ways but also the abstract force of Love itself. Indeed, for all of Venus' follies the figure of Venus Genetrix evidently lies behind her. Yet facts like these need not, of course, preclude a portrait that is mimetic in broader senses of the word—a portrait that mirrors the ways actual people think, feel, and talk—any more than the allegorical significance with which Cordelia or Britomart are weighted precludes their being representational as well.[8]

Venus plucks Adonis from his horse at the beginning of the poem just as, symmetrically, she plucks the flower that represents him at the end (in the world of *Venus and Adonis*, as in the *Metamorphoses*, one may be literally as well as symbolically carried away by love). It is evident, then, that Venus connects loving Adonis with controlling him, mastering him; indeed, so deep is the connection as to make us suspect

[7]For such parallels see, e.g., Adrien Bonjour, "From Shakespeare's Venus to Cleopatra's Cupids," *Shakespeare Survey*, 15 (1962), 73–80; Robert Grudin, *Mighty Opposites: Shakespeare and Renaissance Contrariety* (Berkeley: Univ. of California Press, 1979), pp. 171, 207; Prince, "Introduction," p. xxxii.

[8]For an opposing view, see Clark Hulse, *Metamorphic Verse: The Elizabethan Minor Epic* (Princeton: Princeton Univ. Press, 1981), p. 155. Also compare Lennet J. Daigle, "Venus and Adonis: Some Traditional Contexts," *Shakespeare Studies*, 13 (1980), 31–46, on the combination of realistic and allegorical elements in her character. James J. Yoch ("The Eye of Venus: Shakespeare's Erotic Landscape," *SEL*, 20 [1980], 59–71) discusses characterization in terms of Venus' approach to the landscape.

that even had he been less reluctant her impulse would have been to assert sovereignty by grasping and entrapping him. Yet her concern for mastery is more pervasive than it might at first appear: that concern shapes how she perceives many situations and how she reacts within them.

The goddess of love, like that other impresario Prospero, is prone to describe events, especially those involving love, in terms of mastery. She narrates her relationship with Mars in those terms:

> Yet hath he been my captive and my slave,
> (101)

> Thus he that overrul'd I oversway'd,
> Leading him prisoner in a red rose chain:
> Strong-temper'd steel his stronger strength obey'd,
> Yet was he servile to my coy disdain.
>   Oh be not proud, nor brag not of thy might,
>   For mast'ring her that foil'd the god of fight!
> (109–114)

That extraordinary line "Leading him prisoner in a red rose chain" (110) draws attention to the moral ambiguities we so often find in her behavior: on the one hand, a chain of roses charms us more than it troubles us, and yet even in this image Venus is stressing her own power and control (notice, for instance, that she chooses the verb "Leading" rather than "making"). Similarly, Adonis is called "love's master" (585). When she sings of the effects of love, she describes "How love makes young men thrall, and old men dote" (837). (It is suggestive, too, that the subject of this ditty is the power of women over men even though the most recent events in Venus' own past have illustrated how love makes *women* thrall and makes them dote.)[9] Even when she is soliciting agreement from Adonis, the verb she chooses suggests domination: "But if thou needs wilt hunt, be rul'd by me" (673). And it is telling that this same phrase, "be ruled by me," is used by other Shakespearean characters enamored by power, notably the Bastard in *King John* (II.i.377).[10] In other words, in a few instances

---

[9]William Keach notes in a different context that Shakespeare realizes that the wooer is really more dependent than the person being wooed (*Elizabethan Erotic Narratives: Irony and Pathos in the Ovidian Poetry of Shakespeare, Marlowe, and Their Contemporaries* [New Brunswick: Rutgers Univ. Press, 1977], p. 59).

[10]All citations from Shakespeare's plays are to William Shakespeare, *The Complete Works*, ed. Alfred Harbage (Baltimore: Penguin, 1969).

Venus' preoccupation with power is manifest in her desire to submit to that of Adonis; but more often she is concerned to assert her own power.

The troubling undertones in the passages we have been examining lead us to reflect on how Venus' character has been shaped, and misshaped, by her tendency to see love not as "mutual render" (Sonnet 125.12) but rather as an aggressive struggle for domination. And since her vocabulary of mastery and captivity is drawn from the stock language of love poetry, our reflections on her aggressiveness generate literary questions as well. On one level, it is merely amusing to encounter a putative goddess who sounds like an Elizabethan sonneteer, much as we enjoy Leander's predilection for the tones of a university orator. But on another level the frequent echoes of Elizabethan poesy are disturbing: we again think about the underlying assumptions of that literary system (or, more precisely, systems) and in so doing wonder in particular whether it breeds in its speakers, fictional or otherwise, the tendency to conjoin and confound the sexual and the aggressive that we find in Venus. That tendency provides, as we shall see, a more intimate link between *Venus and Adonis* and *The Rape of Lucrece* than we generally acknowledge.[11] In both a central character connects passion and power; in both the conventions of love poetry express—and, more disturbingly, perhaps encourage—that connection.

Many of Venus' habits, whether they are linguistic gestures or psychological patterns, are a way of achieving and asserting domination. Writing in a genre that traces metamorphoses of all kinds, Shakespeare characteristically focuses on the transformations his heroine performs through her words: much as she appropriates Adonis, so she appropriates language itself. And much as her assertions of power over Adonis often generate subtle reminders of his power over her, so her attempts to impress language into her service often lead us to recognize that she is herself imprisoned by it, once again a captive victor.

It is suggestive, to begin with, that she talks as much as she does: of the 1,194 lines in the poem, 537 are spoken by the goddess of love. The only analogues to this garrulity that we can find in other epyllia are passages anchored in the complaint tradition, such as the laments

---

[11]Though his psychoanalytic reading of the poem is on the whole unconvincing, Alan B. Rothenberg offers the interesting observation that *Venus and Adonis*, *The Rape of Lucrece*, and *The Taming of the Shrew* all involve types of rape ("The 'Speaking Beast'; A Theory of Shakespearean Creativity," *Psychocultural Review*, 3 [1979], 239).

intoned by Lodge's Glaucus and Heywood's Oenone. But Venus is not delivering a complaint: she is cajoling, insisting, insinuating. Her talkativeness, like that of the Wife of Bath, reflects her desire to impose her presence, to dominate the conversation just as she dominates in so many other ways.

Assuming Adam's function, this postlapsarian Eve repeatedly names—or, more to the point, renames—the objects around her:[12]

> With this she seizeth on his sweating palm,
> The precedent of pith and livelihood,
> And trembling in her passion, *calls it* balm,
> Earth's sovereign salve to do a goddess good:
> (25–28; italics added)

> Panting he lies and breatheth in her face.
> She feedeth on the steam as on a prey,
> And *calls it* heavenly moisture, air of grace.
> (62–64; italics added)

To name something is to assert one's power over it—as Hal recognizes when he festoons Falstaff with epithets and as Petruchio acknowledges when, in one of his most subtle but most effective gestures of domination, he insists that his future wife be called not Katherine but Kate. Another function of Venus's naming, however, is to attempt to change the nature of sweat and breath. The earthiest of heroines, she is transforming both into something more ethereal, a habit in her to which I will return shortly. The ambiguity of "calls it" emphasizes the same issue we encountered in the deer park stanzas: does she believe in the transformation she is effecting, or is it merely another way of flattering Adonis? The fact that we cannot know for certain reflects, I would suggest, a telling confusion in Venus herself: she, no less than Richard II, is prone to become carried away by her own words.

In the second passage I quoted, the dramatist who wrote *Venus and Adonis* plays two voices against each other in one of the ways nondramatic poetry permits: he establishes a dialogic tension between the speaker's "as on a prey" (63) and the goddess' "And calls it heavenly moisture" (64). That speaker's honest appraisal of the situation contrasts with her self-serving one. It is suggestive, too, that the more

---

[12]On naming in the plays, see, e.g., Joseph A. Porter, *The Drama of Speech Acts: Shakespeare's Lancastrian Tetralogy* (Berkeley: Univ. of California Press, 1979), esp. pp. 12–19.

honest and more objective of the observers relies on a simile, "*as* on a prey": rather than transforming the steam into something else, he is respecting and retaining its individuality, its identity. In a sense, then, Venus substitutes a metonymic approach for the speaker's metaphoric one: unlike him, she attempts to change the identity of the breath as totally as Petruchio tries to change his Kate.

Venus' predilection for renaming the world typically assumes one form in particular: she tries to transform the material into the spiritual. The poem in which she appears insistently bodies forth the details of the natural world: people sweat and lust, aggressive eagles demonstrate that nature is indeed red in tooth and claw, and divedappers and rabbits remind us that it includes gentleness and frailty as well. Against this complex vision of the physical world is played Venus' distortion of it.[13] We have already observed the ways she uses language in an attempt to effect transformations, turning steamy breath into "heavenly moisture" (64). And she attempts to reshape her own image along similar lines. This earthy goddess unpersuasively insists on the spirituality of love and on her own virtual lack of corporeality:

> Love is a spirit all compact of fire,
> Not gross to sink, but light, and will aspire.
>
> Witness this primrose bank whereon I lie:
> These forceless flowers like sturdy trees support me.
> Two strengthless doves will draw me through the sky
> From morn till night, even where I list to sport me.
>
> (149–154)

Attuned to this habit in her, we find its analogue in her repeated descriptions of the earth as Adonis' lover:

> And therefore would he put his bonnet on,
> Under whose brim the gaudy sun would peep:
> The wind would blow it off, and being gone,
> Play with his locks; then would Adonis weep.
>
> (1087–1090)

---

[13]Lucy Gent also observes this habit in Venus but interprets it differently, concentrating particularly on the use of hyperbole ("'Venus and Adonis': The Triumph of Rhetoric," *MLR*, 69 [1974], 721–729).

And she interprets the boar's attack as a kiss: "If he did see his face, why then I know / He thought to kiss him, and hath kill'd him so" (1109–1110). While in these instances she is not spiritualizing the natural world, she is performing a comparable travesty by idealizing it and by attributing her own emotions to it.

Such travesties serve as a commentary not only on Venus' artifices but also on Shakespeare's art. For many of her conceits exemplify one of his most familiar tools of trade, the pathetic fallacy. By placing it in Venus' mouth rather than that of a narrator, the poet leads us to evaluate that rhetorical technique more critically than we would otherwise do (in fact, in the lines from the poem in Theocritus' *Sixe Idillia* that may have influenced Shakespeare, the speaker, not Venus, attributes an amatory motive to the boar).[14] We recognize, in other words, that the pathetic fallacy may reflect the pathetic self-centeredness of its proponent. Shakespeare is dramatizing a rhetorical pattern by associating it with a psychological one, a habit we shall observe repeatedly in his major poems. And in so doing he is also problematizing a literary convention that is uncritically adduced in many other epyllia—an approach to genre that we will also meet many times in *The Rape of Lucrece* and the sonnets.

Another way in which Venus uses language to create a fictitious and factitious world is by telling stories—her habit of naming and renaming writ large. Like the improvisator figure whom Stephen Greenblatt has anatomized for us,[15] she turns the facts about her relationship with Mars into a scenario more attractive to herself—and more amenable to her aim, persuading Adonis to succeed the god of war in her bed. Thus she defines the relationship in terms of mastery—but then, as if realizing that this may not be the best strategy for wooing Adonis, she ends on a suggestion that the roles have been reversed, that he has mastered her: "Oh be not proud, nor brag not of thy might, / For mast'ring her that foil'd the god of fight!" (113–114). Most revealing, however, is her omission of the humiliating conclusion of her liaison with Mars: they were both mastered, both caught in a net.[16] And by alluding to that type of trap in a different context only forty lines earlier ("Look how a bird lies tangled in a net" [67]), Shakespeare subtly reminds us of the very fact Venus is attempting to conceal: the

---

[14]Theocritus, *Sixe Idillia* (London, 1588), "The XXXI Idillion," 27–31.

[15]Stephen Jay Greenblatt, *Renaissance Self-fashioning from More to Shakespeare* (Chicago: Univ. of Chicago Press, 1980), pp. 227–228.

[16]Compare Robert P. Miller, "The Myth of 'Mars Hot Minion' in 'Venus and Adonis,'" *ELH*, 26 (1959), 470–481.

net result, as it were, of her involvement with Mars. Later, too, the goddess of love is characterized as a storyteller: her song is compared to the "copious stories" (845) of all lovers, she whispers "a heavy tale" (1125) to the dead Adonis, and, of course, she recounts the story of Wat.

But if Venus is a narrative poet, she is also a lyric one: her delivery of an elegy on Adonis is the appropriate culmination of her recurrent tendency to adopt the conventions of Elizabethan art, especially the traditions of love poetry. As many readers have observed, she repeatedly deploys hyperbole, the figure that Puttenham terms the "loud lyar":[17] "More white and red than doves or roses are" (10), "A thousand kisses buys my heart from me" (517), and so on.[18] And her courtship of that "lifeless picture, cold and senseless stone" (211) evidently parallels the situation of the Petrarchan lover—with the important difference, of course, that the sex roles are reversed. We may suspect that the exaggerations of her language not only reflect but also encourage the unhealthy emotiveness of her own character—yet another reminder that rhetoric can be as dangerous for its speaker as its victim. Moreover, we never forget how self-serving her poesy is: Adonis' accusation that her speeches are "full of *forged* lies" (804; italics added) underscores the link between the artistic and fraudulent connotations of that adjective.

Venus' aim, like that of other love poets, is less *educere* or *delectare* than *permovere*, and much of her language is directed toward persuading Adonis by flattering him. Because her initial words in the poem are devoted to such flattery, just as the *The Rape of Lucrece* opens on Collatine's tributes to his wife, the reader's attention is immediately focused on the problems of praise:

> "Thrice fairer than myself," thus she began,
> "The field's chief flower, sweet above compare;
> Stain to all nymphs, more lovely than a man,
> More white and red than doves or roses are."
>
> (7–10)

---

[17]George Puttenham, *The Arte of English Poesie*, ed. Gladys Doidge Willcock and Alice Walker (1936; rpt. Cambridge: Cambridge Univ. Press, 1970), p. 191.

[18]Though Venus' rhetoric has been neglected by most readers, a few have commented sensitively on it from perspectives different from my own. See Gent; Richard A. Lanham, *The Motives of Eloquence: Literary Rhetoric in the Renaissance* (New Haven: Yale Univ. Press, 1976), pp. 82–94. The latter analysis, though useful, is limited by its exclusive emphasis on the negative aspects of her rhetoric.

The first of Venus' many attempts to seduce Adonis, this passage reminds us how much of her behavior is in fact self-centered and self-serving. That self-centeredness is especially evident in her line, "Thrice fairer than myself" (7): she is really lauding her own beauty even while seemingly concentrating on his, presenting herself as the measure of all loveliness. In another sense, too, the passage, like Venus' other compliments, reverses the hierarchies that it ostensibly establishes and in so doing fulfills a function opposite from the one it apparently assumes. If on the most overt level her paeans are a tribute to the power of Adonis—he is beautiful enough to evoke such glowing tributes—on another level they are, as we have observed, an attempt to assert power over him. In short, Venus is preoccupied with mastery even when delivering lines that are seemingly self-effacing.

Nor is it an accident that, though the passage labels Adonis "sweet above compare" (8), it in fact incorporates no fewer than three explicit comparatives: "Thrice fairer than myself" (7), "more lovely than a man" (9), and "More white and red than doves or roses are" (10). Furthermore, behind the epithet "The field's chief flower" (8) lie comparisons with other flowers that have been found wanting in contrast to Adonis, just as "Stain to all nymphs" (9) establishes his superiority over those maidens. Venus' preoccupation with mastery, we come to realize, encourages her to cast relationships in terms of competition. We find allusions to competition, too, in some of the conventional imagery of the poem, such as, "To note the fighting conflict of her hue, / How white and red each other did destroy!" (345–346). And of course two actions in the physical world—the hunt for the boar, and Wat's attempts to escape—involve the competition between hunter and hunted. Venus' predilections, then, are mirrored in the world she inhabits. And they also find echoes in the competitive behavior of the characters in Shakespeare's other major poems.

We observed earlier that some of her tributes to Adonis unpersuasively claim to be self-effacing. Other compliments she delivers, however, are not even nominally self-effacing: she blatantly flatters herself as well as Adonis. In Fletcher's *Venus and Anchises*, for example, the goddess of love is praised by the narrator, whereas in Shakespeare's poem Venus describes her own beauty: "My eyes are grey and bright and quick in turning" (140), and so on. Though such tributes may well be objectively true, they make us uneasy. The oddity of complimenting oneself alerts us to the general problems involved in compliments, and we have more reason to distrust Venus' rhetoric than that of Fletcher's speaker. Hence the passage from *Venus and Adonis*, unlike the blazons in *Venus and Anchises* and other epyllia, again draws our attention to the moral dangers of flattery.

Given how characteristic a mode flattery is for Venus, we should not be surprised that she not only opens on it but also returns to it in a moment of crisis: fearing for Adonis' well-being, she attempts to insure his future by flattering death:

> And that his beauty may the better thrive,
> With death she humbly doth insinuate;
>   Tells him of trophies, statues, tombs, and stories
>   His victories, his triumphs and his glories.
>
> (1011–1014)

The jingly feminine rhyme in the final two lines reflects the mechanical quality of her compliments.

If Venus' compliments to Adonis function centripetally, directing our attention to the nuances of her own psyche, so too do they move centrifugally, highlighting the broader social ramifications of her epideictic mode. A number of scholars have recently demonstrated that Elizabethans were keenly aware of the parallel between courtiership and courtship.[19] Shakespeare activates that awareness by comparing his heroine to a "bold-fac'd suitor" as early as line 6 of the poem, and a subsequent allusion to a "suit" (336) reinforces the parallel. One effect of these references is to underscore Venus' ambiguous and tenuous grasp on power. In the first quotation, "suitor" (6) evidently suggests the efforts of the powerless to ingratiate themselves with the powerful, while "bold-fac'd" is the earliest of many indications in the poem that the goddess of love cannot or will not acknowledge that in certain regards she is indeed powerless. But the lines also serve to comment on the nature of romantic love and its analogue of courtly service: coming to see Venus' flattery as courtly in several senses of the term, we are reminded that the compliments delivered by courtiers are as self-serving as those delivered by lovers. In both instances flattery functions as an implicit bargain—"I will give you praise in return for your favors"—a function very different from the nobler one of inspiring virtue assigned to it by classical rhetoricians.[20]

We encounter lines that introduce these issues, notably Venus' initial tributes to Adonis, very shortly after we read the author's own

---

[19]See esp. Arthur Marotti, "'Love Is Not Love': Elizabethan Sonnet Sequences and the Social Order," *ELH*, 49 (1982), 396–428; Leonard Tennenhouse, "Sir Walter Ralegh and the Literature of Clientage," in *Patronage in the Renaissance*, ed. Guy Fitch Lytle and Stephen Orgel (Princeton: Princeton Univ. Press, 1981).

[20]On attitudes to epideictic oratory, see O. B. Hardison, Jr., *The Enduring Monument: A Study of the Idea of Praise in Renaissance Literary Theory and Practice* (Chapel Hill: Univ. of North Carolina Press, 1962), chap. 2.

[33]

sally into courtiership, his dedication to Southampton. Perhaps the necessity of praising a patron encouraged the young Shakespeare to think further about the issues raised by flattery. But if biographical experiences lie behind his interest in those issues, so too do literary ones; he repeatedly, perhaps even obsessively, explores flattery in his plays. In particular, in the personages of that triad Bushy, Bagot, and Green we find the clearest embodiment of a dramatic convention and political problem that runs throughout the other history plays as well: kings are susceptible to the compliments of bad advisers, prone to be infected by "the monarch's plague, this flattery" (Sonnet 114.2).

We are now in a position to address a question that has long troubled readers of the poem: why did its author make Venus the aggressor? Though that decision may have been influenced by pictorial or literary treatments of the story (scholars have enumerated parallels ranging from Titian's *Venus and Adonis* to Abraham Fraunce's *Amintas Dale* to putative hints of a reluctant Adonis in Ovid himself),[21] the mere presence of such models cannot, as some have asserted, explain Shakespeare's reinterpretation of the goddess of love. After all, also accessible to him were a far greater number of versions in which the two lovers retain traditional sex roles.

Certain answers lie instead in the same impulse that, as we will see, led other epyllion writers to create aggressive women: the aim of commenting on the chaste heroines of Elizabethan love poetry. And politics in the narrower sense of the word lies behind the sexual politics of the poem: Venus' assertions of power may well reflect resentment of Elizabeth herself.[22] The sexually forward women in sixteenth-century epyllia reverse the customary roles of man and woman, much as a female monarch reverses those same roles. Hence in this epyllion, as in many others, ambivalence about an unsuccessfully manipulative heroine encodes ambivalence about a brilliantly manipulative queen.

Yet in this instance—as in many other recent scholarly discussions of the interplay between social history and literature—the vocabulary of encoding is potentially misleading: it can imply that all meanings

[21]On these precedents, see Bush, *Mythology and the Renaissance Tradition*, p. 143; Keach, pp. 53–56.

[22]The ways Elizabeth I affected literature have, of course, been exhaustively studied, both by traditional literary critics and by proponents of the "new historicism." On the tensions generated by the presence of a powerful female monarch, see esp. Louis Adrian Montrose, "'Shaping Fantasies': Figurations of Gender and Power in Elizabethan Culture," *Representations*, 1 (1983), 61–94.

save the covert political one are mere decoys. The political resonances that I am attributing to *Venus and Adonis* and other epyllia are no doubt present, but they do not subsume the more obvious significances of the poem. In this case, while Shakespeare's preoccupation with powerful women may initially have been sparked by the Britomart on England's throne, it is also likely that he had a deep and sustained interest in such temperaments for other reasons as well. In Venus we encounter a preliminary study of a character type that, as his later works testify, intrigued him: the heroine who, refusing to be daunted by literal or metaphoric shipwrecks, energetically attempts to take control of her destiny. But the obvious contrasts between the realization of that figure in Rosalind or Portia and in Venus herself indicate yet another facet of Shakespeare's interest in this plot. Accustomed to power, evaluating experience in terms of it, Venus is confronted by her own powerlessness, engendered first by the unwilling Adonis and then by the willful boar. She reacts by desperately adducing the strategies that have helped her to assert and maintain her power before, such as renaming the objects around her and flattering his opponents. Shakespeare's concern with the powerlessness of the erstwhile powerful, a preoccupation embodied in the phrase, "She's love, she loves, and yet she is not lov'd" (610), recurs in the other nondramatic poems as well and, of course, in many of the plays, testifying to his attraction to this situation.

Venus' most characteristic speech mannerism is one that critics have neglected, her reliance on conditionals:

> If thou wilt deign this favour, for thy meed
> A thousand honey secrets shalt thou know.
>
> (15–16)

> If thou wilt chide, thy lips shall never open.
>
> (48)

> If they burn too, I'll quench them with my tears.
>
> (192)

> But if thou needs wilt hunt, be rul'd by me.
>
> (673)

In addition to this list—and one could extend it—Venus formulates many sentences that are implicit conditionals. "Is thine own heart to thine own face affected? . . . Then woo thyself" (157, 159), for example, can be transformed into "If thine own heart is to thine own face affected, then woo thyself." "Give me one kiss, I'll give it thee again" (209) implies the conditional formulation, "If you give me one kiss. . . ."

Venus' conditional mode is the syntactical manifestation of habits of mind that emerge in many other ways as well: her propensity for establishing bargains and her closely related tendency to see one action as a payment for another. As "Give me one kiss, I'll give it thee again" (209) would suggest, she uses kisses as counters in her bargains. Similarly, when she tries to arrange another meeting with Adonis, she selects a phrase that has connotations of bargaining: "wilt thou make the match" (586). And she bargains even with death, in effect proffering the boar as a target for his rage.

The tendency we are observing, like so many of Venus' other predilections, is not wholly negative. In a sense, in fact, Venus' conditionals assume the function of the etiological myths that Shakespeare, unlike other practitioners of his genre, virtually omits: they symbolize a world of order, of rules—a world that is played against the irrational sphere of the boar, who respects no rules at all. Hence Venus' ability to shape sentences into conditionals—and the ability to promulgate rules, to predict patterns that it implies—breaks down when she fears Adonis' death: "If he be dead,—O no, it cannot be" (937).

In practice, however, this speech mannerism generally manifests the darker, more dangerous tendencies in the goddess of love. First of all, it again signals the issue of power: when her conditionals involve a threat ("If thou wilt chide, thy lips shall never open" [48]), they are evidently an attempt to dominate, to manipulate. This aspect of bargaining becomes explicit in an allusion to ransom that figures in the most negative description of Venus that we find in the whole poem:

> Now quick desire hath caught the yielding prey,
> And glutton-like she feeds, yet never filleth.
> Her lips are conquerors, his lips obey,
> Paying what ransom the insulter willeth.
>
> (547–550)

And if Venus' conditionals in theory attest to at least a modicum of trust and communication between her and her listener, in fact they more often manifest the dissolution of both social and linguistic norms. For example, "If thou wilt deign this favour, for thy meed / A thousand honey secrets shalt thou know" (15–16) not only implies that Adonis has the choice of doing the favor or not but also stresses his authority and autonomy through the strikingly courtly, humble formula, "If thou wilt deign." But in truth he has no choice at all: without even giving him a chance to reply, Venus drags "the tender boy" (32) from his horse.

Other conditionals rank as infelicitous speech acts in the sense Austin and Searle have defined: they violate one of the essential conditions for promising. In Searle's schema, one of the preparatory rules for promising is: "*Pr* is to be uttered only if the Hearer H would prefer S's doing A to his not doing A, and S believes H would prefer S's doing A to his not doing A."[23] Often, however, Venus promises something that Adonis does not want at all. Thus in "Here come and sit, where never serpent hisses, / And being set, I'll smother thee with kisses" (17–18), her promise to kiss him must in fact seem more of a threat to her listener.[24] Nor would he necessarily welcome the promise she bestows on him later: "If they burn too, I'll quench them with my tears" (192).

The violation of the normal rules for promising reflects the instability of a world in which generic and other stylistic rules break down as rapidly and as unpredictably as social ones. We may recall 2 *Henry IV*, where Prince John's violated pledge to the rebels is merely the most overt manifestation of a society in which Diogenes would grow cold and weary roaming the streets. But Venus' untrustworthy promises also serve to reflect her characteristic self-centeredness: unable to admit that Adonis is radically different from herself, she cannot recognize that he will not appreciate the sexual favors she promises him. The same type of self-centeredness is reflected in the rhetorical questions on which she so often relies: "Then why not lips on lips, since eyes in eyes?" (120) and "Is thine own heart to thine own face affected?" (157). Sentences like this imply that their answer is obvious—but Adonis would not in fact give the answer that Venus wants.

The self-centeredness of Venus' linguistic mannerisms is mirrored

---

[23]John R. Searle, *Speech Acts: An Essay in the Philosophy of Language* (Cambridge: Cambridge Univ. Press, 1969), p. 63.

[24]Jerome Schneewind argues that we must distinguish offers and promises ("A Note on Promising," *Philosophical Studies*, 17 [1966], 33–35); in the case of a promise, he contends, the promiser must have good reason to think the promisee wishes the act to be done. Even if one accepts this delimitation of the speech act of promising, however, my general argument about Venus remains valid: rather than suggesting that her infelicitous speech act reflects her self-centeredness, one could maintain that her inability to recognize that Adonis does not want what she promises, her unwillingness to distinguish offer from promise, itself demonstrates self-centeredness.

throughout the poem. We have already observed that her first words measure her beloved against her own beauty: "Thrice fairer than myself" (7). As many readers have noticed, her repeated conceits about the earth and the boar kissing Adonis also represent a kind of self-centeredness: here, as in her conditionals and her rhetorical questions, she is refusing to acknowledge the Other, metonymically making the world over in her own image. And, as petulant and vengeful as an Ovidian god, after Adonis' death she prophesies that all lovers will suffer as she has done: "It shall be fickle, false and full of fraud" (1141). The echoes with which she is surrounded the night before Adonis dies are an externalization, a bodying forth, of her tendency to live in a house of mirrors.

Venus' deceptive rhetoric exemplifies one of the broadest—and deepest—issues in the poem: failures of speech and of language itself. *Venus and Adonis* is concerned with faulty or failed communication, as well as with faulty or failed perception; the one isolates us from the people around us, the other from the world we inhabit. The significance of communication in the poem is reflected in the fact that here, as in Shakespeare's other major poems and, indeed, in the *Metamorphoses*, the inability to speak repeatedly symbolizes other losses, other griefs; Adonis' initial silence aptly represents his loss of power, and even Venus herself is temporarily rendered speechless, first by impatience and then by grief.

One reason communication is problematical, Venus' behavior reminds us, is that language can serve multiple and often contradictory ends. In particular, its expressive and its persuasive aims may be at odds; in describing her love for Adonis the goddess of love in fact weakens her case, repelling rather than persuading him. And the poem plays on the paradox that Adonis' demurrals actually render him more, not less, attractive, much as Elizabeth Bennet finds that her most serious protests are merely interpreted as the coquetry of an elegant female. The failure of words to say what the speaker intends is one more breakdown in expectations and one more collapse of social codes in a poem that depicts so many of these failures. But if verbal signs cannot always be trusted to communicate as intended, neither can their gestural equivalent. The gestures of the horses, their tailwaving, stamping, and biting, effectively prevent a nascent breach between them. Yet in the human semiotic system gestures can be misleading in much the same way as words: though the red and white hues of Adonis' face in fact express his shame and grief, Venus finds them attractive.

Sexual gestures, too, can be an antithesis to communication rather than an extension of it:

[38]

And kissing speaks, with lustful language broken,
"If thou wilt chide, thy lips shall never open."

(47–48)

He saith she is immodest, blames her miss;
What follows more, she murders with a kiss.

(53–54)

On one level, of course, we should not take all this too seriously: Venus is again indulging in playful sexual games, and one would have to be as "unmoved, cold, and to temptation slow" as Adonis himself wholly to disapprove. The word "murders" (54), however, reminds us that serious issues are at stake. The way kissing interrupts language in these instances is a microcosm of the way sexuality bars genuine communication between Venus and Adonis throughout the poem.

But much as Venus' aggressiveness does not preclude tenderness, so the violence that she inflicts on language does not preclude her using it with more respect and to more respectable ends.[25] Venus approaches rhetoric much as she approaches people: overwhelmingly, disturbingly, and yet with a type of vitality and verve that qualify the negative judgments we are tempted to make. As we saw, the deer park episode reflects not only her intention of manipulating Adonis but also the delighted and delightful fluency of her imagination. It is, however, the Wat incident that best exemplifies the positive uses to which she can put language. Though the iconographic association between Venus and hares may explain some of her interest in the unfortunate Wat,[26] in her precisely realized, sympathetic observations we find the very ability to transcend her own interests, look beyond her own mirrors, that she elsewhere lacks:

By this, poor Wat, far off upon a hill,
Stands on his hinder-legs with list'ning ear,
To hearken if his foes pursue him still.
Anon their loud alarums he doth hear.

(697–700)

[25]Compare Coppélia Kahn's point that Venus' sexuality itself is both healthy and destructive ("Self and Eros in *Venus and Adonis*," *Centennial Review*, 20 [1976], 360–364). An abbreviated version of the article appears in *Man's Estate: Masculine Identity in Shakespeare* (Berkeley: Univ. of California Press, 1981), with the relevant section on pp. 33–34.

[26]On the iconographical connections between Venus and the hare, see, e.g., Don Cameron Allen, "On *Venus and Adonis*," in *Elizabethan and Jacobean Studies Presented to Frank Percy Wilson* (Oxford: Clarendon, 1959), pp. 109–110.

It is the process of storytelling, elsewhere used for self-serving ends, that here allows both Venus and her listeners to empathize with Wat. In fact, so involved are we with her descriptions that even after repeated readings we are startled when we are reminded of the framing story of Venus and Adonis by the line: "Lie quietly, and hear a little more" (709).

The acuity of Shakespeare's portrayal of Venus is manifest not only in the broader psychological patterns we have been sketching but also in more isolated reactions. As one editor has noted, the multiple images of Adonis that she sees are a recognizable symptom of hysteria;[27] since the incident reminds us also that she has never seen him clearly, it functions symbolically as well as psychologically. At one point she is so involved in her own world that she forgets what she is saying ("'Where did I leave?' 'No matter where,' quoth he" [715]), a moment that may well remind us of our own responses to stress. Also acute are Venus' rapid transitions from depression to anger. Grieving at Adonis' death, she vents her spleen by mocking the rest of the world:

> Bonnet nor veil henceforth no creature wear:
> Nor sun nor wind will ever strive to kiss you.
> Having no fair to lose, you need not fear.
>
> (1081–1083)

A little later her sorrow is transformed into the anger of her prophecy: "The bottom poison, and the top o'erstraw'd / With sweets that shall the truest sight beguile" (1143–1144).

If Venus' opening words aptly introduce her, her concluding ones are equally characteristic. So revealing is the final passage in the poem, in fact, that it demands to be cited in full:

> She bows her head, the new-sprung flower to smell,
> Comparing it to her Adonis' breath,
> And says within her bosom it shall dwell,
> Since he himself is reft from her by death.
>> She crops the stalk, and in the breach appears
>> Green-dropping sap, which she compares to tears.
>
> "Poor flower," quoth she, "this was thy father's guise,—
> Sweet issue of a more sweet-smelling sire,—

[27]Prince, p. 57.

For every little grief to wet his eyes;
To grow unto himself was his desire,
   And so 'tis thine; but know, it is as good
   To wither in my breast as in his blood.

"Here was thy father's bed, here in my breast;
Thou art the next of blood, and 'tis thy right.
Lo in this hollow cradle take thy rest;
My throbbing heart shall rock thee day and night:
   There shall not be one minute in an hour
   Wherein I will not kiss my sweet love's flower."

Thus weary of the world, away she hies,
And yokes her silver doves, by whose swift aid
Their mistress mounted through the empty skies,
In her light chariot quickly is convey'd,
   Holding their course to Paphos, where their queen
   Means to immure herself and not be seen.

(1171–1194)

The repetition of "compare" in the first stanza I quoted draws our attention to the fact that Venus, like Richard II, is responding to grief by assuming the role of poet. Unlike that monarch, however, she also reacts with violence, plucking the flower much as she had plucked Adonis. In the next stanza, she develops the conceit that the flower is Adonis' son, an image that evidently reflects her maternality. But that maternality involves little genuine concern for the flower and less yet for the truth. When, for example, she claims that it is the flower's "right" (1184) to wither in her breast, she is making the same mistake that marked and marred her promises to that fair flower Adonis: she implies that the blossom is grateful to have the right, that it would wish to wither in her breast. In another way, too, she is twisting facts: if her breast was Adonis' "bed" (1183), he allowed it to be so only very briefly and unwillingly. But if our reactions up to this point have been negative, the assertion "There shall not be one minute in an hour / Wherein I will not kiss my sweet love's flower" (1187–1188) confounds our responses by increasing our pity for her. On the one hand, we have learned by now to distrust Venus' promises, and the hyperbolic vocabulary of this one makes it seem especially unreliable. Yet in this case we also feel that the extravagance of her language reflects the depth of her emotion, and we sympathize with her in her grief.

[41]

Captive Victors

It is instructive to read through the ending of *Venus and Adonis* twice, once pretending that its penultimate stanza in fact terminates the poem and the second time including the actual ending. The difference is striking. First of all, had Shakespeare ended on "Wherein I will not kiss my sweet love's flower" (1188), our final reactions to Venus would have been involvement and sympathy, though a sympathy laced with distrust of her hyperboles. The actual conclusion, however, distances us from her and in so doing enforces more negative moral judgments, a seesawing between sympathy and judgment that characterizes the whole poem. Moreover, by including the final stanza the poet reinforces certain points about Venus' temperament that have emerged throughout the poem. She is enacting her ability to avoid realities she does not wish to face; having escaped into an airy world of words earlier, now she is quite literally escaping into the air. And if her desire to "immure herself" (1194) once again testifies to her genuine sorrow, the preceding phrase in the line, "means to," surprises us by its ambiguity. It can, of course, merely function as a neutral announcement of her intentions—but as we read about her flying away we reflect that the intentions of this, as it were, highly volatile character are not always to be trusted. We may even suspect that her immuring herself is the last of many vows she does not keep, conditions she does not meet.

But these doubts necessarily cannot be confirmed: the poem is over. Hence our responses to the ending are uncertainty and even dismay, reactions all the more intense because they conflict with the aesthetic finality we associate with closure; the text no less than Venus is breaking a promise.[28] Venus' statements and actions represent an unreliable form of closure, an assertion of finality that jars against the irresolution introduced by "means to" (1194). We react rather as we do at the end of *Measure for Measure*, where the sense of finality that the comedic conclusion offers conflicts with our expectations about how Isabella would really respond to the proposal. In short, then, Shakespeare is conjoining an aesthetic and a psychological problem here, as he so often does elsewhere in the poem: he is examining the issue of closure by associating that literary question with his heroine's sensibility.

Venus' inability to effect a satisfactory conclusion to her experiences is in fact foreshadowed a few stanzas earlier in one of the most revealing changes Shakespeare makes in his sources. In both Ovid

[28]For an overview of poetic closure, see Barbara Herrnstein Smith, *Poetic Closure: A Study of How Poems End* (Chicago: Univ. of Chicago Press, 1968).

and Golding, Venus wills the flower into being and in so doing creates an apt symbol for her grief as well as an apt ending for the story. Here, however, the blossom merely springs up unaided:

> By this the boy that by her side lay kill'd
> Was melted like a vapour from her sight,
> And in his blood that on the ground lay spill'd,
> A purple flower sprung up, checker'd with white.
>
> (1165–1168)

If we cannot trust the actions and reactions of Venus, those of Adonis are also problematical. Though he is less fully realized than Venus, his behavior manifests some of the same intriguing ambiguities.[29] In other epyllia, the few ambiguous moments we encounter typically reflect simple hypocrisy—Hero says *"Come thither"* (I.358) because she is more interested in sex than she cares to admit—while in the case of both of Shakespeare's title characters such moments reveal more complex ethical and psychological problems. Adonis' youthfulness is a case in point. Emphasized by Shakespeare's repeated references to him as a boy (for example, 32, 95, 344), his immaturity represents a striking deviation from the sources. Though Golding once calls his Adonis a "tender youth" (634), elsewhere he indicates that he has reached manhood, and Ovid explicitly states that he was "iam iuvenis, iam vir" ("now a youth, now man," *Metamorphoses* X, 523).[30] On the one hand, the youthfulness of Shakespeare's Adonis breeds sympathy for him, encouraging us to cast him as a victim of a scheming older woman and, in particular, providing at least a partial explanation for his reluctance. On the other hand, however, his chronological age also reflects his emotional immaturity, the callowness manifest in such dialogue as his comically petulant excuse, "Fie, no more of love! / The sun doth burn my face, I must remove" (185–186).

But we cannot rest satisfied that his youthfulness justifies his rejection of Venus; like the goddess of love herself, we are confused by his behavior. For one thing, that rejection is explained too frequently and too contradictorily: here, as with the plethora of motives that Iago

---

[29]Most studies of Adonis interpret him allegorically rather than psychologically. For a psychological reading different from my own but not incompatible with it, see Kahn, "Self and Eros in *Venus and Adonis*"; this article focuses on his narcissism.

[30]All citations from Ovid are to *Metamorphoses*, trans. Frank Justus Miller, 2d ed., 2 vols. (Cambridge, Mass., and London: Harvard Univ. Press and Heinemann, 1966).

announces, the very abundance of rationales leads us to distrust all of them—and to distrust the character who is so profusely offering them. In the opening stanza, the narrator clearly announces that "love he laugh'd to scorn" (4), while later in the poem Adonis himself as firmly asserts, "I hate not love, but your device in love / That lends embracements unto every stranger" (789–790). Similarly, he declares that he hates love because "it is a life in death" (413) but only a few lines later implies that it is not the nature of love but rather his own youthfulness that impels him to scorn it (415–420). Recognizing that Adonis does not fully understand his own behavior, we begin to suspect subterranean motives that he cannot or will not face, such as the narcissism of which Venus accuses him. The poem nowhere confirms those suspicions—Venus, herself narcissistic, is not the most reliable of judges on this issue, as on so many others—but they remain a troubling undertone as we read.

Evaluating Adonis' ethical position is as complicated as assessing the reasons he assumes it. There is no question but that his coy, petulant tone leads us to distrust his moral stance.[31] At times asyndeton contributes to the impression of abruptness and churlishness:

> You hurt my hand with wringing, let us part,
> And leave this idle theme, this bootless chat;
>
> . . . . .
>
> Dismiss your vows, your feigned tears, your flatt'ry,
> For where a heart is hard they make no batt'ry.
>
> (421–422, 425–426)

Like the academicians in *Love's Labour's Lost*, he sounds a little too smug and self-righteous when he dismisses love's "batt'ry" (426).

---

[31]On this and other faults in Adonis, cf. J. D. Jahn, "The Lamb of Lust: The Role of Adonis in Shakespeare's *Venus and Adonis*," *Shakespeare Studies*, 6 (1970), 11–25. Norman Rabkin suggests that the imagery associating him with animals, as well as his own perspiration, belie his attempts to escape the flesh (*Shakespeare and the Common Understanding* [New York and London: Free Press and Collier Macmillan, 1967], p. 161). For an earlier version of this chapter, see "*Venus and Adonis* and the Myth of Love," in *Pacific Coast Studies in Shakespeare*, ed. Waldo F. McNeir and Thelma N. Greenfield (Eugene, Oreg.: Univ. of Oregon Press, 1966). These and other arguments about Adonis' faults call into question G. P. V. Akrigg's assertion that Shakespeare's epyllion compliments Southampton by implicitly rebutting the portrait of him in John Clapham's *Narcissus* (*Shakespeare and the Earl of Southampton* [Cambridge, Mass.: Harvard Univ. Press, 1968], pp. 33–34, 195–196). Other possible connections between *Narcissus* and *Venus and Adonis*, however, deserve more attention than they have received.

The smugness finds its rhetorical equivalent in the aphorisms that characterize his speech:

> The colt that's back'd and burden'd being young,
> Loseth his pride, and never waxeth strong.
>
> (419–420)

> Love comforteth like sunshine after rain,
> But lust's effect is tempest after sun;
> Love's gentle spring doth always fresh remain,
> Lust's winter comes ere summer half be done.
>
> (799–802)

As we read these lines, we sense a tension between their neatness, the sense of intellectual and poetic stasis that they convey, and the rapidly moving, unpredictable world we encounter elsewhere in the poem.[32] As we will see, the couplets in Shakespeare's sonnets function in much the same way. The fact that Adonis' sentiments were Elizabethan truisms does not prove that Shakespeare was endorsing them, as some readers have assumed; rather, the author of the poem is holding these conventional "forms" up for our scrutiny, a scrutiny that would become all the more charged for a reader who had accepted and even repeated such aphoristic sentiments unthinkingly. Nor, however, should we assume that Shakespeare is merely mocking the conventional wisdom of his culture. Venus, surely a "tempest" (800) as well as a temptress, exemplifies many of the points Adonis is making. And however suspicious his neat truisms may make us, they clearly provide him with an important bulwark against her attacks.

Where other epyllia typically assign aphorisms to an undramatized, vaguely defined narrative voice, Shakespeare places them in the mouth of one of his principal characters. Similarly, the hyperbolic language in which the narrators in other epyllia revel is here primarily associated with Venus. By dramatizing linguistic behavior in this way, he is highlighting the psychological traits that it reflects—an issue that he was, of course, exploring at roughly the same time in *Love's Labour's Lost* and in so many of his later works.[33] Both in the

---

[32]Lanham (pp. 82–94) argues that he is being criticized for his aphoristic rhetoric; Franklin M. Dickey, in contrast, maintains that he speaks "rather nobly" (*Not Wisely but Too Well: Shakespeare's Love Tragedies* [San Marino: Huntington Library, 1957], p. 50). This chapter suggests that the truth lies somewhere in between.

[33]On attitudes to language in *Love's Labour's Lost*, see esp. William C. Carroll, *The Great Feast of Language in "Love's Labour's Lost"* (Princeton: Princeton Univ. Press, 1976).

plays and in *Venus and Adonis* itself, one effect of this dramatization is to encourage us to question patterns of speech and thought that we might otherwise too readily accept; similarly, it is precisely because they are spoken by a Jacques or a Polonius that we reconsider our attitudes to the moral truisms those characters convey.

However antithetical the ethical positions of Shakespeare's two title characters may be, Adonis adopts some of the linguistic patterns we also found in Venus, demonstrating that here, as in *The Rape of Lucrece* and the sonnets, the lovers share deeper affinities than they themselves would care to admit. Adonis too is very concerned with naming and misnaming: "Call it not love, for love to heaven is fled, / Since sweating lust on earth usurp'd his name" (793–794). Our first impression may be that he, unlike the huntress who pursues him, is assigning names correctly. But in him as well as her the process is self-serving in its aims, deceptive in its effects. Though lust is Venus' primary motive, it is by no means her only one and by no means an adequate label for her behavior: tender maternal love is commingled with her lust, as certain images testify ("Like a milch doe, whose swelling dugs do ache, / Hasting to feed her fawn, hid in some brake" [875–876]). And Adonis too makes and breaks promises, though not as frequently as Venus:

> So offers he to give what she did crave,
>> But when her lips were ready for his pay,
>> He winks, and turns his lips another way.
>>> (88–90)

> Now let me say good night, and so say you;
>> If you will say so, you shall have a kiss.
>>> (535–536)

It is by subtly but significantly recasting his sources that Shakespeare develops another facet of Adonis: he is figured as entrapped, enclosed—sometimes by Venus but sometimes by his own chastity. When recounting the story of Salmacis and Hermaphroditus, Ovid writes, "in liquidis translucet aquis, ut eburnea si quis / signa tegat claro vel candida lilia vitro" (IV.354–355). Golding renders this as, "As if a man an Ivorie Image or a Lillie white / Should overlay or close with glasse" (IV.438–439).[34] But in Shakespeare's hands the image becomes:

[34] All citations from Golding are to *Shakespeare's Ovid Being Arthur Golding's Translation of the Metamorphoses*, ed. W. H. D. Rouse (Carbondale, Ill.: Southern Illinois Univ. Press, 1961).

> Full gently now she takes him by the hand,
> A lily prison'd in a gaol of snow,
> Or ivory in an alabaster band.
>
> (361–363)

The charged word "prison'd" (362) serves to develop the imagery of entrapment that runs throughout the poem (compare the deer park stanzas with which we began: "Since I have hemm'd thee here / Within the circuit . . . Within this limit" [229–230, 235]).[35] Later in the poem, however, Adonis speaks of a very different type of enclosure:

> Lest the deceiving harmony should run
> Into the quiet closure of my breast,
> And then my little heart were quite undone,
> In his bedchamber to be barr'd of rest.
>
> (781–784)

Here the protective custody of the breast displaces imprisonment. While Shakespeare does not recur to these figures or the implicit relationship between them elsewhere in *Venus and Adonis*, it is telling that they were present in his imagination this early in his career. They surface in the other nondramatic poems (as well as in several plays), and there they assume a more central role.

However we interpret Adonis' behavior, it is difficult to consider the boar a fitting punishment for it.[36] Those readers who have argued that the natural world is punishing him for his rejection of naturalistic love neglect the fact that the poem is ambivalent about that rejection. In any event, the punishment does not seem to fit the crime, even if we concentrate on its symbolic ramifications. Its inappropriateness is, I would suggest, the very point: Shakespeare is stressing the randomness, the injustice of fate. There is at times no providence in the fall of a sparrow. That randomness renders Venus' and Adonis' efforts to order experience, whether by renaming it or forcing it into the mold of aphoristic or conditional utterances, all the more understandable—but also all the more foolish.

---

[35]For a different but not incompatible reading of the image, see M. C. Bradbrook, *Shakespeare and Elizabethan Poetry: A Study of His Earlier Work in Relation to the Poetry of the Time* (London: Chatto and Windus, 1951), p. 64.

[36]The significance of the boar has been discussed by many readers. The thesis of Don Cameron Allen's "On *Venus and Adonis*" is that Shakespeare is contrasting the soft hunt of love with the hard hunt for the boar; A. C. Hamilton interprets that destructive beast as the forces that threaten beauty ("Venus and Adonis," *SEL*, 1 [1961], 13).

Though they are alike in that "blessed rage for order," Venus and Adonis evidently differ from each other in their approach to morality. In anatomizing that difference, Shakespeare once again couples the formal and the psychological. Adonis not only subscribes to the conventional pieties, he repeatedly expresses them in a series of sententiae that would make even *A Mirror for Magistrates* look like an exemplar of amoral naturalism by comparison. What results is a poem in which one character bodies forth an amoral delight in sexuality, while the other both symbolizes and expresses a rejection of it in the name of higher philosophical verities. Hence *Venus and Adonis*—and Venus and Adonis themselves—dramatically enact a tension in the generic potentials of Ovidian mythological poetry. Venus stands for the amoral eroticism so common in the mythological narratives of Ovid himself, while Adonis represents the pieties of *Ovide moralisé*. The tension between Venus and Adonis is in effect also a tension between two possible ways of imitating and adapting Ovid, two potential metamorphoses of the *Metamorphoses*: the amoral, Italianate narrative and the pious commentary on human follies. Rosalie Colie has shown us how often Shakespeare's plays envision literary problems in terms of human psychology;[37] the same is no less true of his Ovidian narrative. By thus relating the literary to the psychological in *Venus and Adonis*, he deepens the resonances of his characters—we become aware that they represent distinctive responses to literary dilemmas as well as nonliterary ones—and also enlivens and dramatizes the questions raised by his genre. To be sure, other sixteenth-century Ovidian epyllia are packed with sententiae, but their truisms are normally assigned to the narrator, not one of the personages. Since these narrators are not fully realized characters, the conflict between the two approaches to Ovid is not enacted dramatically as it is in Shakespeare's poem. Shakespeare is, in other words, interpreting his genre and its mode very differently from the way his contemporaries do.

III

Conscious that *Venus and Adonis* is not only one of the most interesting English epyllia but also one of the earliest, scholars have typically stressed the ways it influenced other Ovidian mythological poems rather than the qualities that distinguish it from them. We are often reminded, for example, that Venus is a precursor to the sexually

---

[37] *Shakespeare's Living Art*, esp. chap. 1.

forward women in other epyllia. Yet a comparison between Shakespeare's narrative and other works in its genre suggests that the differences are more telling than the similarities: the author of *Venus and Adonis* approaches the Ovidian mythological poem very idiosyncratically. Determining the intentions or motivations that led him to do so is problematical, but describing the effect of his generic decisions is not. The primary result of many of these decisions is to create a medium singularly well suited to exploring human behavior in general and evoking a temperament like that of Venus in particular.

To understand how Shakespeare's approach to the epyllion differs from that of his contemporaries one must, of course, delineate the contours the genre normally assumes, an apparently straightforward task that proves surprisingly complex. Readers of epyllia are as prone to bewilderment as the hapless lovers in those poems, and much of our confusion originates in the challenge of enumerating the characteristics of the genre. If defining literary types is often difficult, the problems are compounded in this instance: the superficial resemblances between poems in this tradition—all recount mythological stories, all concern love—may tempt us to ignore the differences between them. In addition, any attempt at definition is complicated by the fact that classicists disagree about whether the classical epyllion even exists.[38] And seventeenth-century epyllia often differ significantly from the sixteenth-century versions on which this chapter will focus: some are more allegorical than their Elizabethan counterparts, some more blatantly obscene (the jokes in the anonymous poem *The Loves of Hero and Leander*, for instance, make Arabella's initial greeting to Jude look positively modest by comparison). But even if we concentrate on sixteenth-century contributions to this genre, we find significant variations; the narrator in Lodge's *Scillaes Metamorphosis* is actually a participant in the action, the dramatist Heywood includes in his *Oenone and Paris* less description than many other writers in the tradition, and so on.[39]

These variations reflect not only the individual approaches of the authors in question but also the ambiguous nature of their genre. As many theorists of literary form have reminded us, generic norms, like linguistic ones, evolve only over a period of time. Hence the practi-

---

[38]See Walter Allen, Jr., "The Non-Existent Classical Epyllion," *SP*, 55 (1958), 515–518; Paul W. Miller, "The Elizabethan Minor Epic," *SP*, 55 (1958), 31–38.

[39]The problem of classifying these poems is further complicated if we accept Clark Hulse's thesis that the epyllion and the historical narrative essentially belong to the same genre, the minor epic (*Metamorphic Verse*, chap. 1).

tioners of a genre, again like the speakers of a language, may view their enterprise very differently from the way later students of it will do.[40] Political history offers another parallel; the significance of World War I will inevitably appear differently to those living through it than to historians analyzing it in the light of the Second World War. Thus the poets who composed epyllia early in the 1590s, notably Marlowe and Shakespeare himself, must have seen themselves as experimenting with characteristics the Ovidian mythological narrative might assume in English, not as responding to or rejecting generic norms.

Yet even if modern critics delight in theories of mimetic form, students of English epyllia need not imitate the helpless and pointless peregrinations of their heroines. Adducing the Wittgensteinian concept of family resemblances is, as Alastair Fowler has recently pointed out,[41] a healthy corrective to rigid and frigid attempts to define genres by enumerating their necessary elements. When we do so we can in fact discern the contours of the sixteenth-century English epyllion—and hence can come to understand how Shakespeare's own methods of characterization are related to those contours.

Many of the family resemblances uniting the works in this genre can be traced back to the physiognomy of their common progenitor, Ovid. As eager as Chaucer to claim that poet as their "owne auctor," the authors of English epyllia borrow many strategies and techniques from the *Metamorphoses*.[42] Their most significant legacy from their Roman predecessor is his tone. As William Keach's important study has reminded us, snakes lurk in these gardens: English epyllia, like Ovid's *Metamorphoses*, do not let us forget the darker side of sexuality, its turmoil and pain.[43] From Ovid these poems also borrow rapid, dazzling shifts in mood: the antitheses that dominate their rhetoric

[40]On such difficulties, see Alastair Fowler, *Kinds of Literature: An Introduction to the Theory of Genres and Modes* (Cambridge, Mass.: Harvard Univ. Press, 1982), esp. pp. 156–159; Claudio Guillén, *Literature as System: Essays toward the Theory of Literary History* (Princeton: Princeton Univ. Press, 1971), chap. 4.

[41]*Kinds of Literature*, pp. 37–44.

[42]For useful summaries of the basic characteristics of the genre, see Elizabeth Story Donno, "The Epyllion," in *English Poetry and Prose, 1540–1674*, ed. Christopher Ricks (London: Barrie and Jenkins, 1970), and "Introduction," *Elizabethan Minor Epics* (London: Routledge and Kegan Paul, 1963); Hulse, esp. chap. 1; Keach, esp. chap. 1; Miller, "The Elizabethan Minor Epic," and "Introduction," *Seven Minor Epics of the Renaissance*, (Gainesville, Fla.: Scholars' Facsimiles and Reprints, 1967), pp. xvi-xviii; Hallett Smith, *Elizabethan Poetry: A Study in Conventions, Meaning, and Expression* (Cambridge, Mass.: Harvard Univ. Press, 1952), chap. 2.

[43]See Keach, chap. 1.

reflect not only the antithetical debates between their lovers, as most readers have assumed, but also antithetical movements in the poem itself and the seesawing effect we experience when reading it.[44] Indeed, if we follow Todorov (or, indeed, Aristotle himself) and define a genre in terms of its effect on its audience,[45] English epyllia are characterized by the sense of disorientation they produce in us.

Another characteristic of these poems is their propensity for commenting on other literary traditions. In place of—and in reaction against—pious allegorical commentaries on what Golding terms Ovid's "dark Philosophie of turned shapes" (Epistle, 7) they, like Ovid himself, offer a cynical vision of the gods "Committing headdie ryots, incest, rapes" (*Hero and Leander*, I.144). And they enjoy a relationship with Petrarchism as complex and ambivalent as that between Petrarchan lovers and their ladies.[46] Ovidian mythological poems unabashedly borrow from Petrarchism in particular and Elizabethan love poetry in general a whole store of images and rhetorical devices: characters sport red and white complexions, love is variously compared to a hunt and a ship, and oxymora abound. Yet the authors of these poems are not merely borrowing such rhetoric, nor, as one recent study has asserted, are they fashioning a world of wish fulfillment, a world in which the unsatisfied sexual desires of Petrarchan lovers can be released.[47] They are attempting to exorcise Petrarchan conventions more than to exercise them. The aggressive women who populate these poems function as an implicit critique of the less realistic vision of woman in the Petrarchan tradition: scholars often assume that such heroines merely represent unthinking imitations of Shakespeare's Venus, but in fact these figures are shaped as much or more by their authors' reaction against the author of the *Rime*. The more open and realistic treatment of sex that we encounter in these mythological poems is, too, a subterranean criticism of the reticences and

---

[44]Many critics have noted these antitheses but have explained them differently. See, e.g., Bush, *Mythology and the Renaissance Tradition*, p. 142.

[45]On affective definitions of genre, see esp. Tzvetan Todorov, *The Fantastic: A Structural Approach to a Literary Genre* (Cleveland: Case Western Reserve Univ. Press, 1973), chap. 2.

[46]Many readers have commented on the Petrarchan elements in the epyllion. See, e.g., Bush, *Mythology and the Renaissance Tradition*, pp. 83–84; Philip J. Finkelpearl, "From Petrarch to Ovid: Metamorphoses in John Marston's *Metamorphosis of Pigmalions Image*," *ELH*, 32 (1965), 333–348, and the abbreviated version of that article in *John Marston of the Middle Temple: An Elizabethan Dramatist in His Social Setting* (Cambridge, Mass.: Harvard Univ. Press, 1969); Hulse, chap. 2.

[47]See Hulse, esp. pp. 46–47, 69–70.

indirections that characterize the English Petrarchan tradition. The authors of epyllia, like the authors of formal verse satires, delight in rubbing *sal* in the wounds of Petrarchan lovers.[48]

Indeed, perhaps the epyllion is, as its name suggests, a "little epic" principally in that it, like epic, contains a whole range of generic motifs and allusions. In the *sal* of their aphoristic asides, Ovidian narrative poems incorporate the epigrammatic; in the *mel* of their sensuous descriptions they include many lyric conventions, especially those of the sonnet. But their primary debt is, of course, to the pastoral mode. Though they may feature sophisticated narrators and clothing as elaborate and artificial as the language used to describe it, most epyllia are situated in "the realm . . . of Flora, and old Pan." Heywood's Oenone bemoans her fate among "verdaunt flowers"(5),[49] Edwards' Procris, less ecologically sensitive than Oenone, actually tears the flowers "that hurteth not" (604)[50] as she laments; and Drayton's Phoebe sports in a grove whose flora and fauna are catalogued at some length.

Venus too plucks a flower of course—but her relationship to the natural world is very different from that of the other nymphs in the English epyllion. Indeed, an enumeration of the qualities shared by *Venus and Adonis* and other Ovidian narratives makes the distinctions between Shakespeare's poem and those of his contemporaries all the more striking; if, as I suggested, family resemblances unite the progeny of the *Metamorphoses*, Shakespeare's contribution to the tradition is at best a half-sister. And ranking his poem in comparison to its counterparts is in many respects as invidious as offering qualitative judgments on siblings: though *Venus and Adonis* is superior to other epyllia in some ways, a number of the contrasts we will note represent differences not in quality but rather in purpose and effect.

We are conscious of these contrasts—and conscious of their relevance to the portrait of Venus—from the moment we open his poem. Here Marlowe and Beaumont provide the most pertinent foils:

> On *Hellespont* guiltie of True-loves blood,
> In view and opposit two citties stood,
> Seaborderers, disjoin'd by *Neptunes* might:

[48]On the division of sonnets into *sal* and *mel*, see Rosalie L. Colie, *The Resources of Kind: Genre-Theory in the Renaissance* (Berkeley: Univ. of California Press, 1973), pp. 68–75; *Shakespeare's Living Art*, pp. 96–134.

[49]Heywood is quoted from Donno, ed., *Elizabethan Minor Epics.*

[50]All citations from Edwards are to Donno, ed., *Elizabethan Minor Epics.*

The one *Abydos*, the other *Sestos* hight.
At *Sestos*, *Hero* dwelt; *Hero* the fair,
                    (*Hero and Leander*, I.1–5)

My wanton lines doe treate of amorous loue,
Such as would bow the hearts of gods aboue:
Then *Venus*, thou great Citherean Queene,
That hourely tripst on the Idalian greene,
Thou laughing *Erycina*, daygne to see
The verses wholly consecrate to thee;

. . . . .

There was a louely boy the Nymphs had kept,
That on the Idane mountaines oft had slept,
Begot and borne by powers that dwelt aboue,
By learned *Mercury* of the Queene of loue:
A face he had that shew'd his parents fame,
And from them both conioyned, he drew his name.
              (*Salmacis and Hermaphroditus*, 1–6, 13–18)[51]

We are distanced from the worlds of Marlowe and Beaumont spa-
tially: they specify their locales as Hellespont and Mt. Ida, both far
removed from the experience of most of their readers. This spatial
effect mirrors a temporal one: Beaumont's "There was" (13) firmly
locates his poem in a distant time. That phrase, like "Once upon a
time," also serves to signal the fictiveness of the tale; it aptly prepares
us for a story that the narrator will interrupt with self-conscious allusions to his own art. But if we feel detached from the world that is
being evoked, we experience even more detachment from the lovers
within it. Both poets precede the first encounter of their principal
characters with lengthy descriptions and narratives only tangentially
related to the main story—Marlowe does not even turn to the feast at
which his star-crossed lovers will meet until line 91 of the poem, while
Beaumont embroiders his introduction of Hermaphroditus with so
many descriptive details and so many related myths that we do not
hear of Salmacis until line 103.

---

[51]Beaumont is quoted from *Salmacis and Hermaphroditvs* (London, 1602). Though the
authorship of this poem has been questioned, I accept Philip J. Finkelpearl's persuasive
attribution ("The Authorship of 'Salmacis and Hermaphroditus,'" *NQ*, n.s. 16 [1969],
367–368). For an opposing argument see Roger Sell, "The Authorship of 'The Metamorphosis of Tabacco' and 'Salmacis and Hermaphroditus,'" *NQ*, n.s. 19 (1972), 10–
14.

Captive Victors

Shakespeare's poem opens on a very different note:

> Even as the sun with purple-colour'd face
> Had ta'en his last leave of the weeping morn,
> Rose-cheek'd Adonis hied him to the chase;
> Hunting he lov'd, but love he laugh'd to scorn.
> Sick-thoughted Venus makes amain unto him,
> And like a bold-fac'd suitor 'gins to woo him.
> *(Venus and Adonis, 1–6)*

This narrative could take place anywhere; it is not rooted in a particular locale. And the present tense to which the speaker soon switches intensifies our impression that the scene is being enacted not at some distant time, not in some idyllic Never-Never Land, but rather right in front of our eyes. That switch in tenses parallels another change: even Shakespeare's syntax becomes increasingly immediate as the sixain progresses. In lines 1 through 4 we find a lengthy left-branching modifier and two syntactical inversions; the epithets and the use of antithesis and polyptoton heighten the formal mood. Venus' entrance affects the style of the poem much as she attempts to affect the life of her beloved; diction and syntax become earthier, simpler, more direct. These forms of stylistic immediacy prepare us for the immediacy of dialogue, and in fact Venus begins to speak in the opening of the second stanza.

These passages suggest, then, one of the principal distinctions between Shakespeare's epyllion and other Ovidian mythological narratives: most poets in the tradition, unlike the author of *Venus and Adonis*, delight in distracting attention from the main events and the characters in their poems. To be sure, we are drawn in by the surfaces of their narratives, which have all the immediacy, all the overwrought vividness of a Pre-Raphaelite canvas: we learn exactly what Hero's buskins look like, precisely which flowers adorn the bower in which Paris encounters the abandoned Oenone. Yet the authors of English epyllia, as reflexive and self-conscious as Ovid himself, abruptly remind us of the fictiveness of those precisely detailed surfaces with lines like "And what in vision there to him be fell, / My weary Muse some other time shall tell" (Drayton, *Endimion and Phoebe*, 991–992)[52] or "Confounded with descriptions, I must leave them; / Lovers must

---

[52]I quote Drayton from *The Works of Michael Drayton*, ed. J. William Hebel, 5 vols. (Oxford: Basil Blackwell, 1931–1941).

thinke, and Poets must report them" (Lodge, *Scillaes Metamorphosis*, 319–320).[53]

We are diverted from their characters, too, by rapid changes in focus. The heavily embroidered clothing with which the denizens of epyllia are decked could serve as an emblem for the narrative texture of these poems: the primary narrative is decorated with a series of inset stories, often quite tangential to the main one. Thus Beaumont incorporates a long digression about Astraea, while Marlowe concludes his first sestiad by telling us why the Fates dislike Cupid. On the syntactical level this digressiveness is mirrored in a tendency to parenthetical asides and to right-branching sentences that distract our attention from the principal clause:

> When Ioue ambitious by his former sinnes,
> (From him al Muses, so my Muse beginnes)
> Deposde his Syre *Saturnus* . . .
> (Weever, *Faunus and Melliflora*, 1–3)[54]

> Her wide sleeves greene, and bordered with a grove,
> Where *Venus* in her naked glory strove,
> To please the carelesse and disdainfull eies,
> Of proud *Adonis* that before her lies.
> (Marlowe, *Hero and Leander*, I.11–14)

Often, as in the first of these instances, the disjunctive effect of such interruptions is intensified by the fact that they separate subject and predicate, much as our initial introduction to the characters is often separated from the accounts of their activities by lengthy descriptions or one of those digressive stories. If epyllia typically evoke frustration, passion aroused but not fulfilled, so too do they rely on narrative techniques that frustrate our syntactical expectations.

Shakespeare, in contrast, resists the temptation to distract attention from his principal characters in any of these ways. He omits the reflexive allusions to his own poem that repeatedly distance us from the personages in other epyllia. And he approaches the digressiveness that he inherited from Ovid very differently from the way his contemporaries do. With the single exception of that "mortal butcher" (618)

---

[53]Lodge, *Scillaes Metamorphosis: Enterlaced with the vnfortunate loue of Glaucus* (London, 1589), sig.B2ʳ. All citations are from this edition.

[54]*Favnvs and Melliflora, or, The Original of Our English Satyres* (London, 1600), sig.B.

the boar, the landscape and its inhabitants are described only in brief and general terms. Nor does he devote attention to the clothing of his characters. We have no idea of what Venus wears, while the costumes of her counterparts in other epyllia are detailed with a precision worthy of a commentator at a fashion show. Shakespeare is concerned instead with "that within which passeth show." His epyllion hardly has a visual surface, whereas some of those written by his contemporaries are, in more senses than one, virtually all surface.

His treatment of inset digressive episodes further distinguishes his poem—and, in particular, our responses to its characters. Indeed, the term "digression" does not even seem apt for the three incidents to which it might be applied: the story of Mars and Venus, the encounter of the horses, and the description of Wat. They are digressive only to the extent that the subplots in works like *1 Henry IV* or *King Lear* are: their action mirrors and comments on that of the main plot. All are, in short, far more closely linked to the central story than, say, Beaumont's description of Astraea's court is. Moreover, the narrative about the god of war and the goddess of love, occupying as it does only three stanzas, is far shorter than most of the digressions slotted into the other poems in the genre. Hence we can focus almost all of our attention on the behavior of Venus and Adonis themselves.

The three openings we juxtaposed point to another contrast between Shakespeare's Ovidian narrative and those of his contemporaries: *Venus and Adonis* is more dramatic in several senses of that term.[55] One reason Shakespeare's epyllion is so dramatic is that he in effect writes stage directions; where the other authors in the tradition present us with static tableaux, he is less concerned to set the scene for the encounter of Venus and Adonis than to set it in motion. Returning to the opening of the poem and comparing it this time to the beginning of Drayton's *Endimion and Phoebe* clarifies these distinctions:

> Even as the sun with purple-colour'd face
> Had ta'en his last leave of the weeping morn,

---

[55]A few readers have briefly observed that the poem is dramatic but have developed the point in ways different from mine. T. W. Baldwin notes that Shakespeare borrows the dramatic practice of opening in medias res (*On the Literary Genetics of Shakspere's Poems and Sonnets* [Urbana: Univ. of Illinois Press, 1950], p. 113). Also see Huntington Brown, "*Venus and Adonis*: The Action, the Narrator, and the Critics," *Michigan Academician*, 2 (1969), 85; Louis R. Zocca, *Elizabethan Narrative Poetry* (New Brunswick: Rutgers Univ. Press, 1950), p. 253.

Venus and Adonis

Rose-cheek'd Adonis hied him to the chase;
Hunting he lov'd, but love he laugh'd to scorn.
  Sick-thoughted Venus makes amain unto him,
  And like a bold-fac'd suitor 'gins to woo him.

"Thrice fairer than myself," thus she began,
"The field's chief flower, sweet above compare;
     . . . . .
With this she seizeth on his sweating palm,
The precedent of pith and livelihood,
And trembling in her passion, calls it balm,
Earth's sovereign salve to do a goddess good:
  Being so enrag'd, desire doth lend her force
  Courageously to pluck him from his horse.
               (*Venus and Adonis*, 1–8, 25–30)

Drayton, in contrast, opens on a long description of a paradisial grove:

In *I-ONIA* whence sprang old Poets fame,
From whom that Sea did first derive her name,
The blessed bed whereon the Muses lay,
Beauty of *Greece*, the pride of *Asia*,
Whence *Archelaus* whom times historifie,
First unto *Athens* brought Phylosophie.
In this faire Region on a goodly Plaine,
Stretching her bounds unto the bordring Maine,
The Mountaine *Latmus* over-lookes the Sea,
Smiling to see the Ocean billowes play:
     . . . . .
Upon this Mount there stood a stately Grove,
Whose reaching armes, to clip the Welkin strove,
Of tufted Cedars, and the branching Pine,
Whose bushy tops themselves doe so intwine,
As seem'd when Nature first this work begun,
Shee then conspir'd against the piercing Sun;
Under whose covert (thus divinely made)
Phoebus greene Laurell florisht in the shade.
               (1–10, 23–30)

He then proceeds to explain its significance:

[57]

For which fayre *Phoebe* sliding from her Sphere,
Used oft times to come and sport her there.
And from the Azure starry-painted Sky,
Embalmd the bancks with precious lunary:
That now her *Menalus* shee quite forsooke,
And unto *Latmus* wholy her betooke,
And in this place her pleasure us'd to take.

(75–81)

If, as Coleridge asserts, we are conscious of Shakespeare's "endless activity of thought" as we read *Venus and Adonis*,[56] one might add that we are no less conscious of the "endless activity" of the characters themselves. Shakespeare's is a vision of rapid, often chaotic motion. Within these fourteen lines alone, Venus "makes amain" (5) "gins to woo" (6), "seizeth" (25), "trembles" (27), "calls" (28) and "pluck[s]" (30). In contrast, while the banks in Phoebe's stately pleasure-dome are "Embalmd" (78), that adjective might almost be a fit description of the lovers in the poem. Admittedly, we are told that Phoebe is prone to "sport her" (76) on the banks, but phases like "betooke" (80) and "her pleasure us'd to take" (81) obviously do not suggest the liveliness of the several sports in which Shakespeare's characters participate. The intellectual and emotional tension we experience in reading the poem has its analogue in the frenetic movements of the heroine herself.

As the poem progresses we quickly realize that Venus' rapid actions in the opening stanzas are very characteristic of the restless energies of the world she inhabits. When the principal characters are not actually seizing or running from each other, they are engaged in a whole series of gestures; Venus pushes off Adonis' hat and touches his cheek; Adonis, symmetrically, claps her cheek in the mistaken belief that she has fainted. Moreover, while the lesser denizens of other epyllia typically include languorous nymphs and those conventional props of pastoral, flowers and streams, their counterparts in *Venus and Adonis* are the energetically strutting horses and the frantically darting hare. The world of *Venus and Adonis* is Dickensian not only in its emphasis on the revealing gesture but also in the virtually ceaseless motion of which those gestures are but one part.

The nature of the activity that takes place in *Venus and Adonis* further distinguishes this poem from other epyllia. By and large the

[56]Samuel Taylor Coleridge, *Coleridge's Shakespeare Criticism*, ed. Thomas Middleton Raysor, 2 vols. (Cambridge, Mass.: Harvard Univ. Press, 1930), I, 217.

protagonists in Ovidian narratives are immune from such everyday discomforts as perspiring and tripping. The characters in these poems are more likely to break their hearts than to stub their toes. They weep, but they do not sweat. We find exceptions—the earth-shaker, Neptune, for example, is cursed with physical as well as emotional clumsiness in two epyllia[57]—but they are comparatively rare. In contrast, this is but one of several occasions on which Shakespeare's protagonists perspire. The lovers fall down, kisses produce not bliss but breathlessness, and Venus hurts Adonis' hand when she grasps it too tightly. The poem tends to read as if Shakespeare were directing the scenario he evokes or as if he were writing stage directions for it. Prosody, too, builds the impression of a dramatically realized encounter: the strophic divisions of the poem often serve to divide its action into distinct episodes, while a stichic form would have suggested the continuous seam of a narrative.

The characters in *Venus and Adonis* delight in verbal action as well as physical; throughout the poem, dialogue creates the effect of an actual encounter. Admittedly, the direct discourse in this poem, as in other Ovidian narratives, sometimes merely assumes the form of lengthy set speeches. But at a number of points Shakespeare's characters, unlike their counterparts in most other epyllia, participate in a rapid give-and-take that mimes the rhythms of a real conversation:

> "Where did I leave?" "No matter where," quoth he;
> "Leave me, and then the story aptly ends:
> The night is spent." "Why, what of that?" quoth she.
> "I am," quoth he, "expected of my friends,
>   And now 'tis dark, and going I shall fall."
>   "In night," quoth she, "desire sees best of all."
>
> (715–720)

Throughout *Venus and Adonis*, then, the dramatic mode heightens our engagement with the characters. For Shakespeare's poem offers us a very different type of realism from that in other English epyllia—and in so doing demonstrates yet again the complexities of the term "realism." Where the other epyllia resemble a Pre-Raphaelite canvas, *Venus and Adonis* is more reminiscent of a German Expressionist painting. At first glance one would label the Pre-Raphaelite work more realistic; we would, after all, prefer to teach a botany lesson

---

[57]He is struck with his own mace in Marlowe's *Hero and Leander* (II.211) and bumps his head in Chapman's continuation of the poem (VI.197–198).

from Millais' "Ophelia" than from Kirchner's "Mountain Landscape from Clavadel." And yet the very vividness and precision of the Millais painting distance us from it: we do not experience the world in detail that exact, and so the canvas is an odd blend of the familiar and of the improbable landscape associated with a dream. Our encounter with the German Expressionist painting reverses that process: our initial consciousness of its stylization quickly yields to a recognition of the ways in which it accords with our own deepest experiences. It is not surprising that a young playwright should cast his epyllion in a dramatic mode. But his skill in doing so is worthy of remark; it again discredits the assumption that the young poet's infatuation with rhetorical flourishes precluded his involvement with a whole host of other literary interests and techniques.

Shakespeare's approach to another generic potentiality further distinguishes his epyllion from those of his contemporaries—and further complicates his portrayal of its characters. The tragic elements in *Venus and Adonis* are at once more prominent and more discordant than those in other English Ovidian narratives. We do not, of course, know how Marlowe would have handled the unhappy denouement of his tale, but in the case of the other epyllia the sense of waste and loss on which they conclude is often mitigated or sublimated. Hermaphroditus, for example, is transformed into that sinister stream as he has requested, and, similarly, Chapman's Hero and Leander are apotheosized into birds. And a number of epyllia do end happily; Pygmalion, for example, actually realizes his fantasy. But Shakespeare does not soften the blow. The flower that grows from Adonis' blood is hardly much of a consolation, especially since it too dies young, plucked by Venus virtually as soon as it appears.

Our reactions to the tragic elements in *Venus and Adonis* are, however, complicated by the farcical episodes at the beginning of the poem: Venus tucks Adonis under her arm, they stumble all over each other, he reacts frenetically to her feint of a faint.[58] While we do occasionally encounter farcical moments in certain other epyllia, such as Hero's sliding out of bed or Salmacis' falling down, these incidents are too infrequent to establish a tone or expectations about future action, as they do in Shakespeare's narrative. In *Venus and Adonis*, in contrast, the mood of amoral glee engendered by such incidents

---

[58]On the nature of farce see, e.g., Eric Bentley, *The Life of the Drama* (New York: Atheneum, 1964), chap. 7; Jessica Milner Davis, *Farce* (London: Methuen, 1978), esp. chap. 1; J. L. Styan, *Drama, Stage, and Audience* (Cambridge: Cambridge Univ. Press, 1975), esp. pp. 77–80.

clashes with our knowledge of the tragic fate that awaits their protagonists. Shakespeare's experiments with New Comedy may well lie
behind the farcical elements here. Indeed, in his early comedies, as in
Venus and Adonis, discordant generic motifs and emotional tonalities
sometimes conflict with the farce—witness, for example, the ship-
wreck and the threat of death in *The Comedy of Errors*. But for a
generic conflict as violent as the one we experience at the beginning
of *Venus and Adonis* we need to turn not to its author's own canon but
to two plays he might even have seen around the time he was writing
Venus and Adonis, namely *The Jew of Malta* and *Arden of Feversham*.
Both of these works, like *Venus and Adonis*, provoke laughter that is in
part nervous, defensive: our generic expectations tell us that people
do not get hurt in farce, but we have good reason to suspect that those
expectations will be violated here.

However we define the sources and analogues of the curious interplay of genres in *Venus and Adonis*, its relationship to Shakespeare's
portrait of Venus is manifest.[59] The unstaled and infinite variety of
her behavior is expressed though a variety of generic motifs. Having
boasted early in the poem of her ability to change her form, Venus at
least manifests a tendency to change her moods and her behavior.
From projecting an air of authority, she slips into routines straight out
of the vaudeville hall; from boasting of her victories over the god of
war, she becomes a desperate suppliant to death. And the rapid
movements from farce to tragedy in the poem generate rapid changes
in our own responses to Venus, a point to which we will return shortly.

Venus and Adonis also differs from other epyllia in how it incorporates pastoral motifs. Though other Ovidian narratives skirt the ethical questions often associated with pastoral, they do exemplify its
predilection for presenting an idealized natural world from the viewpoint of a sophisticated observer. Indeed, in the interplay between
their lyric descriptions and cynical, epigrammatic observations, we
find an enactment of the pastoral dialogue between country and
court. These poems incorporate, too, the stage props of pastoral—the
catalogued flowers, the nymphs, the purling streams. Shakespeare's

[59]For different but not incompatible interpretations of genre and mode in *Venus and
Adonis*, see Allen, "On *Venus and Adonis*," p. 101; James H. Lake, "Shakespeare's Venus:
An Experiment in Tragedy," *SQ*, 25 (1977), 351–355; Kenneth Muir, "*Venus and
Adonis*: Comedy or Tragedy?" in *Shakespearean Essays*, ed. Alwin Thaler and Norman
Sanders (Knoxville: Univ. of Tennessee Press, 1964); Rufus Putney, "Venus Agonistes,"
Univ. of Colorado Studies—Series in Language and Literature, 4 (1953), 52–66.

epyllion is pastoral in the very loose sense that it takes place in a country landscape, but this is a landscape more precisely observed and less ideally rendered than the one ordinarily associated with pastoral. Where other epyllia create a Golden World, Shakespeare insistently portrays postlapsarian nature, a world in which animals no less than human beings and goddesses fall inevitably into the roles of hunter and hunted. This element is not wholly absent from all other epyllia—the protagonist in Edwards' *Cephalus and Procris*, after all, is killed in a hunt—but it is far less prominent. In short, while not wholly omitting pastoral motifs, Shakespeare signally omits the values and moods those motifs often connote. In so doing he establishes a generic coordinate for the insistent realism of his poem: in particular, his rejection of pastoral idealism reflects his desire to evoke a goddess who perspires and trips.

IV

We have repeatedly touched on one of the sharpest and yet most subtle distinctions between *Venus and Adonis* and other epyllia: the audience's reactions to their respective characters. Recent students of reader response criticism have offered salutary warnings about the difficulties of mapping those reactions; we are not, so to speak, all surprised by sin at the same time or in the same way or to the same extent.[60] In this instance, it is certainly true that the sex of the reader—or, indeed, his or her attitudes to sex—may influence the relevant responses to Shakespeare's characters. But such factors are more likely merely to affect the intensity of our responses to Venus and Adonis than to determine their nature, for, as we will see, on the whole the language of the poem effectively guides our reactions to its protagonists. And its success in doing so emerges clearly if we once again play Shakespeare's Ovidian narrative against those written by his contemporaries.

Despite all the other shifts in tone and attitude that characterize the work of those writers, they only rarely invite us to experience real sympathy for their characters.[61] The poems most closely modeled on

[60]For a useful summary of these and other issues in reader-response criticism, see Jane P. Tompkins, "Introduction," *Reader-Response Criticism: From Formalism to Post-Structuralism* (Baltimore: Johns Hopkins Univ. Press, 1980).

[61]A few critics have argued that we do feel some sympathy for Marlowe's Hero. M. C. Bradbrook maintains that Marlowe's ruthless portrayal of her is laced with some sympathetic identification ("Hero and Leander," *Scrutiny*, 2 [1933], 63). Also see Keach, pp.

complaints, *Scillaes Metamorphosis* and *Oenone and Paris*, are, predictably enough, exceptions, but in a sense they are exceptions that prove the rule: here the appeals for sympathy are so frequently and so clumsily extended that for this reason alone we do not feel very much of it. In any event, in most epyllia we are distanced from the situations by blatant reminders of their fictionality. Above all, however, we sympathize only rarely with the characters in these poem because we are invited instead into a kind of complicity with the superior, even supercilious, narrators. At times this complicity is anchored in a knowing distrust of women.[62] Marlowe establishes the trend, and many of his followers participate in it:

> Still vowd he love, she wanting no excuse
> To feed him with delaies, as women use:
> Or thirsting after immortalitie,
> All women are ambitious naturallie:
> (Marlowe, *Hero and Leander*, I.425–428)

> Tut, women will relent
> When as they finde such mouing blandishment.
> (Marston, *The Metamorphosis of*
> *Pigmalions Image*, 173–174)

> In womens mouths, No is no negative.
> (Weever, *Faunus and Melliflora*, sig.C2)

Nor do the male characters escape the ironic appraisal of the narrator, and in this too the reader participates: the speaker's wry judgments on them, like some of the asides Richard III addresses to the

---

105, 112; Harry Levin, *The Overreacher: A Study of Christopher Marlowe* (Cambridge, Mass.: Harvard Univ. Press, 1952), p. 140. C. S. Lewis, however, finds no tenderness in Marlowe's portrait (p. 26).

[62]Most of the original readers of Elizabethan epyllia were presumably male. The question of how female readers (or, indeed, males unsympathetic to the narrators' attitudes) would react to this invitation to complicity is an intriguing issue, though it lies outside the scope of this study. The most influential study of the cooption of female readers is Judith Fetterley, *The Resisting Reader: A Feminist Approach to American Fiction* (Bloomington: Indiana Univ. Press, 1978). Any application of her ideas to the Ovidian narrative poem would need carefully to distinguish the ways such cooption functions in different cultures and, indeed, in different individuals within the same culture; for instance, how would sixteenth-century ambivalences about moral truisms affect the process in the case at hand?

audience, encourage us to contrast our own knowingness with the inexperience of the blinded characters before us. One thinks above all of the dramatic irony established by Leander's sexual innocence—"he suspected / Some amorous rites or other were neglected" (II.63–64) or, similarly, of Dunstan Gale's "But let her lye alone, / For other pastime *Pyramus* knew none" (*Pyramus and Thisbe*, 51–52).[63]

If these poems do not invite sympathy toward their characters, neither do they encourage reflection on most of the issues those personages might raise. William Keach is quite right that English authors of epyllia adopt Ovid's preoccupation with the darker side of sexuality and in so doing lead us to think about the nature of love,[64] but here too we encounter significant differences among the poems: while Beaumont's *Salmacis and Hermaphroditus*, for instance, is laden with reminders of the price we pay for love, few such ripples disturb the smooth surface of Drayton's *Endimion and Phoebe*. More to the point, even the poems that do explore the complications of sexuality generally skirt other ethical and psychological issues.[65] Their characters are too sketchily drawn to invite moral questions about any aspect of their behavior save their responses to love (one reader aptly terms Marlowe's unheroic Hero "a majolica sheperdess").[66] And, with the exception of the treatment of love, their plots are too far removed from realities (whether they be the realities of everyday experience or the type of emotional and moral realities so evident even in *The Faerie Queene* despite its dark conceits) to generate serious reflection. What we typically encounter in these poems, in short, is Ovide amoralisé.

Wen we read *Venus and Adonis*, in contrast, our responses to the characters seesaw as rapidly as the tenses do.[67] As my analyses have suggested, within a stanza, or even within a line, we may move back

---

[63]The citation from Gale is to *Pyramus and Thisbe* (London, 1617), sig.A4. I am including this work despite its date of publication because Paul W. Miller has argued persuasively for a sixteenth-century date of composition (*Seven Minor Epics*, pp. xix-xx).

[64]See Keach, chap. 1.

[65]Compare Bush, *Mythology and the Renaissance Tradition*, p. 244. Certain critics, however, have argued for the presence of a serious and sustained moral vision in particular epyllia. See, e.g., Eugene B. Cantelupe, "*Hero and Leander*, Marlowe's Tragicomedy of Love," *CE*, 24 (1963), 295–298; John Scott Colley, "'Opinion' and the Reader in John Marston's *The Metamorphosis of Pigmalions Image*," *ELR*, 3 (1973), 221–231.

[66]Levin, p. 141.

[67]For an opposing interpretation, see, e.g., Beauregard. On the literary practice of pulling the reader back and forth between involvement and detachment, see Wolfgang Iser, *The Implied Reader: Patterns of Communication in Prose Fiction from Bunyan to Beckett* (Baltimore: Johns Hopkins Univ. Press, 1974), esp. pp. 111–112, 116.

and forth between sympathetic identification and intense repulsion. Yet we never read on for long without feeling a surge of sympathy: for much of the poem it is a kind of basso continuo against which our other reactions are played. Given how readily both characters would lend themselves to cold caricature—Adonis' sexual innocence, for example, would be a ready target for the knowing narrators in other epyllia—creating and maintaining this sympathy are among the principal achievements of the poem. No less of an achievement, however, is its ability to elicit from us trenchant ethical judgments on the very characters with whom we are sympathizing.

Several sections of the poem aptly exemplify the way we commingle emotional and ethical reactions to the characters. Compare, for example, seemingly similar passages from Shakespeare and Marlowe:

> Look how a bird lies tangled in a net,
> So fasten'd in her arms Adonis lies;
> Pure shame and aw'd resistance made him fret,
> Which bred more beauty in his angry eyes:
>
> (*Venus and Adonis*, 67–70)

> Even as a bird, which in our hands we wring,
> Foorth plungeth, and oft flutters with her wing,
> She trembling strove, this strife of hers (like that
> Which made the world) another world begat,
> Of unknowne joy.
>
> (*Hero and Leander*, II.289–293)

At first glance, it would seem that Marlowe evokes more sympathy in his reader: after all, his bird is being wrung, Shakespeare's merely entrapped. But in fact just the opposite is the case. Marlowe undermines any impression of the bird's suffering: "like that / Which made the world" (291–292) distances us from that bird, and in any event we are quickly reminded that her trembling soon issues in "unknowne joy" (293).[68] Moreover, that "unknowne" once again pits the speaker and worldly reader against the sexually inexperienced Hero. In contrast, we do not stop sympathizing with Adonis: only two stanzas earlier Shakespeare has even more graphically described him as a prey ("Even as an empty eagle, sharp by fast, / Tires with her beak on

---

[68]A number of scholars have analyzed this image from angles different from mine. See, e.g., S. Ann Collins, "Sundrie Shapes, Committing Headdie Ryots, Incest, Rapes: Functions of Myth in Determining Narrative and Tone in Marlowe's *Hero and Leander*," *Mosaic*, 4 (1970), 120.

feathers, flesh and bone" [55–56]), and the image of the bird deepens our sense that he is a hapless victim. Nor, however, are we wholly free of sympathy for the person who is victimizing him: the allusion to his beauty reminds us again that she too is entrapped. And "angry" (70) may perhaps elicit another moment of sympathy for her, demonstrating as it does that all of her attempts to engage his affections are counterproductive.

The passage from *Hero and Leander* does not invite ethical responses: Marlowe's attitude to Hero's sexual excitement exemplifies the amoral naturalism that is so characteristic of his genre. The lines from *Venus and Adonis*, in contrast, evoke a whole series of ethical judgments from the reader. Whereas a generalized "we" (289) wrings the bird's neck in the Marlovian image, in Shakespeare's version Venus creates the destructive net. And whereas our knowledge that she herself was once caught in a net elicits another measure of sympathy for her, it also makes her willingness to trap someone else seem more culpable. Moreover, Adonis' "*aw'd* resistance" (69; italics added) intensifies our negative judgments by reminding us that it is a goddess who is behaving in this all too human way.

Or take the moments in which Marlowe and Shakespeare describe their heroines' grief:

> To *Venus*, answered shee, and as shee spake,
> Foorth from those two tralucent cesternes brake,
> A streame of liquid pearle, which downe her face
> Made milk-white paths, wheron the gods might trace
> To *Joves* high court.
> (Hero and Leander, I.295–299)

> Upon his hurt she looks so steadfastly
> That her sight dazzling makes the wound seem three;
> And then she reprehends her mangling eye,
> That makes more gashes, where no breach should be.
> His face seems twain, each several limb is doubled,
> For oft the eye mistakes, the brain being troubled.
> (Venus and Adonis, 1063–1068)

If the gods might trace a thoroughfare on Hero's tears, they also form a milk-white path that directs the reader's attention away from the person shedding them; it is hard to sympathize with Hero's emotion when the symbol of that emotion is associated not with grief but with fanciful beauty. Shakespeare is not above using the common image of tears as pearls elsewhere in the poem, but when describing the moment of Venus' deepest grief he chooses a very different type of image. Although his figure is more overdrawn in some senses than Marlowe's, including as it does not only the elaborate initial conceit but also the idea of Venus' reprehending her eye, it is also more firmly anchored in actual emotion. Tears, or even a state of intense grief that does not issue in tears, would indeed dazzle the sight in this way, as Shakespeare's final line reminds us.

Once again, however, the sympathy we feel for Shakespeare's character complicates but does not preclude our ethical responses. We feel no such responses when we peruse Marlowe: what she is weeping for is her potential loss of chastity, but both the beauty and the playfulness of the imagery defuse that explosive issue. As we read the lines from *Venus and Adonis*, our wish to condemn Venus is as strong as our desire to console her. Her faulty sight has been an issue throughout the poem, after all; this passage is the culmination of her inability to see Adonis as he really is, though previously that problem was caused by her self-centered desire, while here it is occasioned by her sorrow. The allusion to her "mangling eye" (1065) reminds us that her destructiveness threatened Adonis long before the boar's destructiveness actually killed him.

Far briefer passages, too, evoke the same combination of sympathy and judgment. Again referring to her eye, Shakespeare writes, "Whose beams upon his hairless face are fix'd, / As if from thence they borrow'd all their shine" (487–488). We realize that Adonis does not welcome such an intense gaze, and the adjective "hairless" (487) reminds us just how inappropriate Venus' choice is. We know, too, that she has recently pretended to faint. Yet the intensity of her glance echoes the intensity of her devotion, and we are conscious that behind the hypocrisy of that faint lies genuine emotion. Or take a passage that we have already examined from a different perspective:

> Her song was tedious, and outwore the night,
> For lovers' hours are long, though seeming short.
> If pleas'd themselves, others they think delight
> In such like circumstance, with such like sport.
>   Their copious stories oftentimes begun,
>   End without audience, and are never done.
>
> For who hath she to spend the night withal,
> But idle sounds resembling parasites.
>   (841–848)

The first sixain intensifies the criticisms of Venus that we have been making earlier in the poem: she is self-centered, and she repeats the same actions, whether they are pleading with Adonis or rehearsing her own story, without recognizing their futility. The couplet at the end of the sixain increases our sense of detachment: encouraged to do so by the third-person plural pronoun, we join the speaker in looking at—and looking down at—the boring lovers he evokes. Yet immediately afterward our sympathy surges up again: we are reminded that Venus is condemned to spending the night alone, and spending it alone in an environment that is in some senses unfriendly, populated by parasitical sounds.

The seesawing pattern of responses that we have been charting is, however, superimposed on a broader one: though at any given moment we are likely to experience a volatile admixture of reactions, on the whole our sympathy for Venus increases as the poem progresses. If we read the first twelve stanzas of *Venus and Adonis* in isolation, we might almost be tempted to classify it as a farce or fabliau. Venus grabs her beloved from his horse, tucks him under her arm, and pushes him to the ground. Neither the imperiousness of the grabbing and pushing nor the implausibility of the tucking encourages the reader to identify or sympathize with her. Though we may even experience some disapproval of her actions, we feel pulled toward the detached, amoral laughter of farce.

In contrast, we experience an upsurge of sympathy for her during the interval from the story of Wat to the moment when Venus discovers Adonis' dead body, a shift in our responses that prepares us to identify with her in her grief. Her evocation of Wat demonstrates her most appealing traits. Moreover, while earlier in the poem the narrative had been omniscient, after Adonis' departure the poet switches to Venus' point of view. In his sources, in contrast, the omniscient viewpoint is retained throughout the tragic conclusion to the tale. The effect of Shakespeare's alteration is to bring us closer to his heroine: conscious of what Adonis' fate will be, we identify with her hopes and fears.

Shakespeare's imagery, too, reinforces our growing sympathy for her. Previously depicted as the aggressor, in this section of the poem Venus is typically described as a victim. Running in response to the dogs' cry, she is attacked by the bushes. In the line "As falcons to the lure, away she flies" (1027), she is compared not to a predatory falcon but to one that is itself being mastered ("to the lure" may refer either to a stage in the bird's training or to its responding to its master's call).[69] And this pattern of imagery culminates in the precisely ob-

[69]Prince, p. 56.

served comparison between the distraught Venus and a snail: "Or as the snail, whose tender horns being hit, / Shrinks backward in his shelly cave with pain" (1033–1034). Transforming the hunter into the hunted, Shakespeare is invoking an old cliché of love poetry.[70] But he revivifies and reshapes that cliché as completely and as successfully as Wyatt does in "Whoso list to hunt": by describing two actual hunts, the pursuit of Wat and of the boar, he reminds us of the pain and violence inherent in the metaphor, and by intensifying our sympathy for Venus as the poem progresses, he deepens our compassion for the hunted.

That compassion signals yet another distinction between Shakespeare's mode of characterization and that of most other epyllia, the treatment of women. In some senses Shakespeare intensifies the rejection of Petrarchan idealism that characterizes those Ovidian mythological narratives: if other authors in the genre insistently demonstrate that women feel desire, Shakespeare renders that desire even more comic, less dignified. And he takes the debunking of the ideal and idealizing Petrarchan vision one step further by reminding us that if women lust, they also sweat. Venus would seem to be a ripe target, then, for just the sort of cynical comments that we have observed in other epyllia ("she (as some say, all woemen strictly do,) / Faintly deni'd what she was willing too" [Edwards, *Cephalus and Procris*, 435–436]). Yet asides like these are signally and significantly absent from Shakespeare's poem. The effect of omitting them, as we have already seen, is to confound the reader's responses. We are not encouraged to retreat to the disdainful, superior pose that such generalizations exemplify. Nor are we encouraged to entertain prejudices about female sexuality.

Shakespeare deploys certain recurrent strategies to elicit the reactions we are charting from his audience. Though the speaker's voice is not distinctive enough or developed enough to invite us to see him as a dramatized character, his commingling of sympathy and judgment serves as a model for our own responses.[71] If his metaphoric criticisms of the characters invite us to share his detached appraisals of their behavior, typically he moves rapidly from those criticisms to apostrophes that, like their analogues in the *Metamorphoses*, express real compassion. Thus the imagery of mastery reaches its climax in

---

[70]Geoffrey Bush observes that she begins to behave like the hare (*Shakespeare and the Natural Condition* [Cambridge, Mass.: Harvard Univ. Press, 1956], p. 25).

[71]In contrast, Lanham argues unconvincingly that the speaker is being criticized (pp. 89–90). The moral reverberations of that speaker's similes alone give the lie to this critic's claim that he does not think at all about the issues raised by the story he recounts.

the disturbing portrait of Venus as a rampaging military conqueror: "With blindfold fury she begins to forage; / Her face doth reek and smoke, her blood doth boil" (554–555). Shortly afterward, however, the speaker treats her efforts at seduction very differently: "But all in vain; good queen, it will not be" (607). At times, too, the speaker blends dispassionate rebuke and compassionate regret in the same phrase. Surely one reason he describes Adonis as a "silly boy" (467) is that that adjective carried with it denotations as diverse as "deserving of pity," "helpless," "weak," "unlearned, unsophisticated," and "evincing or associated with foolishness"[72]—all of which can aptly describe Adonis' actions.

Defamiliarization is another strategy through which Shakespeare evokes emotional and ethical reactions from us. One consequence of reversing the usual sex roles of pursuer and pursued is to force readers to see their own behavior from new perspectives. Though partly identifying with Venus since she assumes the typically masculine role of hunter, male readers are nonetheless distanced from her because she is actually female, a distance that aids in judging what is exploitative about her behavior. Similarly, these same readers are likely to identify with the male character in the poem enough to share the pain and entrapment of the pursued—and hence to acknowledge some of the possible effects of their own pursuits. For women readers, of course, the process is reversed, with similar results.

The primary effect of many of Shakespeare's poetic techniques, however, is to modulate our compassion with more detached evaluations of his characters' failings. In the deer park episode that I analyzed at the beginning of this chapter, we witnessed an instance of one method by which a type of distancing is effected: Venus repeatedly uses words of whose destructive or threatening connotations she, unlike the reader, is unaware, and the distinction between her limited viewpoint and our own reminds us how blinded and blinding her love for Adonis is. Thus her fond "I'll smother thee with kisses" (18) signals the fact that she does not realize how smothering her love really is. In the next stanza she declares, "A summer's day will seem an hour but short, / Being wasted in such time-beguiling sport" (23–24). Though, as one of Shakespeare's editors points out, "wasted" (24) could be employed with no derogatory associations,[73] surely those associations are very much to the point: the contrast between the neutral sense in which Venus is using the term and the negative

[72]*Oxford English Dictionary*, s.v. "silly."
[73]Prince, p. 4.

connotations of which the reader is at least aware is one measure of our distance from her. Similarly, when she describes herself as "light" (150, 155), Shakespeare's readers cannot forget that the term had connotations of sexual promiscuity in Elizabethan England; hence it supports an interpretation of Venus' wooing of which we remain cognizant even if we do not wholly subscribe to it. (One might add, too, that Venus' internal audience would be as attuned to these negative associations as the external audience: the fact that she does not realize that words like "wasted" and "light" in effect provide Adonis with ammunition against her once again demonstrates her inability to acknowledge that his perspective is radically different from her own.)

Indirect discourse is another closely related strategy through which Shakespeare encourages us to pass judgment on the goddess of love.[74] Much as Mr. Collins' phrase "his amiable Charlotte" seems especially ludicrous when delivered by Jane Austen's narrator, so Venus' hyperboles seem all the more absurd reported by Shakespeare's speaker: the fact that he would never use such phrases draws our attention to what is distinctive—and destructive—about Venus' own voice:

> Look how he can, she cannot choose but love;
> And by her fair immortal hand she swears,
> From his soft bosom never to remove
> Till he take truce with her contending tears,
>   Which long have rain'd, making her cheeks all wet:
>   *And one sweet kiss shall pay this comptless debt.*
>   (80–85; italics added)

Similarly, later in the poem indirect discourse highlights the gap between Venus' hope that Adonis is alive and the knowledge of his fate shared by the narrator and reader: "Now she unweaves the web that she hath wrought: / Adonis lives, and death is not to blame" (991–992). The fact that the speaker would not himself voice the hope that he is reporting reminds us of Venus's propensity to deceive herself. Trapped by a net during her liaison with Mars, she is here trapped by her attempt to unweave one.

Elsewhere in the poem indirect discourse complicates our responses even more:

[74]For a linguistic analysis of indirect discourse, see Janet Holmgren McKay, "Some Problems in the Analysis of Point of View in Reported Discourse," *Centrum*, 6 (1978), 5–26.

Till breathless he disjoin'd, and backward drew
The heavenly moisture, that sweet coral mouth,
Whose precious taste her thirsty lips well knew,
Whereon they surfeit, yet complain on drouth.
    He with her plenty press'd, she faint with dearth,
    Their lips together glued, fall to the earth.

                                        (541–546)

Even if we do not recall the revealing line, "And calls it heavenly moisture" (64), we recognize that this hyperbolic description of human breath is more characteristic of the goddess of love than of the narrator. Once again we are aware that Venus is behaving more like a Peter De Vries character than a superhuman luminary. Our responses to "sweet" (542) and "precious" (543) are, however, more divided because these adjectives are a little less extreme. On the one hand, we recognize that such terms, like "heavenly moisture" (542), indubitably reflect Venus' histrionic perspective. On the other hand, we may speculate that his mouth would indeed be "sweet" (542), his kisses indeed "precious" (543) even from a more objective viewpoint, a recognition that makes us better able to understand her passion. Then the poem once more jolts us: the comically ignominious concluding line reminds us yet again of what is farcical about these lovers' behavior. The purveyor and the admirer of that "heavenly moisture" (542) are quite literally brought down to earth, and we are again keenly conscious of the ironies in the phrase.

When reading *Venus and Adonis*, then, we are neither permitted to rest content with a wholly dispassionate judgment on the characters nor, conversely, allowed to indulge in a sympathy that is not tinged with some admixture of moral judgment. At various points in our experience of the poem, however, we may temporarily yield to the temptation to oversimplify our responses: we may grasp at neat categorizations that conveniently filter out some of the complexities of the poem. That temptation is the affective analogue to one of the work's major preoccupations, the way the imagination variously shapes, reshapes, and misshapes events.

For *Venus and Adonis* complicates our reactions to its protagonists in another way as well: our behavior mimes theirs. At several key points in the poem, we make perceptual and conceptual mistakes very like those we have traced in Venus' or Adonis' own behavior. Hence the poem is dramatic in yet another sense of that word: the central intellectual and moral issues it raises are not presented through sententious asides but rather acted out by both characters and readers. This process further confounds our responses to Venus and Adonis: if we are prone to sympathize with manifestations of our own failings, we also, of course, tend to reject in others what we fear to find in ourselves.

First of all, *Venus and Adonis* anatomizes distortions in perception, charting their sources as well as their results. Shakespeare's epyllion resembles *A Midsummer Night's Dream* not only in its Ovidian genealogy but also in its concern for the workings of the imagination—though in this poem a bush is more easily supposed an insubstantial cloud than a bear. One source—and one symptom—of these faulty perceptions is the tendency to impose easy generalizations, particularly moral axioms, on the complexities of human behavior.[75] Though that tendency is by no means wholly rejected, its dangers are exposed throughout. Adonis' aphorisms are an explicit manifestation of it within the world of the poem. And Ovide moralisé is implicitly invoked as another instance of the habit; as we read we contrast the ethical complexities of the poem with the allegorical summaries of them that Ovid's commentators have provided.

But above all it is in the reader's own experience that the tendency in question is enacted. One effect of stressing the less attractive sides of Venus' behavior at certain points in the poem is to tempt us to arrive at simple judgments on her behavior—judgments that are then immediately undermined. We learn we must move from those monolithic evaluations to a complex interplay between acceptance and disapproval, sympathy and cynicism—and in so doing we ourselves exemplify one of the values implicit in *Venus and Adonis*, the need to temper generalizations with an awareness of the individual situation and the individual actor within it.

It would be virtually impossible to compose a poem about Venus and Adonis in the 1590s without invoking the familiar Neo-Platonic interpretations of that story.[76] But the main function of Neo-Platonism in this poem, I would suggest, is affective: it represents a reading that tempts us into oversimplifications not unlike Adonis'. The poem is less a study of Neo-Platonism than of the tendencies that attract us

[75]Compare Barry Pegg's suggestion that the poem travesties the medieval morality tradition ("Generation and Corruption in Shakespeare's *Venus and Adonis*," *Michigan Academician*, 8 [1975], 114).

[76]For the argument that *Venus and Adonis* should be read Platonically see, e.g., Asals; Baldwin, chap. 2. For an interpretation of the Platonic elements similar to my own, see Eugene B. Cantelupe, "An Iconographical Interpretation of *Venus and Adonis*, Shakespeare's Ovidian Comedy," *Shakespeare Quarterly*, 14 (1963), 141–151; Keach, pp. 59–60.

to it. On one level, of course, Platonic readings of the plot do work well: Venus is Love, Adonis is in some sense Beauty, and the poem charts their relationship. But when we attempt to apply the Platonic paradigms more closely, they are undercut or even, as a few readers have claimed, parodied by the action of the poem. If the attraction of Love to Beauty is in some sense as natural as sexuality itself, in another sense it is ludicrous, unfortunate in its immediate consequences and tragic in its conclusion. Nor can we find in the poem any evidence that Love is climbing the Platonic ladder, as one critic has asserted.[77] When we read of Venus' final ascent to heaven ("Thus weary of the world, away she hies, / And yokes her silver doves" [1189–1190]), we are aware of the goddess' very human desire to escape a painful situation, a desire that is at once understandable and suspect. This interpretation of the incident makes it hard to cram it into the mold of the obvious Platonic interpretation: the apotheotic final spiritualization of love.

Similarly, the reader, like Venus herself, is tempted into another form of oversimplification by the horses, the most prominent members of the veritable zoo evoked in this poem. These animals serve one function that critics have neglected: they offer us another perspective on mastery. Ironically, passion literally liberates them—the stallion breaks out of his chains when he sees the mare—whereas it entraps human lovers. More to our purposes here, however, the horses evidently provide an analogy to Adonis' reluctance about sex[78]—but an analogy that we are prone to misinterpret. Our initial impression when we read the incident may well be that Shakespeare is in fact invoking them in the service of a naturalistic moral: their frank and energetic sexuality—"Imperiously he leaps, he neighs, he bounds" (265)—makes Adonis' refusal seem ludicrous. And this is, of course, the very moral that Venus herself adduces:

> Let me excuse thy courser, gentle boy,
> And learn of him, I heartily beseech thee,

[77]Asals. In particular, she argues unconvincingly that Venus' final ascent to heaven reflects her new unearthly nature (p. 49).

[78]Critics have disagreed sharply on whether or not the horses represent a paradigm for the human lovers. On their Platonic significance as unbridled desire, see Allen, "On *Venus and Adonis*," pp. 107–108 (this article also suggests that the animals serve to satirize courtly love [106]); Ian Donaldson, "Adonis and His Horse," *NQ*, 19 (1972), 123–125. The studies arguing that the horses function as a critique of Adonis include Robert P. Miller, "Venus, Adonis, and the Horses," *ELH*, 19 (1952), 249–264. Keach, pp. 64–65, agrees with my contention that the distinctions between the horses and the title characters are significant.

To take advantage on presented joy;
Though I were dumb, yet his proceedings teach thee.
(403–406)

But the episode effectively undermines this interpretation. For one thing, the horses do not in fact love frankly and freely: they indulge in some of the same flirtatious pretenses that we associate with human lovers:

Being proud, as females are, to see him woo her,
She puts on outward strangeness, seems unkind,
Spurns at his love, and scorns the heat he feels,
Beating his kind embracements with her heels.
(309–312)

More to the point, though, just when we are making the obvious comparisons between the human and the equine lovers, we are confronted with Shakespeare's blazon:

Round-hoof'd, short-jointed, fetlocks shag and long,
Broad breast, full eye, small head, and nostril wide,
High crest, short ears, straight legs and passing strong,
Thin mane, thick tail, broad buttock, tender hide.
(295–298)

Similarly, a little later we read:

He vails his tail like a falling plume
Cool shadow to his melting buttock lent;
He stamps, and bites the poor flies in his fume.
(314–316)

Such lines affect us in just the way Chaucer's splendid blazon on Chaunticleer does: we are abruptly reminded of how much roosters and horses differ from our own species at the very point when we are most engaged with the similarities. Whereas in *The Nun's Priest's Tale* that reminder accentuates the pretensions of the cock, here it draws attention to our own failure in crafting too precise a comparison between the two sets of lovers. We learn, in other words, that we have reacted to the horses and to the Neo-Platonic interpretations of the incident in much the same way; we have been tempted to make a

[75]

comparison that does not completely work, to reshape and misshape our reading of the poem to force it to fit into a neat interpretation. Misprision is, after all, a type of misreading, and like the characters themselves we may at times be guilty of it. Shakespeare is not, of course, suggesting that comparisons are inherently fallacious; his speaker's trenchantly observed similes themselves exemplify the potential virtues of this rhetorical and logical technique. But the poem does warn us against comparisons that are too precise or too facile, ones that, like Venus' own metonymic temperament, neglect or subvert distinctions in identity.

Though Shakespeare's commentary on this issue speaks to a general tendency in human nature, it also has more local applications. Comparison and contrast were well-established topoi. As Quintilian puts it, "I consider, however, that there are four principal methods of *amplification: augmentation, comparison, reasoning* and *accumulation* . . . the form which depends on comparison seeks to rise from the less to the greater, since by raising what is below it must necessarily exalt that which is above" (*Institutio Oratoria*, VIII.iv.3,9).[79] Similarly, classical and Renaissance rhetoricians enumerate in detail the advantages of sententiae: "the hearers . . . are pleased if an orator . . . hits upon the opinions which they specifically hold. . . . This is but one of the advantages of the use of maxims, but another is greater; for it makes speeches ethical" (Aristotle, *Rhetoric*, II.xxi.15–16).[80] In other words, if the young poet is polishing and displaying the tools of his trade in this early poem, he is at the same time examining them with a critical eye. We observed this, too, when noting Venus' use—and misuse—of the pathetic fallacy. In both instances, Shakespeare in effect warns us against our tendency to divorce the rhetorical from the mimetic: he himself characteristically embeds literary problems in human psyches, translating aesthetic issues into psychological ones.

V

The best way to summarize what we have been observing about the interplay between formal decisions and psychological complexities in *Venus and Adonis* is to return to the *Metamorphoses* itself. Many critics

[79]I quote Quintilian from *The Institutio Oratoria*, trans. H. E. Butler, 4 vols. (London and New York: Heinemann and G. P. Putnam, 1921–1922).

[80]The citation from Aristotle is to *The "Art" of Rhetoric*, trans. John Henry Freese (Cambridge, Mass.: Harvard Univ. Press, 1926).

have stressed the distinctions between Shakespeare's poem and Ovid's, but in fact it is their affinity that is most striking.[81] For Shakespeare shares his predecessor's interest in a whole range of psychological problems and predilections and shares, too, the acuity with which Ovid anatomizes those issues. It is one measure of the achievement of *Venus and Adonis* that its author compresses so many of those concerns in Venus' own sensibility—and in so doing creates so complex and so credible a character.

In the *Metamorphoses* Shakespeare found a preoccupation with the uses and abuses of language that accorded to—and no doubt helped to develop—the concerns in his own temperament that shape his portraits of Venus and Adonis.[82] Ovid too is intrigued by the power of language. The dangers of slander and gossip haunt many of his characters (Diana turns Actaeon into a stag not as a punishment for having seen her but as a precaution against his reporting that he has done so). The loss of speech reflects the loss of other powers (the fact that Io, attempting to respond to her fate, can only moo is at once one of the most comic and one of the most poignant moments in the *Metamorphoses*. And Ovid too recognizes that language may be no less dangerous a weapon for the teller than for the hearer; carried away with their own stories, the daughters of Minyas fail to see how those narratives in fact prefigure their sorry fate. In short, that supreme storyteller Ovid is so reflexive that if he did not exist, contemporary critics would surely have invented him;[83] this self-consciousness itself must have appealed to a young poet like Shakespeare, who, as *Love's Labour's Lost* among other plays testifies, was very engaged in thinking about his own art at this point in his career.

---

[81]In contrast, W. B. C. Watkins maintains throughout chapter 1 of *Shakespeare and Spenser* (Princeton: Princeton Univ. Press, 1950) that one reason the poem fails is that Shakespeare was temperamentally too different from Ovid; he argues that Marlowe had a far deeper affinity for the author of the *Metamorphoses*. I would contend that both Shakespeare and Marlowe were temperamentally close to Ovid but close to different aspects of him; Marlowe may have been drawn to him by his wry cynicism, while, as I have suggested, Shakespeare was particularly attracted by Ovid's interest in language. Donald G. Watson notes that Shakespeare closely resembles Ovid in his vision of the animal world and of Venus' "manhandling of Adonis" but does not develop the comparison from other angles ("The Contrarieties of *Venus and Adonis*," *SP*, 75 [1978], 56).

[82]Many scholars have analyzed Ovid's attitudes to language. See, e.g., Robert M. Durling, *The Figure of the Poet in Renaissance Epic* (Cambridge, Mass.: Harvard Univ. Press, 1965), esp. p. 40; B. R. Fredericks, "Divine Lust vs. Divine Folly: Mercury and Apollo in *Metamorphoses* 1–2," *CJ*, 72 (1977), 244–249.

[83]On Ovid's reflexiveness, cf. Charles Altieri, "Ovid and the New Mythologists," *Novel*, 7 (1973), 31–40.

Another affinity between Shakespeare and Ovid lies in their treatment of love. For Ovid is far more concerned with power and control
than any of his English imitators save the author of *Venus and Adonis*.
The *Metamorphoses* repeatedly returns to a paradox that also concerns
Shakespeare in his epyllion: the member of a couple who loves more
deeply than the other has less power, however much of it he or she
may be able to exercise in other spheres. It is not surprising that the
Metamorphoses, like *Venus and Adonis*, is crammed with images of birds
of prey. This is not to say that Ovid's figures are necessarily Shakespeare's source: most of the images in question are commonplaces
that it would be impossible to trace back to a single work. Rather, the
recurrence of these tropes reflects the preoccupation with power that
led both poets to choose them.

Shakespeare's portrait of Venus testifies that he also shared Ovid's
fascination with deception, especially self-deception.[84] In Book II of
the *Metamorphoses*, for example, we encounter a crow who recounts
stories about the dangers of gossip even as he himself starts to indulge
in it. Likewise, Venus repeatedly fails to perceive the actual implications and consequences of her own actions. These instances of self-
deception exemplify a broader issue that also concerns both Ovid and
Shakespeare: the ways the mind reshapes experiences and perceptions.

Many of the distinctions that we have noted between Shakespeare's
epyllion and those of other Renaissance writers, then, reflect the fact
that he was reading Ovid from different angles and to different ends:
he was far more involved both in exploring certain psychological
subtleties and in bodying them forth dramatically. For him the
epyllion is above all a vehicle for studying human behavior.

Understanding Shakespeare's approach to that genre helps us to
resolve the problem on which we began: why the deer park passage,
Venus' extraordinary persuasion poem, is so distinctive. For Shakespeare the Ovidian mythological narrative represents not an escape
from most moral complexities but rather an avenue toward exploring
them; hence he packs ethical problems even—or especially—into the
goddess of love's sensuous evocation of the grazing deer. Indeed,
much as the types of moral concerns he brings to comedy during a
later period in his career generate the subgenre of problem comedy,
so here in some senses he may be said to be writing a problem

---

[84]Compare John M. Fyler's suggestion that Ovid, "the Freud of the Middle Ages," is
especially concerned with the instability of the lover's mind (*Chaucer and Ovid* [New
Haven: Yale Univ. Press, 1979], p. 1).

epyllion: like the problem comedies, this work studies ethical issues that trouble the reader because they do not admit of clear solutions, and, again like those comedies, it calls many of the assumptions of its own genre into question.[85] And for Shakespeare the epyllion provides a structure for investigating not only love but also a wide range of other emotional states and psychological proclivities; hence he is concerned to offer us an intimate view of his heroine's patterns of thought at the moment when she herself is evoking the deer park in the hope of achieving a different type of intimacy.

The author of *Venus and Adonis* is, as we have seen, particularly interested in one aspect of psychology that is manifest in Venus' description of that park: the way the persuasive rhetoric of lovers leads them to deceive others as well as themselves. Yet we find in her words another range of qualities, qualities that counterbalance the troubling ethical and psychological dimensions of the lines. A vitality, a joie de vivre, a delighted and delightful comic voice are also wholly characteristic of Venus, of the passage in question, and of the poem as a whole.

[85]On the characteristics of Shakespeare's problem plays, see esp. William Witherle Lawrence, *Shakespeare's Problem Comedies* (New York: Macmillan, 1931), chap. 1; Ernest Schanzer, *The Problem Plays of Shakespeare: A Study of "Julius Caesar," "Measure for Measure," "Antony and Cleopatra"* (London: Routledge and Kegan Paul, 1963), pp. 1–9; E. M. W. Tillyard, *Shakespeare's Problem Plays* (London: Chatto and Windus, 1950), pp. 1–11.

[2]

"Full of forged lies":

The Rape of Lucrece

Our fathers . . . fenced their gardens
with the Redman's bones.
                              Robert Lowell

I

The discords of syneciosis, observes the Elizabethan rhetorician
John Hoskyns, express "a strange harmony."[1] Defined by Hoskyns'
contemporary Angel Day as "when one contrary is attributed to another, or when two diverse things are in one put together,"[2] the figure
may assume several different forms. In one of its most familiar manifestations, the oxymoron, syneciosis typically produces its strange
harmony by linking together an adjective and noun of opposing
meanings. But the label also applies to a statement that uncovers
similarities in two seemingly dissimilar things; thus Day cites "Pleasure it selfe is sometimes a labour, and labour also is often a pleasure"
as an instance of the trope.

Students of Renaissance rhetoric themselves more often generate
disagreements than harmonies, strange or otherwise, and their observations on syneciosis are no exception: though some classify it as a
form of antithesis, many others distinguish those two figures, pointing out that antithesis merely opposes its terms, while syneciosis also

[1]John Hoskyns, *The Life, Letters, and Writings of John Hoskyns 1566–1638*, ed. Louise
Brown Osborn (New Haven and London: Yale Univ. Press and Humphrey Milford,
1937), p. 150.
[2]Angel Daye, *The English Secretorie* (London, 1595), p. 95.

conjoins them.[3] However one resolves that problem of categorization, it is telling that while some readers have noted that *The Rape of Lucrece*, like many of its author's early works, abounds in antitheses, they have been prone to ignore how often the contrasts in the poem in fact assume the form of syneciosis.[4] First of all, *The Rape of Lucrece* contains enough oxymora to satisfy even a sonneteer—"niggard prodigal" (79), "naked armour" (188), "living death" (726), and so on. Certain of these tropes employ the privative suffix "-less," as in "helpless help" (1056) and "lifeless life" (1374); the presence of such privatives is especially striking when one realizes that, for all the oxymora in *Venus and Adonis*, none involves this "x-less x" formula. The line on which I have based the title of this book, "A captive victor that hath lost in gain" (730) unites contraries not only in the initial phrase but also in the one that succeeds it: losing can be gaining and gaining losing, the line informs us, much as pleasure may be a labor and vice versa in the example Day adduces. Elsewhere in the poem, too, we encounter a number of figures that link together opposites in much the same way syneciosis does, even though they would not be classified as such. Thus in the pun "for his prey to pray" (342) semantic conflict between praying and preying is set against the homophonic similarity.

As my examples of the figure would suggest, syneciosis describes—and evokes—tension. To be sure, in *The Arte of English Poesie* Puttenham claims that the trope "takes me [*sic*] two contrary words, and tieth them as it were in a paire of couples, and so makes them agree like good fellowes, as I saw once in Fraunce a wolfe coupled with a mastiffe, and a foxe with a hounde."[5] But the figure he terms the "crosse copling" in fact often produces unions that at best seem in urgent need of a marriage counselor: a phrase like "A captive victor that hath lost in gain" (730) not only describes Tarquin's emotional

[3]See, e.g., Hoskyns, pp. 150–151.

[4]After completing this book I heard the paper Joel Fineman delivered at the 1984 Modern Language Association convention, "The Temporality of Rape"; he too notes the presence of syneciosis in the poem but interprets it very differently, relating it primarily to the nature of sexuality. On antithesis in Shakespeare, see, e.g., Rosalie L. Colie, *Paradoxia Epidemica: The Renaissance Tradition of Paradox* (Princeton: Princeton Univ. Press, 1966); Robert Grudin, *Mighty Opposites: Shakespeare and Renaissance Contrariety* (Berkeley: Univ. of California Press, 1979), esp. chap. 1; Rabkin, *Shakespeare and the Common Understanding*, esp. chap. 1. These studies, however, focus primarily on the plays. One of the best summaries of the rhetorical theories behind antithesis is Sister Miriam Joseph, C.S.C., *Shakespeare's Use of the Arts of Language* (New York: Columbia Univ. Press, 1947), esp. pp. 322–325.

[5]Page 206.

conflicts but also embodies its own unresolved tensions between subject and modifier, between the past participle "lost" and the prepositional phrase that immediately follows it.

Such disharmonies are heightened in the intriguing type of syneciosis to which I referred earlier: phrases like "lifeless life" (1374), in which opposites have the same etymology.[6] Here, as in other oxymora, we experience a conflict between the expectation of congruity that the syntax creates (adjectives normally do not contradict their nouns) and the incongruity that we in fact encounter. But one need only juxtapose the seemingly synonymous phrase "dying life" to recognize that the effect of Shakespeare's trope is far more intense than that of other oxymora. For in this figure that expectation of congruity is based not only on the customary relationship between subject and modifier but also on the visual and etymological similarities between "lifeless" and "life." Alerted to *discordia concors* in this way, we may even respond to a further instance of it that otherwise we would not notice: the word "lifeless" is a microcosm of the tensions we have noticed in the whole phrase, offering "life" in its prefix and taking it away with its suffix.[7]

The internal tensions in a trope like "lifeless life" (1374) aptly and obviously correspond to the internal tensions in Tarquin, who precedes the rape with enough vacillations to qualify him for a leading role in a Senecan tragedy. But the relationship of syneciosis to *The Rape of Lucrece* is both deeper and broader than a study of Tarquin alone would suggest. Instances of the figure establish a kind of rivalry between their contrary terms—a linguistic analogue to the competitiveness that, as we shall see, is the primary characteristic of the world Shakespeare evokes. Moreover, the poem repeatedly describes ambiguous intermediate states, such as the sensation of being both dead and alive or the dilemma of being at once chaste and unchaste, and these examples of "strange harmony" are mirrored by syneciosis itself. And oppositions break down in other ways as well. For example, Tarquin invades not only Lucrece's body but also her very being, so that, for all the contrasts between them, we see her becoming very like him.

[6]On Shakespeare's attraction to privative prefixes and suffixes like "un-" and "-less," see Alfred Hart, *Shakespeare and the Homilies and Other Pieces of Research into the Elizabethan Drama* (1934; rpt. New York: Octagon Books, 1970), pp. 229, 253–254. Also see contemporary linguistic studies of types of antonymy, such as F. R. Palmer, *Semantics: A New Outline* (Cambridge: Cambridge Univ. Press, 1976), pp. 78–85.

[7]Compare Robert Grudin's suggestion that words employing privatives are "inwardly opposed" (p. 3).

As the affinity of Lucrece and Tarquin would suggest, *The Rape of Lucrece* is very concerned with problems of identity.[8] Throughout the poem, we discover that people, concepts, and emotions that at first seemed simple are in fact polysemous and polymorphous. Names do not necessarily correspond to what they are identifying; the work opens on a confidently ascribed appellation ("Lucius Tarquinius [for his excessive pride surnamed Superbus]") but closes on the revelation that Brutus is not, as his name informs us, foolish. And people turn in on and against themselves—"Myself thy friend will kill myself thy foe" (1196). Implying as it does a threat to identity, a loss of integrity (can one be at once alive and dead? a captive and a victor?), syneciosis is an apt symbol for the dilemmas in the poem.

In a broader sense, too, the figure mirrors the aesthetic techniques of the work. In *The Rape of Lucrece*, as in *Venus and Adonis*, Shakespeare very frequently draws attention to his characters' limitations by combining within the same phrase two disparate meanings, of which they only understand one. Thus Tarquin uses the observation, "All orators are dumb when beauty pleadeth" (268) as a rationalization for rape—but we realize that he is raping logic as well, for if we read "beauty" as a personification of Lucrece, she would evidently plead against, not for, the crime.

Shakespeare's use of syneciosis exemplifies, then, the sophisticated approach to wordplay that we encountered in *Venus and Adonis* as well. This is not to say that the poem is invariably successful in its rhetoric. As I acknowledged in the introductory chapter, Homer, especially the young Homer, does indeed nod; even the most sympathetic of readers might not feel enthusiastic about lines like "A pretty while these pretty creatures stand" (1233). In general, however, the tropes in the poem are more graceful—and more germane to their context. The editor who declares, "Shakespeare's skill of expression is self-defeating"[9] neglects the fact that the central issues in the poem are examined by means of—not in spite of—its rhetorical figures. And even a reader more sympathetic to Shakespeare's rhetoric may misstate its functions: "Shakespeare in *Lucrece* with . . . little more than the same 'literary' impulse to tell the story, makes inimitable poetic adornment justify his work. It is a justification through vir-

---

[8]Compare Robert N. Watson's discussion of the internal divisiveness that threatens Coriolanus' identity (*Shakespeare and the Hazards of Ambition* [Cambridge, Mass.: Harvard Univ. Press, 1984], chap. 3). I am grateful to the author for making his manuscript available to me prior to publication.

[9]Prince, p. xxxiv.

tuosity."[10] In fact, the poem is characterized (and, one suspects, inspired) less by a pleasure in poetic adornment per se than by a preoccupation with the moral and psychological issues expressed through—or even raised by—such adornment.

II

Syneciosis aptly expresses the tensions in the Roman culture that Shakespeare is evoking. The central values of that culture clash with each other; and its inhabitants are in conflict not only with each other but also with themselves.[11] Drawing attention to the phrase by using it twice within a few lines, the Argument informs us that the Romans banished Tarquin "with one consent." But the words are ironic, for as we read the ensuing poem we soon realize that theirs is a society of discordant and distrustful voices, a community with little communication.

The most characteristic quality of this milieu is competitiveness.[12] An instance of what Harry Levin has termed the overplot, the war between Rome and Ardea demonstrates competition in the political and military arenas. And it is competition with Collatine that motivates the rape—a point that Shakespeare emphasizes by making a major though neglected change in his sources.[13]

We know that he consulted Livy's *Historia* I.57–59 and Ovid's *Fasti* II.685–852, in all probability relying on a standard edition annotated by the fifteenth-century editor Paulus Marsus. It is also possible that he was familiar with the version of Livy in Painter's *Palace of Pleasure* and with the tribute to Lucrece in that work of secular hagiography,

[10]Willard Farnham, *The Medieval Heritage of Elizabethan Tragedy* (1936; rpt. Oxford: Basil Blackwell, 1956), p. 324.

[11]Compare T. J. B. Spencer's different but related point that Elizabethans saw quarrels and violence as very typical of Rome ("Shakespeare and the Elizabethan Romans," *Shakespeare Survey*, 10 [1957], 31–33).

[12]Other critics have noted the presence of competitiveness in the poem, though they have generally confined their observations to the competition between Collatine and Tarquin and have analyzed that relationship differently from the way I do (e.g., see Catherine R. Stimpson, "Shakespeare and the Soil of Rape," in *The Woman's Part: Feminist Criticism of Shakespeare*, ed. Carolyn Ruth Swift Lenz, Gayle Greene, and Carol Thomas Neely [Urbana: Univ. of Illinois Press, 1980], p. 58).

[13]On Shakespeare's sources, see Baldwin, *On the Literary Genetics of Shakspere's Poems*, chaps. 4 and 5; Geoffrey Bullough, *Narrative and Dramatic Sources of Shakespeare*, 8 vols. (New York and London: Columbia Univ. Press and Routledge and Kegan Paul, 1957–1975), I, 179–183.

The Legend of Good Women. In any event, Livy's narrative of the episode preceding the rape resembles the accounts we find in the other
retellings of the story as well:

> It chanced, as they were drinking in the quarters of Sextus Tar
> quinius . . . that the subject of wives came up. Every man fell to praising
> his own wife with enthusiasm, and, as their rivalry grew hot, Collatinus
> said that there was no need to talk about it, for it was in their power to
> know, in a few hours' time, how far the rest were excelled by his own
> Lucretia. . . . Arriving there at early dusk, they thence proceeded to
> Collatia, where Lucretia was discovered very differently employed from
> the daughters-in-law of the king. . . . It was there that Sextus Tarquinius
> was seized with a wicked desire to debauch Lucretia by force.[14]

The Argument of *The Rape of Lucrece* follows this narrative quite
closely.[15] Yet the text of the poem nowhere refers to the surprise visit
that resolves the rivalry among the men and inflames Tarquin's passion. The relevant stanzas demand to be quoted in full, for what they
do not say is quite as revealing as what they do:

> For he the night before, in Tarquin's tent
> Unlock'd the treasure of his happy state:
> What priceless wealth the heavens had him lent,
> In the possession of his beauteous mate;
> Reck'ning his fortune at such high proud rate
>   That kings might be espoused to more fame,
>   But king nor peer to such a peerless dame.
>
>   . . . . .
>
> Beauty itself doth of itself persuade
> The eyes of men without an orator;
> What needeth then apologies be made,
> To set forth that which is so singular?
> Or why is Collatine the publisher
>   Of that rich jewel he should keep unknown
>   From thievish ears, because it is his own?

[14]*Livy*, trans. B. O. Foster et al., 14 vols. (1919; rpt. London and Cambridge, Mass.:
Heinemann and Harvard Univ. Press, 1939–1959), I, i.57.6–11.
[15]On the authorship of the Argument, see Rollins, *Poems*, p. 117, and James M.
Tolbert, "The Argument of Shakespeare's *Lucrece*: Its Sources and Authorship," *Studies
in English*, 29 (1950), 77–90. Most recent critics have disagreed with Professor Tolbert's
contention that it is not in fact authorial.

Perchance his boast of Lucrece' sov'reignty
Suggested this proud issue of a king;
For by our ears our hearts oft tainted be.
Perchance that envy of so rich a thing,
Braving compare, disdainfully did sting
    His high-pitch'd thoughts, that meaner men should vaunt
    That golden hap which their superiors want.

But some untimely thought did instigate
His all-too-timeless speed, if none of those;
His honour, his affairs, his friends, his state,
Neglected all, with swift intent he goes
To quench the coal which in his liver glows.
    O rash false heat, wrapp'd in repentant cold,
    Thy hasty spring still blasts and ne'er grows old!

(15–21, 29–49)

Most readers have maintained that Shakespeare assumes and implies the earlier visit in which seeing Lucrece excites Tarquin's desire, even though the text nowhere refers to it.[16] But this is unlikely. It is hard to imagine why he would devote so much attention to the boast itself and none to the visit if indeed he wished us to believe that in this version, as in the Argument, the episode did in fact take place.

Though the speaker falls short of assigning a definitive motive to Tarquin, the speculations in lines 36–42 do suggest that it was his rivalry with Collatine, not the glimpse of Lucrece that resulted from it, that "suggested this proud issue of a king" (37):

Perchance that envy of so rich a thing,
Braving compare, disdainfully did sting
    His high-pitch'd thoughts, that meaner men should vaunt
    That golden hap which their superiors want.

(39–42)

In short, by omitting Tarquin's initial visit, the text foregrounds the competition between the king's son and Collatine, transforming it into

[16]For a statement of this case, see, e.g., Bullough, p. 180. Richard Lanham is one of the few critics who argue that the discrepancy is significant, but his interpretation of it differs from mine (pp. 95–96). R. Thomas Simone suggests that one of the main effects of omitting the first visit is to put more weight on Tarquin's own character (*Shakespeare and "Lucrece": A Study of the Poem and Its Relation to the Plays*, Salzburg Studies in English Literature 38 [Salzburg: Institut für Englische Sprache, 1974], pp. 36–37).

into the primary motive for the rape. This same passage also anatomizes the moral dangers of that competitiveness, drawing attention to the sordidness of Tarquin's rivalry through the sort of double-edged rhetoric that is so characteristic of this poem. His thoughts are "high-pitch'd" (41) in the sense that they are lofty, but they are low morally, and Collatine, if "meaner" (41) in his social status, lacks the mean motivations that drive the king's son.

Even inanimate objects and abstract ideas compete with each other in the milieu the poem evokes. Admittedly, some of the figures are common ones reminiscent of Ovid's own wordplay, but the frequency of such images in Shakespeare's poem is telling:

> The aim of all is but to nurse the life
> With honour, wealth and ease, in waning age;
> And in this aim there is such thwarting strife
> That one for all or all for one we gage:
>
> (141–144)

> Now leaden slumber with life's strength doth fight
>
> (124)

> The wind wars with his torch to make him stay,
>
> (311)

> Conceit and grief an eager combat fight.
>
> (1298)

Recognizing Shakespeare's recurrent emphasis on competition allows us to defend two passages sometimes dismissed as inexcusable blunders. The description of the contending colors in Lucrece's face may well be unnecessarily long and unduly ingenious:

> But beauty in that white entituled
> From Venus' doves, doth challenge that fair field;
> Then virtue claims from beauty beauty's red,
> Which virtue gave the golden age to gild
> Their silver cheeks, and call'd it then their shield;
>   Teaching them thus to use it in the fight,
>   When shame assail'd, the red should fence the white.

> This heraldry in Lucrece' face was seen,
> Argu'd by beauty's red and virtue's white;

Of either's colour was the other queen,
Proving from world's minority their right.
Yet their ambition makes them still to fight;
  The sov'reignty of either being so great,
  That oft they interchange each other's seat.

                (57–70)

But the lines do serve the important function of demonstrating that even beauty is not exempt from the rivalries that dominate the Roman world. And the references to sovereignty and unseating in this metaphoric War of the Roses not only remind us that Tarquin's father unjustly seized power but also anticipate the political change that will occur at the end of the poem.

Similarly, many readers have criticized the way Collatine and Lucretius react to Lucrece's suicide: they indulge in a lengthy rivalry about which of them has a greater right to mourn her.[17] Once again, the passage does continue far beyond the moment when it has made its point. But, like so many other sections of the poem, it reminds us of a psychological truth. Collatine and Lucretius are turning their grief into anger against each other, one of the most common of psychological transformations. And the form that anger takes—competition—is precisely the mode of behavior they have inherited from their society.

In a sense, too, the values of that society are in competition with each other; adopting certain of them renders one liable to violate others, a dilemma very like the one Coriolanus faces in his own Roman milieu.[18] Family bonds, for example, are very important.[19] Tarquin broods on how his actions will affect his own descendants and threatens Lucrece with bringing shame to her children:

    That my posterity sham'd with the note,
      Shall curse my bones,

                (208–209)

---

[17]Coppélia Kahn notes that the competitiveness between Tarquin and Collatine parallels that between Collatine and Lucretius and suggests that the latter rivalry serves to criticize the characters' tendency to see human relationships in terms of property ("The Rape in Shakespeare's *Lucrece*," *Shakespeare Studies*, 9 [1976], 55–56).

[18]On this problem in *Coriolanus*, see Watson, chap. 3.

[19]On the family in *Titus Andronicus* and the relevant implications about Roman society, see G. K. Hunter, "Shakespeare's Earliest Tragedies: 'Titus Andronicus' and 'Romeo and Juliet,'" *Shakespeare Survey*, 27 (1974), 4–5.

Thy issue blurr'd with nameless bastardy.

(522)

And both Tarquin and Lucrece at times imply that Collatine, not his wife, is the primary victim of the rape. While, as many critics have noted, this perspective evidently reflects the assumptions of a patriarchal society, it is also consistent with the emphasis on all types of kinship manifest in this poem, as in its author's Roman plays. Yet the very society that is so committed to the Penates and all they symbolize also worships at the altar of military values that threaten the family.[20] It is symbolically apt that Collatine's absence at war permits the rape to occur; while he is winning honor "in the fields of fruitful Italy" (107), his wife is losing her honor at home. But these implications about the conflict between heroic and familial obligations would remain latent were it not for the fact that Tarquin's military values lie behind his siege of Lucrece, a point to which we will return.

The relationship between the individual and Roman society is also charged with tensions and inconsistencies: Roman citizens are always in the public eye and yet always utterly, tragically alone.[21] Shakespeare emphasizes the former point by the way he adapts one detail from his sources:

> They did conclude to bear dead Lucrece thence,
> To show her bleeding body thorough Rome,
> And so to publish Tarquin's foul offence.

(1850–1852)

Foregrounded by their position in the final stanza of the poem, these lines ensure that the narrative that has opened on a reference to publishing—

> Or why is Collatine the publisher
> Of that rich jewel he should keep unknown
> From thievish ears, because it is his own?

(33–35)

[20]Many critics have noted that Shakespeare's Roman plays stress the militarism of Rome. See, e.g., David M. Bergeron, "*Cymbeline*: Shakespeare's Last Roman Play," *SQ*, 31 (1980), 31.

[21]In *The Rapes of Lucretia: A Myth and Its Transformations* (Oxford: Clarendon, 1982), Ian Donaldson notes that the relationship between public and private behavior is a recurrent concern in the varied versions of the story (p. 8). I am indebted to Inga-Stina Ewbank for suggestions about this and other aspects of slander.

—also concludes on one. The verb "publish" has several possible meanings in these passages, including (as in *Two Gentlemen of Verona*, III.i.47) "proclaim," but one of the most salient glosses is "make public."

Indeed, throughout *The Rape of Lucrece*, as throughout *Troilus and Cressida*, the characters' most private actions (or other people's ill-informed speculations about them) are continually made public through a network of surveillance and slander: images of eyes and mouths reflect a world whose citizens are engaged in gazing on and gossiping about each other. Thus within only a few pages (lines 71–112) Tarquin stares lustfully at Lucrece, she returns his gaze uncomprehendingly, he muses on her husband's boasts about her beauty and in turn praises Collatine to her. And shortly afterward he threatens her with a fate she literally considers worse than death: being the object of slander.

This emphasis on performing in public, under scrutiny, helps to establish Lucrece's Rome as what anthropologists have termed a shame culture.[22] According to traditional definitions, the inhabitants of guilt cultures suffer from the failure to fulfill internalized values, while their counterparts in shame cultures endure disapproval from others. One should not push these parallels too far (not least because anthropologists have themselves engaged in questioning and revising the categories), but it is significant for our purposes that shame is connected to exposure, the very fear that dominates so much of Lucrece's behavior. She often seems more concerned with how the rape will affect her fame than with her own judgments on it. And it is significant, too, that shame is associated with precisely the experience that informs and deforms the milieu that Shakespeare is evoking: a threat to one's identity.

If one lives one's life before spectators, one may come to feel like an actor performing a part. And in fact the poem does adduce theatrical metaphors at a few key moments. Attempting to justify the rape to himself, Tarquin declares, "My part is youth, and beats these from the stage" (278). An appropriate image for his psychomachia, the allusion to acting hints at Tarquin's awareness that the most private actions are in a sense done on a public stage. (The line also exemplifies the flashes of psychological insight that illuminate the characters of this

---

[22]See Helen Merrell Lynd, *On Shame and the Search for Identity* (New York: Harcourt, Brace, 1958), esp. chaps. 1 and 2. Donaldson interprets the negative reactions that readers have had to various versions of the Lucrece story in terms of the change from a shame culture to a guilt culture (pp. 33–34).

poem, often occurring just when Shakespeare's portraits seem to be at their most conventional and least acute: if one is an actor, then one is in some important sense not responsible for one's behavior and not behaving as one would in one's own persona, as it were. Thus the image offers Tarquin a way to distance himself from his crime while at the same time proleptically hinting to the audience the real loss of identity that that crime will generate.) Lucrece herself plans her confession to Collatine almost as though she were going to deliver it on the stage or in a court of law; ironically, in order to convince her husband of her honesty, she must play her part with calculation:

> Besides, the life and feeling of her passion
> She hoards, to spend when he is by to hear her,
> When sighs and groans and tears may grace the fashion
> Of her disgrace, the better so to clear her
> From the suspicion which the world might bear her.
>
> (1317–1321)

She fears, in short, that "To be direct and honest is not safe" (*Othello*, III.iii.378).

But the glare of the footlights can create an odd sense of isolation: the actors cannot see the audience that is so intensely gazing on them. For all their involvement with the society's values and judgments, the characters in the poem seldom enjoy any sense of companionship or communion. Typically, Lucrece, like that other Roman victim Titus, lives "as one upon a rock, / Environed with a wilderness of sea" (*TA*, III.i.93–94). The Argument borrows from the sources the scene in which she sits spinning with her maids, but the poem proper omits this episode; one effect of this change is to avoid even this brief glimpse of a sense of community. And throughout the poem Lucrece's contacts with people are marked more by misunderstandings and misapprehensions than by sociability or solace. Thus when we do view her with one of the maids toward the end of the poem, what is stressed is her inability to explain her grief. Indeed, shortly before that encounter she has drawn attention to her own isolation:

> Where now I have no one to blush with me
> To cross their arms and hand their heads with mine,
> To mask their brows and hide their infamy;
> But I alone, alone must sit and pine.
>
> (792–795)

[91]

The anadiplosis on "alone" underscores her point. This recurrent emphasis on isolation aptly culminates on the image of Lucrece's body "Who like a late-sack'd island vastly stood / Bare and unpeopled in this fearful flood" (1740–1741).

One source of isolation further connects the Rome of *The Rape of Lucrece* to the worlds evoked in its author's Roman plays: here, as in those dramas, a number of characters seem curiously sexless.[23] Lucrece and Collatine share a network of obligations and expectations, and at a few points we sense affection—but never do we find the slightest hint of passion. Indeed, Shakespeare's curious imagery suggests that his heroine is virginal despite her marriage: "Her breasts like ivory globes circled with blue, / A pair of maiden worlds unconquered" (407–408). While "maiden" could merely signify "that has not been conquered, tried, worked, etc.,"[24] it seems more than likely that discordant connotations of virginity continue to adhere to the word. The "bearing yoke" (409) of her husband has not conquered those worlds; like the prelapsarian Adam and Eve of certain Protestant theologians, they make love without lust. But how does this absence of passion accord with a poem that is, after all, about a rape? One answer is that the question itself may not be wholly valid: desire is at best a secondary motivation in Tarquin's brutal conquest of those maiden worlds. A fuller answer, however, involves recognizing that once again we are encountering a contradiction within the society, a tension in its identity and integrity: the king's son, theoretically one of the best representatives of his culture's values, behaves in a way that violates those same values.

Nowhere is the portrait of Rome that we have been tracing better realized than in the central images of the poem. The tensions and threats in this society are manifest in references to robbery and locks:

> The locks between her chamber and his will,
> Each one by him enforc'd, retires his ward;
> (302–303)

> He like a thievish dog creeps sadly thence,
> (736)

[23]On this issue in the Roman plays, see Paul A. Cantor, *Shakespeare's Rome: Republic and Empire* (Ithaca: Cornell Univ. Press, 1976), esp. pp. 22–23.

[24]*Oxford English Dictionary*, s.v. "maiden." Prince unpersuasively suggests that "maiden" merely signifies "chaste" (p. 87).

> . . . robb'd and ransack'd by injurious theft;
>
> (838)

> But thou shalt know thy int'rest was not bought
> Basely with gold, but stol'n from forth thy gate.
>
> (1067–1068)

Such images may well remind us of their counterparts in the sonnets and in *1* and *2 Henry IV*. And just as the idea of competition is extended metaphorically to encompass a whole range of objects in the physical world, so the poem charts even the passage of time in terms of robbery: "Now stole upon the time the dead of night" (162). At other points Shakespeare's narrative takes a more oblique glance at thievery. Thus, as one critic reminds us, the weasel to which the poem refers ("Night-wand'ring weasels shriek to see him there" [307]) is an animal that robs nests.[25] And slander is a kind of robbery: the Lucios of the world steal our reputations.

These allusions to thievery participate in a pattern of ideas that recurs in Shakespeare's later works as well: what is precious is bodied forth as a treasure, especially a treasure that must be locked up, protected against a thievish world. Thus any reader of Shakespeare's sonnets is wise enough to anticipate trouble after hearing that Collatine "Unlock'd the treasure of his happy state" (16). In this case the treasure in question is simply his happiness, but elsewhere the image refers to the source of that happiness, Lucrece herself. Shortly before the rape, for example, she is protected by the curtains that enclose her bed—an image ironically reversed when her attacker "pens" (681) her cries with her clothing.

As that action by Tarquin would suggest, against the idea of Lucrece as an enclosed treasure are played the poem's many allusions to the encirclement of a siege.[26] The metaphor is too common in Renaissance literature to demand a particular source, but it is possible it was initially suggested to Shakespeare by Ovid's use of *cingitur* ("compassed" [721]). Shakespeare, however, develops the idea far beyond this brief hint in his source. Most obviously, the siege of Ardea is compared to the siege of Lucrece, an implication that becomes ex-

---

[25]D. C. Allen, "Some Observations on *The Rape of Lucrece*," *Shakespeare Survey*, 15 (1962), 92.

[26]Sam Hynes also notes the presence of the siege metaphor ("The Rape of Tarquin," *SQ*, 10 [1959], 451–452); he focuses, however, on what it shows about Tarquin himself.

plicit in the line, "This siege that hath engirt his marriage" (221). Similarly, Lucrece describes her soul as a temple "Grossly engirt with daring infamy" (1173).

The nature of those sieges and of the society that not only permits but also in some sense invites them becomes apparent when we examine the image that most clearly links this poem with its author's Roman plays. As many critics have noted, Shakespeare typically presents Rome as "the enclave of civilization ringed round with a protective wall."[27] Barbarians and barbarieties press against its gates. In *Titus Andronicus*, for instance, the rape of Lavinia takes place in the forest outside the city walls. *The Rape of Lucrece*, of course, occurs outside Rome—which is one of the many reasons the symbolism is transposed onto Lucrece herself. Associated with cities at other points in the poem ("so my Troy did perish" [1547]),[28] Lucrece, I would suggest, comes to represent the center of civilization that is threatened by barbarians.

Some of the passages we have been examining acquire new significance when they are viewed in this light. We can, for example, understand why nearly twenty lines are devoted to Tarquin's attempts to enter her chamber (302–315, 337–340, 358–359). The parallel between Lucrece and the walled city of Rome continues after her attacker is in her room: "His hand that yet remains upon her breast,—/ Rude ram, to batter such an ivory wall!" (463–464). By adducing in this very different context the Petrarchan comparison of the lady's skin to ivory, Shakespeare reminds us just how frail the defenses of this beleaguered city are. Tarquin's sexual penetration evidently mirrors the invading army's penetration of the city, a parallel that was anticipated in the line, "And with his knee the door he opens wide" (359). Indeed, given the common association of gates with the vagina,[29] the notion of rape is latent in the image of the attacked city,

---

[27]John W. Velz, "The Ancient World in Shakespeare: Authenticity or Anachronism? A Retrospect," *Shakespeare Survey*, 31 (1978), 11. On Rome as an enclave of civilization, also see Hunter, pp. 5–6, and J. L. Simmons, *Shakespeare's Pagan World: The Roman Tragedies* (Charlottesville, Va.: Univ. Press of Virginia, 1973), p. 166.

[28]Several readers have noted that Lucrece is associated with cities. See, e.g., Donaldson, pp. 9–10. It is suggestive that Lavinia, another victim of rape, is also compared to a city. On this pattern in *Titus Andronicus*, see Tricomi, "The Aesthetics of Mutilation in 'Titus Andronicus,'" pp. 17–18, and Willbern, "Rape and Revenge in *Titus Andronicus*," p. 162. Robert S. Miola's recent study, *Shakespeare's Rome* (Cambridge: Cambridge Univ. Press, 1983), also suggests that Tarquin is portrayed as a barbarian attacking a city (pp. 27–28).

[29]On this association in the Roman plays, compare Watson, pp. 78, 175.

and so in *The Rape of Lucrece* we are encountering less a transposition of that image to the domestic and sexual spheres than an enactment of one of its inherent implications. Furthermore, the banishment of the Tarquins acquires new significance in light of the symbolism we are charting: the barbarians who have forced their way into the walled city are cast outside it.

The image of the besieged city is mirrored in several other passages of the poem. Thus Tarquin envisions his soul as a "spotted princess" (721) whose "subjects with foul insurrection / Have batter'd down her consecrated wall" (722–723), and Lucrece, too, sees her soul as a "mansion batter'd by the enemy" (1171)—an intriguing pair of images to which we will have cause to return several times. And the contrast between the walled city and the violence outside it is a spatial analogue to the temporal contrasts of day and night that run throughout the narrative.[30]

But in a sense that violence is not really outside the wall, and day is not truly distinct from night. Tarquin is a Roman who is, as it were, attacking the city of Rome—a symbolic analogue to what would technically be termed "acquaintance rape," in contrast to rape by a stranger. One reason those paired allusions to battered walls are so significant is that they invite us to compare foreign wars with domestic insurrections and to notice that this rape approximates the latter, not the former, experience. Critics of Shakespeare's plays have observed that threats to the enclave of Rome seem especially disturbing when its enemy is internal,[31] and this, as I have been indicating, is precisely the situation we encounter when Shakespeare writes of Rome in his nondramatic poetry. Its walls battered by competing citizens and competing values, Rome is also ravished by someone who would normally be charged to protect it, the king's son.

The disturbed and disturbing society that Shakespeare evokes does not have its Malcolms or its Edgars; as we will see, Brutus at first appears to fill their function of restoring stability to the state, but his behavior proves more problematical. It is through the poem's images, not the actions of its dramatis personae, that we are afforded glimpses of a better society. This first of these glimpses is very brief indeed, but it is resonant to any reader of Shakespeare's plays: the narrator refers to Lucrece's loyal servant as a "pattern of the worn-out age" (1350).

---

[30]Robert J. Griffin also notes the allusions to night and day but interprets them differently ("'These Contraries Such Unity Do Hold': Patterned Imagery in Shakespeare's Narrative Poems," *SEL*, 4 [1964], 50–51).

[31]See, e.g., Velz, p. 12.

What is happening, I would suggest, is that Shakespeare is thinking in terms of a paradigm that was to find fuller realization later in his career, particularly in *As You Like It* and *King Lear*: a vision of a corrupt and disloyal society typically engenders in his mind an opposing vision of a Golden Age marked not by the classlessness normally associated with that happy time but rather by loyal and unquestioning service. The reference in *The Rape of Lucrece* testifies how early at least a rudimentary version of these ideas was present in Shakespeare's sensibility. But we are conscious as well of a significant difference between this allusion and the form the relevant concepts assume in the plays. The behavior of Adam and Kent reminds us that the values of that ideal age may still be recuperated. The servant in *The Rape of Lucrece*, however, is far too shadowy and minor a figure to represent such a hope—and it is telling, too, that the phrase that introduces him stresses the inaccessibility of the earlier and better age through the adjective "worn-out" (1350).

Similarly, the values of another antique and antiquated world, that of romance, are invoked at a few key points in the poem. In particular, when Lucrece appeals to the Romans to avenge her, she declares:

> For 'tis a meritorious fair design
> To chase injustice with revengeful arms:
> Knights by their oaths should right poor ladies' harms.
> (1692–1694)

The monosyllables in line 1694, as well as the neat couplet on which the passage concludes, provide a sense of simplicity and order very appropriate to the sentiments Lucrece is expressing. But the chivalric vision evoked by the lines, like the occasional allusions to chivalry we find elsewhere in the poem, does not provide a viable alternative to the problems of Rome. As we will see, these loyal knights are in fact skillfully manipulated by Brutus. And so we read this generic motif as yet another symptom of Lucrece's characteristic desire to find simple solutions to the complicated dilemmas she faces. Romance holds out the promise that its blacks and whites can be substituted for the clashing colors of synesiosis, but, like so many other promises in the poem, it is an empty one.

For if the rape in *Titus Andronicus* occurs in a literal forest, Tarquin's attack takes place in a metaphoric "selva oscura," in "a wilderness where are no laws" (544), or, more precisely, where social codes exist but only to clash with one another. The Rome of *The Rape of Lucrece* is a world that values conflict—and a world whose values conflict. Paul Cantor has persuasively demonstrated that Shakespeare's Roman plays embody the tension between the norms of the Republic and those that later characterized Imperial Rome.[32] In *The Rape of Lucrece* Shakespeare also focuses on tensions in Rome, but here they are related to each other not diachronically but synchronically: like the terms in syneciosis, Rome is divided against itself.

III

If Roman society is divided against itself, so too are its principal characters. It is obvious that Tarquin's worst enemy is himself, a traitor within his own walls. But in a sense the same is true of his victim: she is defeated as much by the habits of mind that determine her responses to the rapist as by the attack itself. This is not to say that Shakespeare is blaming her in the way that certain modern critics have done,[33] nor even that he is raising the more tentative and more temperate questions about her chastity posed by St. Augustine;[34] despite the criticisms of its title character that the poem implies, the portrait remains sympathetic and respectful. Through that portrait, however, Shakespeare is exploring the problem to which he was to return at several points in his career and, in particular, some twelve or so years later when he wrote *Othello*: what type of person is prone to be victimized by evil?

Despite—and in some sense because of—the experiences to which she is subjected, two principal characteristics remain constant in Lucrece. The first is that she—like Othello and Desdemona, both of whom she resembles in so many ways—lives in a world of absolutes, of clear and simple values and of constant and comforting pieties.[35]

[32]*Shakespeare's Rome*, pp. 10ff.

[33]See, e.g., Roy W. Battenhouse, *Shakespearean Tragedy: Its Art and Its Christian Premises* (Bloomington: Indiana Univ. Press, 1969), chap. 1. In this controversial study he argues that her behavior is often self-serving and that she manifests a "proclivity to self-pity and evasive argument" (p. 19).

[34]*The City of God*, trans. George E. McCracken et al., 7 vols. (Cambridge, Mass., and London: Harvard Univ. Press and Heinemann, 1957–1972), I, I.xix. Subsequent citations from this edition will appear in my text.

[35]For an argument different from my own, see Bickford Sylvester, "Natural Mutability and Human Responsibility: Form in Shakespeare's *Lucrece*," *CE*, 26 (1965), 505–511; he claims that absolutes are seen as a positive value in the poem, an antidote to the types of impermanence with which it is concerned. A reading related to the one in this chapter may be found in Simone; he suggests that Lucrece is the victim both of dualism and of man's vision of an ideal (pp. 168–169).

Thus, like her predecessors in *A Mirror for Magistrates*, she greets every situation with a sententious generalization:

> For kings like gods should govern everything.
>
> (602)

> The aged man that coffers up his gold
> Is plagu'd with cramps and gouts and painful fits,
> And scarce hath eyes his treasure to behold;
>
> (855–857)

> O opportunity, thy guilt is great!
>
> (876)

Such generalizations are, of course, common in Renaissance poetry,[36] but, as we have already observed, that fact need not preclude their use to characterize an individual temperament. In this case we may remember that classical rhetoricians list adducing the conventional pieties as a way of appealing to common consent.[37] In other words, Lucrece's axioms imply that the members of her society share certain values and codes with her, the very assumption that tragically governs her initial responses to Tarquin.

Another symptom of her belief in absolutes is her reliance on the idea that appearance does indeed reflect reality; prelapsarian in her ignorance of evil, she is persuaded that Tarquin's fair face necessarily guarantees fair behavior. The most revealing—and most psychologically acute—manifestation of this habit of mind is her immediate response when her attacker reveals his true colors:

> In Tarquin's likeness I did entertain thee:
> Hast thou put on his shape to do him shame?
> To all the host of heaven I complain me,
> Thou wrong'st his honour, wound'st his princely name;
> Thou art not what thou seem'st, and if the same,
>   Thou seems't not what thou art, a god, a king.
>
> (596–601)

---

[36]Cantor, pp. 109–110, notes that Shakespeare's Roman characters typically rely heavily on proverbs; his suggestion that this habit reflects a reluctance to think for themselves is, as I am suggesting, as relevant to Lucrece as to her counterparts in the Roman plays.

[37]See, e.g., Aristotle, *The 'Art' of Rhetoric*, II.xxi.11.

Unable to believe that she has so badly misjudged him, unable to accept that sometimes fair is indeed foul and foul fair, she reacts to the realization that he is not what he seems by asserting half in earnest that he is in fact a totally different person.

Lucrece's speech patterns clearly manifest her belief in absolute truths. She delights in antitheses, the ultimate expression of a world of blacks and whites:

> My honour I'll bequeath unto the knife
> That wounds my body so dishonoured.
> 'Tis honour to deprive dishonour'd life;
> The one will live, the other being dead.
> (1184–1187)

> My woes are tedious, though my words are brief.
> (1309)

> Thou worthy lord
> Of that unworthy wife that greeteth thee.
> (1303–1304)

Equally significant is her use of predication:

> My husband is thy friend;
> (582)

> "Thou art," quoth she, "a sea, a sovereign king,"
> (652)

> Time's glory is to calm contending kings.
> (939)

Apposition and certain forms of *copia* function very like predication, for they too equate objects:

> O unseen shame, invisible disgrace!
> O unfelt sore, crest-wounding private scar!
> (827–828)

> O night, thou furnace of foul reeking smoke.
> (799)

[99]

Though her reliance on predication is less pronounced than that of Richard II,[38] it is no less revealing. Like a good scholastic, she is assuming that objects have clear-cut and fixed qualities. And she is also assuming that *res* and *verba* do indeed correspond; she is applying to the world in which Brutus proves to be something other than what his name suggests the more confident approach to naming that is evident in the first line of the Argument ("Lucius Tarquinius [for his excessive pride surnamed Superbus]").

Lucrece's second dominant trait is her passivity. This is most clearly manifest in the plot itself. Like Venus, she lives in a world whose inhabitants are always coming or going: Tarquin rushes to her "all in post" (1); the groom travels away with her message; her father, husband, and a group of knights hasten to her side; and the witnesses of her suicide bear her body to Rome. Unlike Venus, however, Lucrece herself in an important sense does not participate in the movement: she may roam her house in her distraction, but she never actually leaves it until she is carried away. The images associated with her reinforce our impression of passivity: she is the fort that Tarquin invades (for example, 440–441), the monument that he views (391–392), and, more ominously, the plain open to worms (1247). All of these figures imply the danger inherent in her mode of being: she is liable to be the victim of actions by others, and a victim no more able to resist than the plain can resist its worms. Shakespeare renders these implications overt in a passage that at once firmly asserts traditional notions of woman as the weaker vessel and as firmly rejects the misogynist condemnations normally associated with those notions:

> For men have marble, women waxen, minds,
> And therefore are they form'd as marble will;
> The weak oppress'd, th'impression of strange kinds
> Is form'd in them by force, by fraud, or skill.
> Then call them not the authors of their ill,
> No more than wax shall be accounted evil,
> Wherein is stamp'd the semblance of a devil.
>
> (1240–1246)

Even the way she is at first identified draws attention to her passivity; whereas Tarquin's initial epithet is "Lust-breathed" (3), with the past participle associating him with the world of action, she is called "Lucrece the chaste" (7). (That phrase points, too, to the obvious connec-

[38]On Richard II's use of predication, see Porter, chap. 1.

tion between her speech mannerisms and her own mode of being: she not only sees the world in terms of absolute, unchanging attributes but also represents one such attribute herself.)

The rape, then, intensifies the role of passive victim that has been latent in her behavior all along. Hence that crime aptly symbolizes the nature of tyranny itself: we are reminded yet again of the helplessness of its subjects, and of the criminal irresponsibility of the monarch who abuses them.[39] And of course the passivity of her personality has social as well as political implications: as many readers have justly observed, Lucrece is the victim not only of her attacker but also of a society that defines women in terms of their relationships to men and, in particular, assumes that their worth resides in the chastity enjoined by those relationships.[40] Important though these political and social frameworks are, however, they should not tempt us to neglect what is idiosyncratic in Lucrece's behavior; at a few key moments the poem hints that its unhappy heroine is not inevitably and totally conditioned by her culture, that her responses to the rape are but one of the many ways a Roman woman might have behaved.

As *The Rape of Lucrece* progresses, we witness the confrontation between a sensibility predicated on the clarities of antithesis and a world based on the complexities of syneciosis. First of all, what is emphasized most in our initial view of Lucrece is her fugitive and cloistered virtue. If locked-up treasures are protected from evil, they are also, the poem implies, denied the ability to recognize and hence withstand it:

> This earthly saint adored by this devil,
> Little suspecteth the false worshipper;
> For unstain'd thoughts do seldom dream on evil,
> Birds never lim'd no secret bushes fear:
> So guiltless she securely gives good cheer
>   And reverend welcome to her princely guest,
>   Whose inward ill no outward harm express'd.

. . . . .

[39]See Michael Platt, *Rome and Romans According to Shakespeare*, Jacobean Drama Studies, 51, ed. James Hogg (Salzburg: Institut für Englische Sprache und Literatur, 1976), pp. 8–9. An earlier version of his chapter on *The Rape of Lucrece* appeared as "*The Rape of Lucrece* and the Republic for Which It Stands," *Centennial Review*, 19 (1975), 59–79.

[40]See Kahn, "The Rape in Shakespeare's *Lucrece*." Notice, too, that Jane Shore is called "Shore's wife" in the title of her complaint in *A Mirror for Magistrates*, in the title of the expanded version of that complaint that Churchyard published in 1593, and in the subtitle of Anthony Chute's "Beawtie Dishonoured."

> But she that never cop'd with stranger eyes,
> Could pick no meaning from their parling looks,
> Nor read the subtle shining secrecies
> Writ in the glassy margents of such books;
> She touch'd no unknown baits, nor fear'd no hooks:
>   Nor could she moralize his wanton sight,
>   More than his eyes were open'd to the light.
>   (85–91, 99–105)

The allusions to saints and worshippers in the first stanza, like the description of her red and white complexion in the passage that precedes this one, ironically invoke the realm of love poetry. As in *Venus and Adonis*, the simpler and purer world of Petrarchism is contrasted with a vision that permits and even encourages a more disturbing form of desire: a lust uncontrolled by literary convention and unhampered by the power of a chaste maiden. Another contrast stems from the fact that Lucrece's very innocence is seen as dangerous: whereas the purity of the Petrarchan mistress merely frustrates her respectful worshipper, that of Lucrece actually fosters the schemes of her violent adorer. (Compare the earlier suggestion that Tarquin was inflamed by hearing of her very chastity: "Haply that name of 'chaste' unhapp'ly set / This bateless edge on his keen appetite" [8–9].) At the same time, however, these lines, again like those of *Venus and Adonis*, hint at troubling depths behind the traditions of love lyrics, especially Petrarchism itself: they remind us that desire is dangerous, even potentially violent. In any event, however we interpret these subterranean allusions to love poetry, one point is clear: the passage warns us of the perils of unsuspecting innocence. Like Iago, Tarquin makes the net that will ensnare Lucrece out of her own goodness. For if she is literally asleep when he breaks into her chamber, this passage proleptically mirrors that one by portraying her as metaphorically unaware, unawake.

Lucrece's reactions to the threat of rape and to the crime itself are often cited as prime instances of what is wrong with the poem in which she figures.[41] According to these readings, Shakespeare himself gets as carried away with rhetoric as his heroine: he employs the conventions of the set speech with no regard for psychological reality or even common sense, crams in rhetorical tropes with no concern for their appropriateness to the context. To be sure, even the most sym-

---

[41]Compare Farnham on the "temptation to sentimentality" (p. 323) that he finds in many complaints.

pathetic reader will certainly find some infelicitous phrases in this long central section of the poem. But this is not to say that we will or should paraphrase Jonson and wish that all thousand or so of the lines in question had been blotted; indeed, in many regards this section of the poem best demonstrates the neglected strengths of *The Rape of Lucrece*. For here, as in such early plays as *Richard III*, rather than abandoning the formulas of the set speech, Shakespeare infuses them with psychological depth. And rather than substituting a sparer style for the extravagances of Elizabethan rhetoric, he chooses to craft figures that are subtly and surely appropriate to the speaker and the situation.[42]

That achievement is all the more striking when one considers how closely Shakespeare is adhering to elaborate literary conventions unrelated to these particular events. By the time he wrote *The Rape of Lucrece*, the lineaments of a certain type of set speech were well established, as works ranging in quality from *Locrine* to *The Spanish Tragedy* testify; based on a lengthy expression of intense emotion, these speeches typically included such rhetorical devices as the apostrophe and rhetorical question and such formulas as the appeal to the destinies and the curse. Though Seneca is often credited—and even more often blamed—for shaping this literary type, French and Italian models may also lie behind English instances of it.[43]

In many senses, the impassioned monologues that Lucrece delivers immediately before the rape as well as after it are textbook examples of such set speeches. The monologue in lines 764–1036 adopts one of their most familiar structural patterns: it opens on a apostrophe ("O comfort-killing night" [764]) and concludes on a resolution ("Kill both thyself and her for yielding so" [1036]). The intervening lines are crammed with the rhetorical devices most favored by Seneca and the English writers who imitated the set speech. Thus the apostrophe to night is followed immediately by many instances of copia:

[42]Her set speeches are also analyzed in Robert Y. Turner, *Shakespeare's Apprenticeship* (Chicago: Univ. of Chicago Press, 1974), pp. 108–110; he primarily focuses, however, on the aesthetic limitations of those speeches in contrast to the scene in which Lucrece views the depiction of Troy.

[43]On the characteristics of the Senecan set speech, see esp. Wolfgang Clemen, *English Tragedy before Shakespeare: The Development of Dramatic Speech*, trans. T. S. Dorsch (London: Methuen, 1961), pp. 215–252. Other relevant studies include John W. Cunliffe, *The Influence of Seneca on Elizabethan Tragedy* (London: Macmillan, 1893), esp. pp. 14–41; T. S. Eliot, "Seneca in Elizabethan Translation," in *Selected Essays* (New York: Harcourt, Brace, 1932), pp. 52–61; G. K. Hunter, "Seneca and the Elizabethans: A Case-Study in 'Influence,'" *Shakespeare Survey*, 20 (1967), 17–26.

O comfort-killing night, image of hell,
Dim register and notary of shame,
Black stage for tragedies and murders fell,
Vast sin-concealing Chaos, nurse of blame!
Blind muffled bawd, dark harbour for defame,
  Grim cave of death, whisp'ring conspirator
  With close-tongued treason and the ravisher!
                        (764–770)

We also encounter exclamations ("O unseen shame, invisible disgrace!" [827]), rhetorical questions ("Or kings be breakers of their own behests?" [852]), antithesis ("Thy secret pleasure turns to open shame" [890]), and anaphora ("Guilty thou art of murder and of theft, / Guilty of perjury and subornation" [918–919]). And the passage demonstrates virtually every formula through which the speakers of Senecan declamations normally express their tumultuous emotions. Lucrece addresses an apostrophe to her own body: "Poor hand, why quiver'st thou at this decree?" (1030). Accusation and malediction, central topoi in the set speech, are prominent throughout her impassioned lines. She voices the desire to die herself, and in her prayer that the day never come ("Make war against proportion'd course of time" [774]) we encounter a variant on yet another common motif, the plea that the world be annihilated.

But the fact that he is observing literary convention so closely does not, as so many readers have assumed, prevent Shakespeare from observing human behavior equally closely. Indeed, if Lucrece's lines could be cited as examples in a sixteenth-century textbook on rhetorical declamations, they would be no less appropriate in a twentieth-century textbook on the behavior of rape victims. For to a striking degree her reactions are the very ones that contemporary psychologists and sociologists have charted. Applying modern theories of rape victimology to a Roman victim created by an Elizabethan writer is, of course, a potentially hazardous enterprise: to some extent local attitudes to sexuality and morality are bound to affect how the woman responds. (Most obviously, one could relate Lucrece's concern about the relationship of her body and soul to the modern studies in question only by distorting those studies or her words.) Nonetheless, the parallels between her behavior and the responses analyzed in the extensive recent literature on rape are compelling enough to suggest that certain reactions commonly recur, at least in Western culture—and to testify that Shakespeare understood those reactions well. In fact, in his perceptions about how a woman responds to rape we find

[104]

decisive evidence of an observation Coleridge offered about Shakespeare's narrative poems: their author manifests an extraordinary ability to work on subjects distant from his own experience.[44]

Rape victims typically have a great deal of trouble communicating the event to others.[45] A recognition of that fact may lie behind the Philomel myth, which provides a physiological correlative to psychological difficulties in speaking. In any event, Lucrece's lengthy laments about the rape are, significantly enough, monologues, even though the author might easily have portrayed her delivering these same speeches to the maid or to Collatine himself. When she does in fact confront a real audience—the maid, the groom, or Collatine and Lucretius and their retinue—she is rendered virtually speechless.

Women who have been raped characteristically blame themselves for not fighting enough.[46] We have seen that Shakespeare borrows the convention of speakers addressing their own bodies from the well-established formulas of the set speech—but he skillfully adapts that convention to the self-castigation that is so common in the situation he is evoking:

> Poor hand, why quiver'st thou at this decree?
>
> . . . . .
>
> Since thou could'st not defend thy loyal dame,
> And wast afeard to scratch her wicked foe,
> Kill both thyself and her for yielding so.
>
> (1030, 1034–1036)

It is suggestive, too, that, like so many of us, Lucrece attempts both to blame and defend herself: by reproaching her hand she is at once censuring herself and deflecting that censure onto only one part of her body, with the implication that the rest may be less guilty. In a sense she is both using synecdoche and rejecting it through the claim that the part is not in fact the whole. This quotation may well remind us, then, of the way Tarquin's theatrical metaphor serves to deny his

---

[44]*Shakespeare Criticism*, II, 329. Kahn also notes that Shakespeare is very interested in the ways rape affects its victim ("The Rape in Shakespeare's *Lucrece*," p. 46), but she develops the point in terms of the implications about patriarchy.

[45]See Sandra Sutherland and Donald J. Scherl, "Patterns of Response among Victims of Rape," *American Journal of Orthopsychiatry*, 40 (1970), 504, 507.

[46]Many authorities have analyzed this reaction. See, e.g., two studies by Ann Wolbert Burgess and Lynda Lytle Holmstrom, "Rape Trauma Syndrome," *American Journal of Psychiatry*, 131 (1974), 983, and *Rape: Victims of Crisis* (Bowie, Md.: Robert J. Brady, 1974), p. 39.

responsibility. The preoccupation with how people cope with guilt that we find in both of these passages—and at so many other points in *The Rape of Lucrece*—anticipates the subtle anatomies of that emotion that are so central to the sonnets and, of course, to Shakespeare's tragedies.

But Lucrece does not castigate herself unremittingly: throughout her monologues she vacillates between that reaction and blaming her attacker. The most tragic instance of these shifts hints at one of the motivations behind her suicide. Within thirty lines her angry wish that Tarquin kill himself ("Himself, himself seek every hour to kill" [998]) is succeeded by her first reference to self-destruction ("The remedy indeed to do me good / Is to let forth my foul defiled blood" [1028–1029]). It is as though she has transferred not only the guilt but also the "remedy" (1028) for it from him to herself.

When rehearsing the incident, rape victims generally brood on how it could have been prevented,[47] and here, too, Lucrece behaves typically:

> Yet am I guilty of thy honour's wrack;
> Yet for thy honour did I entertain him:
> Coming from thee I could not put him back,
> For it had been dishonour to disdain him.
> Besides, of weariness he did complain him,
>
> (841–845)

And a little later she expresses the obsessive wish, "O this dread night, would'st thou one hour come back, / I could prevent this storm and shun thy wrack!" (965–966). Similarly, while her abrupt changes of mood lend themselves to dismissal as yet another instance of the implausibility of Elizabethan set speeches, the fact remains that such changes are familiar not only in the aftermath of rape but also, of course, in many other kinds of emotional crisis.[48] And if her declaration, "For me, I am the mistress of my fate" (1069) reflects the same Stoicism we find in the tragic heroes of the Roman plays, one should

[47]See Burgess and Holmstrom, *Rape*, p. 41, and Malkah T. Notman and Carol C. Nadelson, "Psychodynamic and Life-Stage Considerations in the Response to Rape," in *The Rape Crisis Intervention Handbook: A Guide for Victim Care*, ed. Sharon L. McCombie (New York: Plenum Press, 1980), p. 136.

[48]On mood swings in rape victims, see Burgess and Holmstrom, *Rape*, p. 39.

add that rape victims also typically manifest a need to reassert control.[49]

Above all, however, it is in her loss of identity—and in the particular form the loss assumes—that Lucrece exemplifies the patterns charted by students of rape. We will look at other manifestations of that loss later, but now it is significant that she experiences a kind of identification with Tarquin.[50] In passages I examined above from a different perspective, the strikingly similar way their souls are described hints disturbingly at the link between the aggressor and his victim:

> Besides, his soul's fair temple is defaced,
>> To whose weak ruins muster troops of cares,
>> To ask the spotted princess how she fares.

> She says her subjects with foul insurrection
> Have batter'd down her consecrated wall.
>> (719–722)

> Her house is sack'd, her quiet interrupted,
> Her mansion batter'd by the enemy,
> Her sacred temple spotted, spoil'd, corrupted.
>> (1170–1172)

Such hints were to be developed in the ambiguities of Middleton's "The Ghost of Lucrece": "Now enters on the stage of Lucrece' heart / Black appetites in flam'd habiliments" (183–184).[51] The literature of rape victimology offers certain explanations for this radical change in Lucrece's identity. The crime is, according to the co-authors of one study of it, "a total attack against the whole person, affecting the victim's physical, psychological and social identity"; they go on to describe a "loss of ideal self," stressing that this loss will be especially

[49]For a summary of Roman stoicism, see Reuben A. Brower, *Hero and Saint: Shakespeare and the Graeco-Roman Heroic Tradition* (Oxford: Oxford Univ. Press, 1971), esp. pp. 141–172. On rape victims' desire to reassert control, see Notman and Nadelson, p. 139; Ellen L. Bassuk, "Crisis Theory Perspective on Rape," in McCombie, p. 127; Elaine Hilberman, *The Rape Victim* (New York: Basic Books, 1976), p. 43.

[50]Other readers have discussed this identification taking a perspective different from mine. See esp. Hynes, pp. 452–453.

[51]*The Ghost of Lucrece*, ed. Joseph Quincy Adams (New York: Charles Scribner's Sons, 1937).

intense in the case of a victim who particularly valued sexual fidelity.[52] More specifically, other authorities have documented an identification with the aggressor that occurs in this crime, as in others.[53]

But Lucrece's own character offers a further explanation for her curious affiliation with Tarquin. For someone so committed to absolutes, to antitheses, there can be no middle ground: if, as she so firmly believes, she no longer merits the epithet "Lucrece the chaste" (7), then she must exemplify the other extreme, the corruption represented by Tarquin himself. The image of the besieged city offers a gloss on this change in her identity: what was outside the walls has entered within them.

As this instance suggests, then, within the apparently rote formulas of Lucrece's speeches we find evidence not only of the actual behavior of rape victims but also of this specific victim's character. In particular, the allusion to her spotted soul is but one of many passages in which the poem charts the ways the crime affects—or, more to the point, fails to affect—her belief in absolutes. To be sure, she occasionally moves toward a vision of greater moral complexity and ambiguity. Witness, for example, her attempts to distinguish between mind and body ("Though my gross blood be stain'd with this abuse, / Immaculate and spotless is my mind" [1655–1656]) or the change from her "Thou look'st not like deceit; do not deceive me" (585) to her recognition that Sinon's looks do not in fact guarantee his virtue. But by and large Lucrece reacts by continuing against all the odds to find evidence of the simpler, clearer world whose existence has been thrown into question by Tarquin's crime; as all of us so often do, she responds to a crisis by intensifying her customary modes of behavior—even though this crisis has shown how inappropriate those modes are. When a crystal is shattered, Freud reminds us, it most clearly reveals its structure.

Lucrece's frequent references to night and day reflect her continuing tendency to think, as it were, in terms of blacks and whites. Thus when she says "But when I fear'd I was a loyal wife: / So am I now,—O no, that cannot be!" (1048–1049), she is demonstrating her inability to define loyalty in terms more complex than the absolute ones she had previously used: she cannot acknowledge that though in one

<hr>

[52]Kurt Weis and Sandra S. Borges, "Victimology and Rape: The Case of the Legitimate Victim," in *Rape Victimology*, ed. Leroy G. Schultz (Springfield, Ill.: Charles C. Thomas, 1975), pp. 92, 128.

[53]See, e.g., Notman and Nadelson, p. 135.

sense she has been unchaste and unfaithful to her husband, those definitions of chastity and loyalty are obviously inadequate to the circumstances of a rape. When she describes herself as "she that was thy Lucrece" (1682) she is not only anticipating her suicide but also manifesting in extreme form her habit of predication; when predication breaks down, when she cannot say "Lucrece is chaste," then in some important sense Lucrece does not exist at all. She is merely, as she herself puts it, a casket emptied of its treasure. And, again demonstrating 'the habits of mind we are examining, she declares, "These contraries such unity do hold, / Only to flatter fools and make them bold" (1557–1558); in other words, she cannot recognize that it is wise men, not fools, who perceive the unity of contraries, that it is syneciosis, not other forms of antithesis, that characterizes the world.

Interpreted by some readers merely as a sign of her changing attitudes, Lucrece's response to Sinon is in a deeper sense the most dramatic evidence of what does not change. To be sure, as I have said, she now acknowledges that a fair exterior does not guarantee a fair character. But the terms in which she does so are very revealing:

> "It cannot be," quoth she, "That so much guile,"—
> She would have said,—"can lurk in such a look."
> But Tarquin's shape came in her mind the while,
> And from her tongue "can lurk" from "cannot" took:
> "It cannot be" she in that sense forsook,
>   And turn'd it thus: "It cannot be, I find,
>   But such a face should bear a wicked mind."
>
> (1534–1540)

In other words, as the final three lines of the passage indicate, she in fact maintains her belief that outward appearances can definitely predict character, merely changing her definition of what type of character they predict. Like Leontes, she has "drunk, and seen the spider" (*WT*, II.i.45)—but in some important regards she is seeing it from the same angle of vision that has defined her perceptions throughout.

In one significant respect, though, she does change. The conventional wisdom informs us that most complaints, rooted as they are in heavy-handed didacticism, adopt the providential approach to history; Frederick Kiefer has recently demonstrated that such poems instead typically trace causality to a volatile admixture of providential intervention and Fortune.[54] While she resembles the heroines of com-

---

[54]"Fortune and Providence in the *Mirror for Magistrates*," *SP*, 74 (1977), 146–164.

plaints in so many other ways, in this regard Lucrece is very different: her declamations both implicitly and explicitly demonstrate her belief that the events in her careening universe may be traced to Fortune's wheel. In particular, her long diatribe on Opportunity, dismissed by many readers as irrelevant to the poem, in fact serves the function of testifying to her belief in chance. Though she attempts in other respects to adhere to her earlier vision of a stable world, in her attribution of causality to Fortune she shows some recognition that that stability was illusory. She attempts to retain in her grammar the copula "is" but questions the conjunction "because."

The imagery in Lucrece's declamations also serves to reveal her angle of vision, with even stock figures acquiring new resonance in light of what we know about the speaker and her situation. Thus she cites a series of instances of virtue being "profan'd" (847):

> Why should the worm intrude the maiden bud,
> Or hateful cuckoos hatch in sparrows' nests?
> Or toads infect fair founts with venom mud,
> Or tyrant folly lurk in gentle breasts?
> Or kings be breakers of their own behests?
>
> (848–852)

The phallic symbolism of the first line is evident. And the second line continues the imagery of foreign invasion while also hinting at one result of that invasion that we know Lucrece fears: giving birth to a child fathered by Tarquin, a hateful intrusion into both the nest of her own body and the nest of her husband's house. Once again, a barbarian intruder has breached the wall. These references to sexuality and procreation continue in the next line, which implicitly alludes to spontaneous generation—compare "or keep it as a cistern for foul toads / To knot and gender in" (*Othello*, IV.ii.61–62). Then, more directly confronting the thoughts behind her previous images, Lucrece bemoans the "tyrant folly" (851) of a king's son.

Not only the content of her declamations but also their very existence contributes to the characterization of Lucrece. The prevalence of this mode of rhetoric in the complaint tradition may originally tempt us to assume that Shakespeare is doing nothing more than borrowing a literary convention. But by referring so explicitly and so frequently to its set speeches, the poem invites us to look more closely at not only how but also why Tarquin and Lucrece deliver them. Thus Tarquin, adopting a technical rhetorical term, asks, "O what excuse can my invention make / When thou shalt charge me with so black a deed?" (225–226). Shortly afterward the narrator glosses his behavior: "Thus graceless holds he disputation / 'Tween frozen conscience and hot burning will" (246–247). Lucrece herself pointedly draws attention to her use of declamations:

> In vain I rail at opportunity,
> At time, at Tarquin, at uncheerful night;
> In vain I cavil with mine infamy,
> In vain I spurn at my confirm'd despite;
> This helpless smoke of words doth me no right.
>
> (1023–1027)

Moreover, because lengthy Senecan speeches are not employed at several points when they might well be—Brutus' oration is strikingly short, and Lucrece's language is more matter-of-fact when she acquaints her husband with the rape than when she rehearses it to herself—we become aware that they represent only one of many possible ways of speaking about and reacting to experience.

Conscious of that truth, we begin to see Lucrece's declamations as symptomatic of her temperament. Her belief in absolutes lends itself naturally to the hyperbolic utterances of the declamation: exclamations, not subjunctives, are her natural mode. And the fact that she criticizes her own rhetoric but continues to employ it is yet another indication of syneciosis, yet another symptom of the divisions in her being. We share her impatience at the length of her speeches, recognizing that she is getting too carried away with emotion, as Venus does under very different circumstances. For Shakespeare is qualifying the common Renaissance belief that language provides a useful purgative for our emotions.[55] When carried to an extreme, he demonstrates through his portrait of Lucrece, rhetoric may exacerbate, not purge the passions: "For sorrow, like a heavy hanging bell / Once set on ringing, with his own weight goes" (1493–1494). The conventional length of those speeches, in other words, comes to seem a sign of something very individual about Lucrece herself.

This is not to say, however, that the text supports Richard Lanham's cynical appraisal of Lucrece's histrionics. To claim, for example, that Lucrece is "seizing the occasion to enjoy a good rant" or to

---

[55]For an analysis of that belief, see Jane Donawerth, *Shakespeare and the Sixteenth-Century Study of Language* (Urbana: Univ. of Illinois Press, 1984), pp. 57–61.

refer to her "elephantine ego"[56] is to ignore the sympathy for his heroine that Shakespeare builds. His detailed anatomies of both the horrors of Tarquin's behavior and the values of Rome make her emotion seem an understandable reaction to the rape, if not an ideal one. And the poem balances its expositions of Lucrece's melodramatic self-absorption against frequent reminders of her unselfish concern for Collatine.

As my earlier reference to Sinon would suggest, not only Lucrece's earlier declamations but also her responses to the portrayal of Troy serve to develop her character.[57] Though Shakespeare apparently added this scene to his narrative for many reasons (its only precedent is a very different episode in which Daniel's Rosamond examines a casket her seducer has bestowed upon her), one of its primary effects is to draw attention to the limitations in his heroine's outlook. In one sense her identification with Hecuba is very natural. To cite that suffering woman as a type of grief was of course a virtual cliché in Renaissance poesy, and Lucrece's own story lends point to her invocation of Hecuba: both of them not only suffer but also suffer sympathetically for someone else's grief (Priam in one case, Collatine in the other), and both of them lose their identities (we are told of Hecuba, "Of what she was no semblance did remain" [1453]). In another sense, however, the identification reflects the same emotiveness and passivity that have characterized Lucrece's behavior all along. Some readers have dismissed the lengthy description of the Trojan scene that precedes the allusion to Hecuba as mere self-indulgence on Shakespeare's part,[58] but in fact these stanzas serve several functions, one of which is to remind us of all the sections of the tableau Lucrece could have scrutinized had she not concentrated on Hecuba. She might, for instance, have found in the fall of Troy a proleptic vision of the fall of

---

[56]Pages 103, 107. Robert L. Montgomery, Jr. also notes that she becomes carried away with her own passion, but his criticism of her behavior is more temperate ("Shakespeare's Gaudy: The Method of *The Rape of Lucrece*," in *Studies in Honor of DeWitt T. Starnes*, ed. Thomas P. Harrison et al. [Austin: Univ. of Texas Press, 1967], esp. pp. 32–33).

[57]Many scholars have studied the iconographical sources of the poem. See esp. Hulse, pp. 175–194 (an earlier version appears as "'A Piece of Skilful Painting' in Shakespeare's *Lucrece*," *Shakespeare Survey*, 31 [1978], 13–22); Elizabeth Truax, "Lucrece: What hath your conceited painter wrought?" in *Shakespeare: Contemporary Critical Approaches, Bucknell Review*, 25, ed. Harry R. Garvin (Lewisburg: Bucknell Univ. Press, Associated Univ. Presses, 1980). Muriel Bradbrook notes that the tapestry functions like a play within a play (p. 112).

[58]For example, Zocca claims the whole scene is hard to justify (p. 49).

the Tarquins—"sic semper tyrannis." She might have seen in "Nestor's golden words" (1420) hints of how her own oratory could serve to denounce her attacker. Instead, however, she concentrates only on the episode that feeds her own despair.

Lucrece's histrionic reactions to the rape render the way she reports the event to Collatine all the more striking. First of all, she uses, as she herself says, "few words" (1613): her summary of her tragedy occupies a little less than seven stanzas, while her major declamation after the rape fills thirty-nine. Similarly, while these seven stanzas are not without rhetorical tropes, by and large their language is much simpler than that of Lucrece's earlier set speeches; indeed, much of her dialogue with Collatine in this scene consists of straightforward narrative statements:

> With this I did begin to start and cry,
> And then against my heart he set his sword,
> Swearing, unless I took all patiently,
> I should not live to speak another word.
> (1639–1642)

The distinctions between her speech mannerisms here and in earlier passages of the poem support my contention that Shakespeare is tailoring literary conventions to the demands of the speaker and the situation. First of all, she wishes to express only briefly what she is ashamed to express at all. And in attempting to reassert control over her destiny during the encounter with her husband, Lucrece is also reasserting control over her language: she substitutes simple narrative statements for the exclamations and copia of her earlier speeches.

What Lucrece says (and does not say) is, however, even more revealing than how she says it. Influenced by the common assumption that Shakespeare's use of language in this poem lacks sophistication, readers have overlooked one detail as psychologically acute as the observations we find in Shakespeare's mature plays. Though she had in fact eloquently and lengthily attempted to defend her honor, Lucrece denies that fact in so many words:

> Mine enemy was strong, my poor self weak,
> And far the weaker with so strong a fear.
> My bloody judge forbod my tongue to speak;
> No rightful plea might plead for justice there.
> (1646–1649)

It is revealing that she sees her helplessness as speechlessness: Shakespeare is again associating language with power. Even more revealing, however, is the very denial that she tried to prevent the crime. Since she would have no reason to deceive her audience, she is evidently deceiving herself. Her deep sense of helpless victimization, her consciousness of the passivity that marks her all along, lead her to block out the fighting that she did in fact do. Another reason she ignores her valiant verbal defenses, I would suggest, is the irrational guilt that characterizes her responses to the rape throughout the poem. Her fear that she did not resist enough leads her to repress the resistance that she did offer.

Though the way Lucrece recounts the rape has been neglected by critics, they have devoted considerable attention to her suicide itself.[59] Like St. Augustine, a number of readers have been troubled by the problem of why an innocent victim should feel impelled to kill herself. The notion that her patriarchal society in effect demands her death, considering her forever corrupted, is not in itself an adequate answer, though it has sometimes been cited as one: after all, the men who hear her story unanimously deny her guilt: "With this they all at once began to say, / Her body's stain her mind untainted clears" (1709–1710). Rather than merely arguing that her culture condemns her to death, one needs at the very least to recognize that on this issue, as so many others, the culture is internally divided. On the one hand, through its emphasis on public opinion and on family obligations it has encouraged her to feel corrupted; it is significant, too, that shame, unlike guilt, is generally seen as irreversible.[60] On the other hand, however, the members of the society evidently value good sense and compassion enough to countermand the accusations that their more rigid values would otherwise lead them to direct toward Lucrece.

If the Romans are not demanding her suicide, why then does she

---

[59]On suicide in Shakespeare's dramatic and nondramatic poetry, see Brower, pp. 46–47; Maurice Charney, *Shakespeare's Roman Plays: The Function of Imagery in the Drama* (Cambridge, Mass.: Harvard Univ. Press, 1961), pp. 209–214; James Holly Hanford, "Suicide in the Plays of Shakespeare," *PMLA*, 27 (1912), 380–397; David L. Krantz, "Shakespeare's New Idea of Rome," in *Rome in the Renaissance: The City and the Myth*, Papers of the Thirteenth Annual Conference of the Center for Medieval and Early Renaissance Studies, ed. P. A. Ramsey (Binghamton: Center for Medieval and Early Renaissance Studies, 1982), pp. 372–374; Derek Traversi, *Shakespeare: The Roman Plays* (Stanford: Stanford Univ. Press, 1963), pp. 176–178, 190–203. The last of these studies offers an argument about the plays that is particularly close to my own reading of *The Rape of Lucrece*.

[60]Lynd, p. 50.

do it? The reasons she cites are in themselves important ones: the fear that her conduct will be misinterpreted and will set a bad example for others, the fear of bearing Tarquin's child. Moreover, the suicide is the final testimony to the depths of her irrational guilt. It is the last extreme gesture of someone who has tended toward such gestures all along. Her medicinal imagery suggests she will cure herself in the very act of punishing and destroying herself, another of the paradoxes that we find so often in this poem: "The remedy indeed to do me good / Is to let forth my foul defiled blood" (1028–1029). Finally, the question of identity is important here, as it is in so many of the other problems raised by *The Rape of Lucrece*. Parolles can announce that he will "eat and drink and sleep" as well as a captain even though he is no longer called one (*AWEW*, IV.iii.309), the grief-stricken Antony can declare, "I am / Antony yet" (*A & C*, III.xii.92–93), but Lucrece, as we observed in another context, has no identity, no life, outside the epithet that she feels she has forever lost, "Lucrece the chaste" (7). Now she is only "she that was thy Lucrece" (1682), in effect a denial of predication that anticipates her denial of life itself.

Within only two years of each other, Rembrandt painted two significantly different Lucreces.[61] In the canvas now in the National Gallery in Washington, though her expression is melancholy she strikes a heroic, defiant pose before she kills herself; in the other, which hangs in the Minneapolis Institute of Art, the figure committing suicide looks like a helpless child. These two paintings define the conflicting views of Lucrece that the suicide produces in the reader. On the one hand, the act is the appropriate culmination to what for all our sympathy we have found pitiful and regrettable about her behavior earlier. Anticipated by her tearing her own skin with her nails, it is part of her histrionic reaction to grief, her inability to assess guilt and innocence clearly because she is so carried away by emotion. Turning anger and violence inward against herself rather than outward against a foe, she exemplifies not heroic action but an alternative to heroism: she becomes, as many readers have observed, an icon or emblem to inspire heroism in others.

On another level, however, the action has the same bravery and nobility that we sense in the suicides of the characters in Shakespeare's Roman plays. This aspect of the deed is reflected in the way she talks of it earlier. Her speech in lines 1156–1211 opens on a series

---

[61]Though the Rembrandt paintings in question are not included in his analysis, Donaldson provides a useful discussion of other pictorial treatments of Lucrece (see esp. pp. 13–20).

of questions ("My body or my soul, which was the dearer, / When the one pure, the other made divine?" [1163–1164]) and passives ("Her house is sack'd" [1170]). As she moves closer to the resolution to kill herself, however, her language itself becomes firmer, relying on commands ("My resolution, husband, do thou take" [1200]) and declaratives ("My blood shall wash the slander of mine ill" [1207]). And at the end the speech invokes military imagery: "Yield to my hand, my hand shall conquer thee: / Thou dead, both die, and both shall victors be" (1210–1211). The neat couplet and the use of anadiplosis in line 1210 reinforce the impression of decisiveness and command. Such changes are also mirrored in the differing ways she talks about Collatine in the course of the speech; in lines 1177–1180 she describes him as her avenger, while in line 1205 she forthrightly and confidently orders him to oversee her will.

But even in such passages, our admiration for Lucrece is not unalloyed. Later we will observe that the poem hints at the dangers inherent in military values, and Lucrece's invocation of them here reminds us uneasily of her identification with her assailant. Moreover, the very neatness of the couplet in 1210–1211 stems from the same troubling process that renders so many of the couplets in Shakespeare's sonnets problematical: not only the lines but also the sentiments they convey have been crammed into a preestablished and confining pattern. In this case, what is omitted, or at least downplayed, is the tragic paradox in her view of death: to rephrase the words of that infamous Vietnam commander, to save herself she must destroy herself.

Our responses to Lucrece's suicide are, then, as ambivalent as our reactions to her behavior earlier. On the one hand, we do experience the same type of approval that marks our interpretation of the suicides of Antony and Cleopatra. Like those characters, Lucrece at once recovers and manifests her self-respect by killing herself, taking control of a situation in which she and those around her have previously lost control. But even in the Roman plays some ambivalence surely complicates our responses to suicide. For one thing, giving notional assent to the fact that pagans need not adopt Christian mores would not completely obviate many Christians' instinctive horror at suicide. For another, in certain plays at least we are aware of troublingly complex motives (thus Cleopatra's self-centered pride is hardly absent even from her final moments, though it is partly subsumed by her dignified love for Antony). But the doubts we experience when encountering suicide in the Roman plays are slight and often subterranean ones. In the case of Lucrece, in contrast, we are in fact at least as conscious of the irrationality behind her act as of the dignity. We are, in short, divided in our responses to an act that is itself the product of a divided society—and, according to some interpretations of suicide, of a divided self.[62]

IV

If Shakespeare's portrait of Venus is more subtle and sophisticated than that of Adonis, the same might well be said of the principal male and female characters in *The Rape of Lucrece*. Perhaps in composing these poems their author was deliberately attempting to develop the very quality that, as we have seen, Coleridge finds in *The Rape of Lucrece*: the ability to write about experiences remote from his own. In any event, it is clear that those who see in Tarquin an important early study for Shakespeare's major tragic heroes are prone to overstate their case.[63] At a few points, in fact, Lucrece's assailant seems like nothing so much as the stock villain of Victorian melodrama; he all but twirls his moustache as he stalks down the corridor in pursuit of his prey. The differing titles of the poem—the title page of the 1594 edition merely calls it "Lucrece," while "The Rape of Lucrece" appears as the heading and running-title—may reflect the author's recognition that he had gradually lost interest in Tarquin, concentrating far more on Lucrece in the latter part of the poem.

Nonetheless, his portrait of the king's son is not without its complexities.[64] His behavior, particularly his use of military language, casts new light on the culture that shaped him. And the way he analyzes his projected crime reveals a great deal about both his nature and the nature of rape. In particular, while the readers who have

[62]In addition to the divisions in Lucrece that we have already noted, compare M. D. Faber's suggestion that Shakespeare's suicidal characters typically experience ambivalence ("Shakespeare's Suicides: Some Historic, Dramatic, and Psychological Reflections," in *Essays in Self-Destruction*, ed. Edwin S. Shneidman [New York: Science House, 1967], pp. 30–58). Shneidman himself notes that in suicide, as in sleep, there is a division between the individual as he experiences himself and as he is experienced by others (*The Psychology of Suicide*, ed. Edwin S. Shneidman, Norman L. Farberow, and Robert E. Litman [New York: Science House, 1970], chap. 3).

[63]Kenneth Muir, e.g., suggests he is among Shakespeare's early tragic heroes ("The Rape of Lucrece," *Anglica*, 5 [1964], 26–27); Harold R. Walley discusses the poem as a whole as an anticipation of tragedy ("*The Rape of Lucrece* and Shakespearean Tragedy," *PMLA*, 76 [1961], 480–487).

[64]For a different analysis of his motives, see Lanham, pp. 95–102; he argues that Tarquin is trapped in feudal attitudes and metaphors.

[117]

noted that the poem links sexuality and competition have focused on the consequences for women, the implications about the rapist himself are no less significant.

Tarquin's language repeatedly testifies to his self-centeredness. In his long debate with himself before the rape he devotes far more attention to its putative effects on him and his descendants than on how it will harm his victim; thus, for instance, a single stanza on how the event will stain Lucrece (190–196) is succeeded by two on how he himself will be stained (197–210). In a sense the rape is the ultimate extension of his tendency to see the world as revolving around his needs.

His conduct alerts us, then, to yet another oxymoron in his milieu: for all their commitment to communal values, many of the Romans are as self-centered and self-regarding as Venus. Lucretius views his daughter's death primarily in terms of its effects on himself:

> Poor broken glass, I often did behold
> In thy sweet semblance my old age new-born;
> But now that fair fresh mirror, dim and old,
> Shows me a bare-bon'd death by time outworn.
> O from thy cheeks my image thou hast torn,
>   And shiver'd all the beauty of my glass,
>   That I no more can see what once I was.
>   (1758–1764)

And Brutus, as we will see, may well be more interested in his own advancement than in the well-being of Rome. Many readers have been puzzled by the functions of one detail in the ecphrasis of the fall of Troy:

> Whose words like wildfire burnt the shining glory
> Of rich-built Ilion, that the skies were sorry,
>   And little stars shot from their fixed places,
>   When their glass fell, wherein they view'd their faces.
>   (1523–1526)

The main purpose of these lines, I would suggest, is to provide an analogue to the kind of self-centeredness being charted in human society: seeing images of themselves in the fall of Troy, the mirrored stars are imitating human behavior, particularly the strikingly similar action of Lucrece when she gazes at a mirror image of herself, the mourning Hecuba.

But Tarquin of course differs from the other characters in the poem in many ways. He is, for example, distinguished from Lucrece in how he uses maxims. Invoking and twisting moral saws quite as frequently as a Marlovian character, he, like many of the villains in Shakespeare's plays, demonstrates that sententiousness is the last refuge of a scoundrel:

> But if thou yield, I rest thy secret friend;
> The fault unknown is as a thought unacted.
> A little harm done to a great good end
> For lawful policy remains enacted.
> The poisonous simple sometime is compacted
>   In a pure compound; being so applied,
>   His venom in effect is purified.
>
> (526–532)

In point of fact, according to traditional theological precepts, whether or not a thought is acted does not determine its sinfulness; what matters is whether it is willed. Even more revealing is the progress of thoughts in the passage: Tarquin is getting carried away with his own distorted logic, much as the speaker in the sonnets is prone to do. Language can help us to reason, as Renaissance rhetoricians often point out;[65] in Tarquin's case it is subverting, not serving, his rational faculties. Thus he moves from calling what he proposes a "fault" (527) (though one from which much of the harm is apparently purged), to describing it as "lawful policy" (529), to claiming that it is medicinal and hence positively beneficial. In other words, the passage attempts to enact the very process of purification that it concerns.

His allusions to the mercantile world are equally distorted:

> Then who fears sinking where such treasure lies?
> (280)

> Huge rocks, high winds, strong pirates, shelves and sands
> The merchant fears, ere rich at home he lands.
>
> (335–336)

Conscious of the contrast between these lines and lengthy references to covetousness in the poem (for example, lines 134–140), we recognize that Tarquin is attempting to transform sordid or even destruc-

---

[65]Donawerth, esp. pp. 20–21.

[119]

tive acquisitive instincts into a heroic adventurousness. By associating some of the mercantile imagery that runs through the poem with Tarquin, Shakespeare is drawing attention to implications latent in the vocabulary of love poetry, much as he did in *Venus and Adonis*.[66] Here he reminds us of a point with very modern resonances: to see a woman as a treasure is to imply that she is a passive object with no control over who garners her. She is, therefore, in constant danger of being seized against her will. Rape is merely the extreme and logical outcome of that danger; the word itself in fact comes from the Latin *rapio*, to seize. And the situation is all the more perilous because the man in quest of treasure may justify and even dignify his violence in the way Tarquin does. Though they remain latent in the imagery, these implications are virtually imperceptible when a speaker with the respectful caution of, say, the persona of the *Amoretti* pursues his quest; it takes a Tarquin—and a Shakespeare—to foreground the troubling resonances of a pattern of thought we often accept unquestioningly.

Tarquin's references to conquest in the mercantile world parallel a more central pattern in his language and character: he repeatedly views his crime as a military campaign and in so doing attempts to imbue it with heroism.[67] Throughout the poem a number of different metaphors for sexual relationships are played against each other— mercantile possession, feudal troth, animal desire, military conquest—but the last of these is most central in the poem and in Tarquin's behavior. The link between making love and making war was, of course, a well-established literary convention by 1594, but Shakespeare leaves us in no doubt that for all their conventionality the references in question signal important truths about Tarquin himself.

The very first stanza of the poem prepares us for the way he will view his attack: its lines remind us of the parallel between the siege of Ardea and his plot to "girdle with embracing flames the waist / Of Collatine's fair love, Lucrece the chaste" (6–7). Many later allusions reinforce the link between the two events; witness, for instance, the reference to her breasts in the line "These worlds in Tarquin new ambition bred" (411). To Lucrece language is a means of venting emotion and communicating events (though she is forced to recognize that it often fails in those functions). In contrast, Tarquin, like

[66]For a different but not incompatible analysis of Elizabethan attitudes to the mercantile, see Kurt Heinzelman, *The Economics of the Imagination* (Amherst: Univ. of Massachusetts Press, 1980), esp. the afterword.

[67]Kahn also notes the presence of this military imagery but interprets it differently (pp. 56–58).

many of the characters in *King John*, sees speech in military terms;[68] it is a maneuver in his campaign against Lucrece ("First like a trumpet doth his tongue begin / To sound a parley to his heartless foe" [470–471]). And if the frequent allusions to Tarquin's falchion are connected through paronomasia to the references to falconry that we find elsewhere in the poem, even more significant is the obvious fact that the falchion, which is clearly phallic, draws attention to the connection between sexuality and military aggression.

But Tarquin does not merely accept that connection; he repeatedly invokes it in order to justify and even glorify his enterprise. Having elsewhere declared that it is wrong for "A martial man to be soft fancy's slave" (200), he proceeds to imply that, thanks to his martial courage, he is a slave to neither fancy nor its object but rather a proud conquering soldier:

> Affection is my captain, and he leadeth;
> And when his gaudy banner is display'd,
> The coward fights, and will not be dismay'd.
>
> Then childish fear avaunt, debating die!
> (271–274)

> Under that colour am I come to scale
> Thy never-conquer'd fort.
> (480–481)

In addition to these explicit invocations of his military heritage, he implicitly refers to it in comments like, "My will is back'd with resolution" (352), where he seems to be congratulating himself on his valor.

Such lines are, of course, a comment on language and poesy themselves, signaling as they do the potentially disturbing and even dangerous underside of familiar imagery. Much as *Venus and Adonis* reminds us that the Petrarchan metaphor of the hunt may reflect real pain and much as other passages in *The Rape of Lucrece* imply that the treasure hunt may not be a happy experience for its object, so Shakespeare is demonstrating here that the conventional literary linkage between warring and loving may conceal—and at the same time reveal—destructive urges. That demonstration also hints at important truths about society and its inhabitants. Here, as when he criticizes heroism in his later plays, Shakespeare is participating in a contempo-

[68]On *King John*, cf. Donawerth, pp. 169–170.

rary debate about military values.[69] In short, writing in and about a culture that celebrated both the older, aristocratic ideal of military adventure and the newer, middle-class ideal of mercantile adventure, he privileges neither, instead adducing Tarquin's metaphors to remind us that both visions can all too easily degenerate into mere opportunism.

But the main effect of the images in question is to deepen our understanding of Tarquin himself. Like so many passages in the sonnets, his invocations of heroic honor show us how readily the self-centered and self-deceiving can twist facts and events to their own ends. Above all, however, the lines in question illuminate Tarquin and men like him by demonstrating that aggression is a central component in their sexuality. Shakespeare is approaching the questions about mastery that he addressed in *Venus and Adonis* from a new and more disturbing perspective: whereas sexual desires generated aggressive ones in Venus, in an important sense for Tarquin and his counterparts that process is reversed.

The discovery that those drives are intimately connected is not, of course, original to Shakespeare: that recognition is, for example, manifest in the imagery connecting love and war in the work of Ovid, Petrarch, and many of their imitators, as well as in the way romance heroes acquire fair damsels in the course of their jousts.[70] Behind such literary references may well lie a acknowledgment of the nature of actual combat; as Shakespeare himself writes in *Coriolanus*, "war, in some sort, may be said to be a ravisher" (IV.v.229–230), and many studies have documented the connection between war and rape.[71]

In *The Rape of Lucrece*, however, Shakespeare traces that common connection with uncommon acuity and precision. While some readers have noted that Tarquin's attack is motivated in part by aggressive urges, they have concentrated only on what that fact shows about Lucrece's role in her society. No less significant, however, is what is revealed about Tarquin: his behavior exemplifies—and in so doing clarifies—what has been termed the "power rape." Though many scholars would second Susan Brownmiller's observation that "All rape is an exercise in power,"[72] a more detailed classification of rapists'

---

[69]On Elizabethan attitudes to the military, see Paul A. Jorgensen, *Shakespeare's Military World* (Berkeley: Univ. of California Press, 1956).

[70]For a useful summary of this literary background, see Allen, "Some Observations," pp. 92–93.

[71]See Susan Brownmiller, *Against Our Will: Men, Women, and Rape* (New York: Simon and Schuster, 1975), chap. 3.

[72]Page 256.

motives has also proved influential among social scientists.[73] Characterized by physical brutality, the anger rape is generally a spur-of-the-moment attack whose main aims are to hurt and degrade the victim. As the name of the second type, the sadistic rape, would suggest, its attacker derives pleasure from inflicting violence. In the third form, the power rape, the rapist wishes to capture or control his victim. His behavior "may be triggered by what the offender experiences to be a challenge by a female or threat from a male, something which undermines his sense of competency and self-esteem."[74] Concerned about his masculinity, this type of rapist needs to believe that his victim wanted or enjoyed the attack.

Tarquin could, then, serve as a case study for the power rapist. First of all, in one of those revealing moments that are so common in the poem, Shakespeare hints at his preoccupation with power. The terms in which he describes lighting his torch are telling: "As from this cold flint I *enforc'd* this fire, / So Lucrece must I force to my desire" (181–182; italics added).[75] Indeed, the very fact that he uses his falchion, evidently an icon of power, to light his torch aptly symbolizes the fact that a concern for power leads him into Lucrece's chamber—a point also implied, of course, by the way he is associated with his sword throughout the poem. But *The Rape of Lucrece* also offers us more direct evidence that his act is a classic instance of the power rape. It is a challenge from Collatine that apparently inspires his ill-fated journey from Ardea ("Perchance his boast of Lucrece' sov'reignty / Suggested this proud issue of a king" [36–37]). By shaking his falchion immediately before the attack (505), at a point in their dialogue where there is no reason for him to threaten his victim, he gratuitously asserts his domination over her. We might even find in his insistence that her beauty not only invites the attack but also pleads for him a version of the power rapist's belief that the woman desired the rape.

Tarquin's references to fear when he is vacillating about his crime (lines 190–245, 253–280) reinforce our reading of his character. The word and its cognates appear no fewer than seven times in the eighty-three lines in question. He starts by speculating that the consequences of the deed will produce great and "coward-like" (231) fear in him:

[73]See two studies by A. Nicholas Groth and H. Jean Birnbaum, "The Rapist: Motivations for Sexual Violence," in McCombie, pp. 17–24, and *Men Who Rape: The Psychology of the Offender* (New York: Plenum, 1979), esp. chap. 2.

[74]Groth and Birnbaum, *Men Who Rape*, p. 30.

[75]It is conceivable that the passage includes an ironic allusion to the torches in wedding processions: the torch here is being used not to celebrate but to destroy a marriage.

"The guilt being great, the fear doth still exceed" (229). Shortly afterward he muses at some length on his putative victim's "loyal fear" (261) that her husband has been killed. These reflections are succeeded immediately by his resolution to muster his courage and perform the rape, a resolution expressed in such lines as "Then childish *fear* avaunt, debating die!" (274) and "Then who *fears* sinking where such treasure lies?" (280; italics added in both quotations). The passage hints that Tarquin finds Lucrece's fears sexually attractive. And it hints, too, that he is threatened by his own fear of performing the deed, viewing that emotion as a sign of shameful cowardice rather than of laudable morality. Indeed, one might almost suggest that he rapes her in part to prove that he is not afraid to do so.

My analysis of Tarquin indicates that the connection between his behavior and that of his counterparts in *Cymbeline* and *Titus Andronicus* is deeper than we have previously acknowledged.[76] In all three works, Shakespeare links rape (or, in the case of *Cymbeline*, intimations of it) not only with a drive for power but also with competitiveness between men. Lavinia's rape occurs in the context of fraternal rivalry that would be comically adolescent were its results less terrifying. Cloten's rape fantasy is closely connected with aggression toward another man; he plans to kill Posthumus and wear his clothes when raping Imogen. His monologue in III.v reveals his motivations as much by what is not said as by what is: he alludes bitterly to Imogen's contempt for him but mentions lust itself only once. And when Posthumus so incautiously displays the jewel to other men, Shakespeare in effect rewrites the opening scene of *The Rape of Lucrece*: if in boasting about Lucrece Collatine was "the publisher / Of that rich jewel he should keep unknown" (33–34), Posthumus is in turn publishing the literal gem that symbolizes the devotion of his own rich gem, Imogen.

Tarquin's behavior may also alert us to further connections between the treatment of rape in Shakespeare's dramatic and nondramatic work. Noting that allusions to dismemberment figure prominently in both *Titus Andronicus* and *Cymbeline*, readers have assumed that such references fill their customary function of, as it were, bodying forth disorder and, in particular, representing the dissolution of that analogue to the human body, the state.[77] I would suggest, however, that the imagery also enacts the rape victim's loss of identity

[76]On rape in *Titus Andronicus*, see esp. Tricomi and Willbern. Miola notes the parallel between the wager scene in *Cymbeline* and the contest in *The Rape of Lucrece* but interprets it differently from the way I do (p. 211).

[77]For discussions of dismemberment from a perspective different from mine, see Tricomi (esp. p. 11) and Willbern (esp. pp. 172–173).

and integrity; the rhetoric of the whole poem is miming the psychological condition of one of its chief characters. *The Rape of Lucrece* does not refer to dismemberment as directly and horrifyingly as the plays in question do: no limbs are lopped off, no bodies butchered and eaten. But the poem invokes with striking frequency common Renaissance images of conflicts between parts of the body or between the body and soul. Tarquin's allusion to his "spotted princess" (721) is one of the most obvious examples. Equally memorable is the description of the warring colors in Lucrece's cheeks. "Their ambition makes them still to fight" (68), as Shakespeare puts it, and his description of that fight occupies no fewer than nineteen lines. Other examples of this type of warfare appear elsewhere in the poem, reminding us yet again just how concerned this poem is with internal divisions:

> Rolling his greedy eyeballs in his head;
> By their high treason is his heart misled,
> (368–369)

> Such shadows are the weak brain's forgeries;
>   Who, angry that the eyes fly from their lights,
>   In darkness daunts them with more dreadful sights.
> (460–462)

>   the fault is thine,
> For those thine eyes betray thee unto mine.
> (482–483)

Similarly, Lucrece accuses her hand of betraying her by not fighting Tarquin, then uses that hand to commit suicide, the final battle of the self against the self. Such passages displace the preoccupation with dismemberment and mutilation that we find in *Titus Andronicus* and *Cymbeline*; they too mirror the loss of integrity suffered by a woman who has been raped, suggesting that in a sense the whole society is enacting that loss through its own disintegrations. And of course the images in question also remind us of the loss of self suffered by the rapist.

If that rapist is an unabated villain, Brutus would at first glance seem to be his opposite number, a hero at a point when we, like his namesake in *Julius Caesar*, would be "glad to learn of noble men" (IV.iii.54).[78] His invocation of religious and patriotic values appar-

---

[78]Many critics do subscribe to this reading. See, e.g., Lanham's claim that Brutus represents a mature personality (p. 108).

ently distinguishes him from the amoral Tarquin. The self-control that he both manifests and advocates ("Courageous Roman, do not steep thy heart / In such relenting dew of lamentations" [1828–1829]) is in sharp contrast to the unrestrained emotion that Lucrece's suicide has called forth from her husband and father. He is associated with effective action, they with pointless reaction, a contrast symbolized by the fact that he responds to the suicide by pulling the knife from the wound while Lucrece's father falls weeping on the body. (In the versions by Livy and Painter, Brutus assumes a comparable role at a second point in the story: after Lucrece's body has been borne to the marketplace, he exhorts his listeners there to control what are termed in Painter their "tears and other childishe lamentacions.")[79]

Brutus' patterns of speech, like those of Tarquin and Lucrece, are revealing. Thus his apparent commitment to forthright and effective action is indicated by the fact that his preferred mode is the command; four imperatives appear in the twenty-four lines that he speaks. Like Venus, he uses rhetorical questions to build an impression of consensus, but unlike Venus he uses them effectively. When he demands of Collatine, "is woe the cure for woe?" (1821) Collatine appears to agree that it is not, for he, like all of Brutus' listeners, abandons his mourning and joins this persuasive orator in banishing the Tarquins.

In fact, however, the man who vows to avenge Lucrece proves to be quite as morally ambiguous—or even dubious—as revengers on the Elizabethan and Jacobean stage.[80] Syneciosis, not antithesis, defines the relationship between Lucrece's attacker and her avenger no less than that between the rapist and his victim. Both Tarquin and Brutus mislead others through their deceptive appearances; and both exploit Lucrece's body for their own ends.

The legends that lie behind Shakespeare's plot prepare us for the ambiguities in the behavior of his ostensible hero; when Brutus becomes consul, for example, he presides over the execution of his own sons, behavior that may variously be read as Stoic self-control or inhuman insensitivity.[81] In any event, Shakespeare's poem itself immediately raises certain doubts about Lucrece's avenger; he never emerges as unambiguously villainous, but unresolved questions at the

---

[79]*The Palace of Pleasure*, ed. Hamish Miles, 4 vols. (London: Cresset Press, 1929), I, 20.

[80]For a different discussion of his problematical behavior, see G. W. Majors, "Shakespeare's First Brutus: His Role in *Lucrece*," *MLQ*, 35 (1974), 339–351.

[81]On these legends, see Donaldson, chaps. 6 and 7.

very least complicate his apparent probity. Notice, first of all, the terms in which he is introduced:

> Brutus, who pluck'd the knife from Lucrece' side,
> Seeing such emulation in their woe,
> Began to clothe his wit in state and pride,
> Burying in Lucrece' wound his folly's show.
> He with the Romans was esteemed so
>   As silly jeering idiots are with kings,
>   For sportive words and utt'ring foolish things.
>
> (1807–1813)

"Show" (1810) has connotations of hypocrisy and manipulation—connotations that link him with the two principal villains in the poem, Tarquin and Sinon. The final lines of the passage remind us that his previous actions have been based on a shrewdness uncomfortably allied to hypocrisy: to avoid the Tarquins' displeasure, he has pretended to be "brutus," a fool. In a sense he is one of the earliest of Shakespeare's Machiavels.

These reservations, at first only faintly troubling, are intensified when we begin to wonder about his motivations in avenging Lucrece. To what extent is he more interested in his own advancement than in her suffering? He was to profit from the Tarquins' banishment, after all, becoming one of the first consuls. With that fact in mind, we may begin to wonder whether the histrionic gestures with which this self-controlled man introduces the idea of revenge—he kisses the knife and urges his listeners to kneel—represent a clever way of manipulating the crowd. And, like Marc Antony, he coopts a dead body as a stage prop in the drama he is staging. In a later age, one suspects, he would have been an excellent advance man—had he not instead schemed to assume the position of candidate.

His ambitiousness suggests yet another parallel with the man he is opposing. At the beginning of the poem we are told that Tarquin's "lightless fire . . . . lurks to aspire" (4–5). The phrase implicitly links the physical rising of the flame with Tarquin's ambition to conquer Lucrece—a connection that may alert us to observe that in ten of the fourteen instances in which Shakespeare uses "aspire" or its cognates in his canon, the word connotes or actually denotes ambition.[82] This

---

[82]Marvin Spevack, *A Complete and Systematic Concordance to the Works of Shakespeare*, 9 vols. (Hildesheim: Olms, 1968–1980), s.v. "aspire." Because of the debate about its authorship, I am omitting *Two Noble Kinsmen* from these statistics.

early description of Tarquin could, then, also apply to Brutus: he lurks in the society in the guise of a fool, preparing to aspire to the role of leader.

The three principal personages in *The Rape of Lucrece* are related in several other important ways as well: the structure of this narrative, like that of its author's dramatic works, depends on a series of mirrored events and characters. Each of the three, for example, represents a different way of dealing with emotion. Thus Tarquin puts himself through the paces of a traditional Renaissance debate between reason and will—but, like the speaker in the sonnets, distorts the facts so that he will get the result he wishes. "Like Niobe, all tears," Lucrece freely expresses her passions. Brutus, who exemplifies Stoic self-control during his consulship, here too controls himself and in so doing provides an opposite pole to Lucrece. And each of the three represents a different perspective on the issues about identity that are so central to the poem. Tarquin, a house divided against itself, loses his identity when he rapes Lucrece—"And for himself himself he must forsake" (157). This mirrors his victim's own loss of identity, suggesting yet another parallel between them. Once again Brutus becomes Lucrece's opposite number. For he finds his identity at just the moment when she loses hers; revealing his true intelligence and acumen, he assumes a well deserved position as one of the leaders of the society. But he also reminds us how slippery the concept of identity is: not only may one's identity change, but it may be deliberately and cunningly concealed. If in one regard the poem's concern for naming culminates when Lucrece reveals the name of her assailant, in another it culminates when Brutus reveals the inappropriateness of his own name and hence draws attention to the difficulties inherent in any form of predication.

V

Throughout *The Rape of Lucrece* Shakespeare manipulates our moral and emotional reactions to his personages. As in the case of *Venus and Adonis* (and, of course, Shakespeare's plays themselves), what we learn about the characters is intimately related to how we learn it. Our judgments on Tarquin are, of course, quite straightforward. In the case of Lucrece, however, our responses become more complex. On the one hand, by defining her own and her society's values as thoroughly as he does, Shakespeare makes clear how and why an event that would be traumatic for any victim is especially dreadful for her; our recognition that she is too innocent even to anticipate evil and the fact that her sense of self is based so totally on her chastity lead us to sympathize with her even more, a response that is heightened by our knowledge of how much her society itself valued that chastity. Yet, as we have seen, we are also very aware of the narrowness of vision symbolized by the fact that she focuses so much attention on Hecuba and so little on the other characters in the Troy tapestry and what they represent. And when she commits suicide we, like Rembrandt, maintain a double vision of what that decision reveals, seeing it at once as a type of heroism that we admire and a type of misguided melodrama that, for all our sympathy, we deplore.

Even more divided are our reactions to Brutus. On one level, we feel grateful when he appears, welcoming this human version of the deus ex machina with a kind of relief that mirrors and helps us to understand the way he is accepted by the "wond'ring" (1845) spectators. One reason our responses are so positive is that his emotional self-control and political shrewdness contrast so strikingly with the helplessness of those around him; in both literal and metaphoric senses, he brings articulateness to the speechless.

What we are experiencing at the end of *The Rape of Lucrece* is, then, the psychological need that corresponds to—and helps to explain— the literary phenomenon of closure: we want tumult to be quieted, pain to be assuaged, and Brutus promises to do all that. In short, we react to him with the pleasure we experience when we encounter the prosodic equivalent to his behavior, the couplet that closes a sonnet or a scene in a play. But if Brutus effects a kind of closure, like the couplet he does so at the price closure so often demands: he conceals the facts that may interfere with the ending he hopes to bring about, reshaping events to conform to the pattern he has predetermined. In this he may remind us of Fortinbras, whose epitaph on Hamlet is as inappropriate on one level as it is reassuring on another. And we may also recall the behavior of Shreve at the end of *Absalom, Absalom!*—or even that of the psychiatrist at the end of *Psycho*. Though their motives are less disturbing than Brutus', these figures are, like him, outsiders who vainly attempt to understand and summarize events very foreign to their sensibilities. Such characters are common enough—and important enough—in literature to merit a category in our anatomy of criticism.

Just as our responses to couplets may be divided, so our judgments on Brutus are very ambivalent; if we seek neat and reassuring conclusions, we also come to distrust them, looking askance at the man who promises to make the trains run on time. Yet the grounds for our distrust remain at best problematical: we need—and do not receive—more information about Brutus' motives in order to reach a balanced judgment. For all its apparent decisiveness, in certain regards the poem ends indeterminately. And so the abruptness of its conclusion both mirrors and intensifies the sense of unease Brutus has produced in us since his initial appearance, much as the ending of *Venus and Adonis* heightens our suspicions about Venus and her mode of effecting closure.

Our ambivalence about Brutus reminds us once more how complex human motivations are—and hence how difficult moral decisions can be. We are, in short, shown yet again that syneciosis is a surer model for the world than Lucrece's forms of antithesis, that predication is likely to be deceptive, and that those who, like Lucrece, attempt to ignore these truths do so at their peril. The poem, then, forces its readers to view, or review, the very truths that its title character is resisting. Another effect of our changing impressions of the principal characters is to lead us to perform a feat that Gestalt psychologists would deem impossible: to see the plot as assuming two different configurations at once. To the extent that we approve of Brutus' actions, the terrible events that preceded them enjoy some sort of resolution at the end of the poem, while to the extent that we distrust him we experience a sense of irresolution again similar to that engendered by Venus' flight at the end of *Venus and Adonis*. This double vision of the contours of *The Rape of Lucrece* parallels a broader pattern in the poem: as we will shortly see, Shakespeare explores historiography and poesy itself by juxtaposing several different modes of writing about Lucrece, each of which is marked by a distinctive approach to closure.

His methods of characterization in his second narrative poem resemble those in *Venus and Adonis* in another way as well: he repeatedly creates what is in effect a dialogic situation by attributing to his characters words with a second meaning of which they are unaware. Through this form of irony he plays two readings against each other—the meaning intended by the personages and the meaning that the reader thinks they should have intended—in much the same way that, as we will see, he plays different versions of the plot itself against each other.

One measure of how much Tarquin deceives himself is that his speech is full of examples of this irony. Take, for instance, a passage we have already examined in a different context:

Quoth he, "She took me kindly by the hand,
And gaz'd for tidings in my eager eyes,
Fearing some hard news from the warlike band
Where her beloved Collatinus lies.
O how her fear did make her colour rise!"

(253–257)

And Tarquin proceeds for nine more lines to anatomize Lucrece's fear. The reader's reaction is that her wifely concern for her husband is—and is being cited as—a telling argument against the rape. Hence we are shocked to discover that Tarquin is in fact employing it in the opposite way; his description of Lucrece is followed immediately by the rhetorical question "Why hunt I then for colour or excuses?" (267). The logical adverb "then" functions ironically, reminding us just how illogical the connection that Tarquin is making really is.

In other instances ambiguities in Tarquin's language create a different but related interplay of meanings. Vacillating about the rape, he exclaims, "O impious act including all foul harms!" (199). While it is impossible to be sure whether he is thinking about harms to himself, to her, or to both, the fact that the two preceding lines have focused on how the rape would hurt the rapist encourages us to accept the first interpretation. In so doing, however, we become acutely conscious of the potential meaning that he is apparently neglecting—the rape will harm its victim—and of the self-centeredness that the neglect manifests. The possibility that he intends to refer to her remains, of course, but even in that case the fact that he chooses a phrase that could apply to his own conduct reveals the underlying self-centeredness that we observed. Similarly, only two lines later Tarquin declares, "True valour still a true respect should have" (201). "Valour" here may retain certain meanings that are now obsolete, such as "discrimination" or "attention given to more than one point"; but its most obvious denotation, "deferential regard or esteem," is surely also present.[83] When read as an allusion to deference, the line lends itself to two very different glosses, "True valour should always receive true respect" and "True valour should always show true respect to others," and in this case the immediate context does not help us choose one over the other. If we assume Tarquin is interested in others' respect for him rather than in his respect for his victim, we are yet again

---

[83]*Oxford English Dictionary*, s.v. "respect." Prince's gloss on this, like several similar lines, claims that one meaning is central rather than acknowledging that the ambiguity is itself part of the meaning (p. 77).

[131]

reminded of how little concern he feels for Lucrece. If instead we assume he is speaking about her, the presence of an undercurrent of self-centered emotion is as revealing as it was in his statement two lines earlier. And if we assume that he intends both meanings, or consciously chooses to express one while unwittingly expressing the other because it is on his mind, then the tension between the two glosses precisely enacts the tension between the arrogant and self-serving side of the king's son on the one hand and the moral principles with which he is struggling on the other.

Shakespeare also uses such interplays of meaning to evoke contradictory impulses within Lucrece or, alternatively, the conflicts between her interpretations of experience and those of the reader. Thus the narrator explains why Lucrece does not mention the rape when she writes to Collatine:

> She dares not thereof make discovery,
>   Lest he should hold it her own gross abuse,
>   Ere she with blood had stain'd her stain'd excuse.
>
> (1314–1316)

He is using indirect discourse to express the way she views her suicide: her blood will "stain" in the sense of mark the deed that is itself stained in that it involves the letting of blood. But the word "stain" and its cognates have resonated through the whole poem, and when we read these lines we are conscious of a meaning that the word often assumes, both in this poem in particular and in speech in general: to blemish or discolor. According to this interpretation, her suicide is a tragic mistake: her blood is, appropriately enough, a blemish on a deed that is already blemished in the sense of being morally ambiguous. Hence this passage, like many of the others we have examined, embodies a conflict between how we perceive the events of the story and how its participants do.

VI

We have observed that Rome is racked by certain forms of syneciosis, while Lucrece, Tarquin, Brutus, and the readers who attempt to interpret their behavior are troubled by other instances of internalized division, of conjoined similarity and dissimilarity. Nor is the text itself immune: as we will now see, Shakespeare's approaches to both generic and historical models also involve versions of syneciosis. But his treatment of those models is best understood against the backdrop of the larger questions about perception and communication raised by the poem.

The Rape of Lucrece is packed with allusions to types of reading or, more often, misreading; *legere* and *intellegere*, like so many other components of the Roman world, are more often enemies than allies. During their initial encounter, Lucrece misreads Tarquin's face. Shortly afterward, he misconstrues the portents warning him against the rape:

> But all these poor forbiddings could not stay him;
> He in the worst sense consters their denial.
> The doors, the wind, the glove, that did delay him,
> He takes for accidental things of trial.
>
> (323–326)

Attempting to explain his behavior, Lucrece claims he is not viewing the situation clearly: "And wipe the dim mist from thy doting eyne, / That thou shalt see thy state, and pity mine" (643–644). She in turn misreads the expression on the groom's face. And the description of the rendition of Troy repeatedly draws attention to the act of viewing it: "There might you see" (1380), "That one might see" (1386), "You might behold" (1388), "That one would swear he saw them quake and tremble" (1393), "might one behold!" (1395). Throughout the poem, too, Lucrece believes that Tarquin's deed can be read on her face; she fearfully predicts, for instance, that,

> Yea, the illiterate that know not how
> To cipher what is writ in learned books,
> Will quote my loathsome trespass in my looks.
> (810–812)

Hence one sign of her attempt to become "mistress of [her] fate" (1069) is her newfound belief that her face can serve a different function than it has previously assumed, becoming a text that will punish, not merely publish, Tarquin's deed: "How Tarquin must be us'd, *read* it in me" (1195; italics added). Notice that even at this point she characteristically maintains that the text will be read correctly.

If Lucrece herself repeatedly reads texts, we are engaged in reading, or at times misreading, the text that is merely called "Lucrece" on its 1594 title page. The final act in *Troilus and Cressida* includes a scene in which the audience watches Thersites watching Troilus and Ulysses watching Cressida and Diomedes. Similarly, in *The Rape of Lucrece* the audience reads the story of Lucrece reading the story of Hecuba.

[133]

That reflexive process is heightened by references that again find an analogue in *Troilus and Cressida* as well as in *Julius Caesar* and *Antony and Cleopatra*: the poem frequently alludes to the fact that later authors will tell the story of Lucrece. On one level, of course, such allusions playfully assert that what we are encountering is not one of those versions but rather the actual, unfolding events. At the same time, on another level we are reminded that what we are reading is indeed an instance of those fictive accounts whose popularity Lucrece so accurately predicts. In other words, such references function very like a phenomenon in the visual arts: a border or frame on which the painting itself intrudes, or from which it extrudes. The fact that the work will not be confined to its border implies that it has a reality beyond that of art—while at the same time we are all the more conscious of that border and hence all the more aware that this is in fact a work of art.

This concern with reading is part of a broader preoccupation with how we communicate. For the poem plays two very different modes of interpretation against each other and in so doing offers a semiotic analogue to the distinction between the simple and innocent world that Lucrece attempts to inhabit on the one hand and the more ambiguous one in which she in fact resides on the other. The first mode of communication typically consists of icons and indexes, signs that by their very nature facilitate clear communication. On the whole heraldry, to which the poem frequently refers, exemplifies this type of sign.[84] Thus when Tarquin predicts "Some loathsome dash the herald will contrive, / To cipher me how fondly I did dote" (206–207), neither he nor the reader has any doubts that the herald's sign would be read correctly; indeed, that is the very thing that makes it so harmful. The faces of Ajax and Ulysses also exemplify this type of communication:

> In Ajax and Ulysses, O what art
> Of physiognomy might one behold!
> The face of either cipher'd either's heart;
> Their face their manners most expressly told.
> (1394–1397)

---

[84]For a different but related interpretation of signs in *The Rape of Lucrece*, see David Bevington, *Action Is Eloquence: Shakespeare's Language of Gesture* (Cambridge, Mass.: Harvard Univ. Press, 1984), pp. 22–26. I am grateful to the author for making his work available to me prior to publication. Hulse (p. 178) also comments on the heraldry, but his interpretation, unlike mine, stresses its ambiguity.

And Lucrece repeatedly expresses the belief that all countenances function like Ajax' and Ulysses'. Thus, for instance, she predicts:

> Reproach is stamp'd in Collatinus' face,
> And Tarquin's eye may read the mot afar,
> How he in peace is wounded, not in war.
>
> (829–831)

But most of the signs in the poem belong to the second mode of communication: they are characteristically ambiguous, even deceptive. The faces outside the depiction of Troy cannot in fact be read as easily as those of Ajax and Ulysses. Lucrece typically assumes that the groom can interpret her expression correctly—an assumption that leads her to misinterpret his:

> The homely villain cur'sies to her low,
> And blushing on her with a steadfast eye,
> Receives the scroll without or yea or no,
> And forth with bashful innocence doth hie;
> But they whose guilt within their bosoms lie,
>   Imagine every eye beholds their blame,
>   For Lucrece thought he blush'd to see her shame:
>   . . . . .
> His kindled duty kindled her mistrust,
> That two red fires in both their faces blazed;
> She thought he blush'd, as knowing Tarquin's lust,
> And blushing with him, wistly on him gazed.
> Her earnest eye did make him more amazed;
>   The more she saw the blood his cheeks replenish,
>   The more she thought he spied in her some blemish.
>
> (1338–1344, 1352–1358)

These stanzas are not wholly successful (an unfortunate and apparently unwitting undercurrent of comedy steals in), but they do draw attention to the type of confusing sign that is so common in the world Shakespeare evokes. Especially common—and especially troubling—are signs that seem to mean one thing while in fact they mean another. Thus Brutus' name appears as translucent as its analogies in the "lingua Adamica"—but both the motives for which it was adopted and the person who adopts it are in fact opaque to the internal audience of the poem.

As the instance of that name would suggest, *The Rape of Lucrece* is particularly concerned with one central component of the interpretative process, language itself. This concern is prominent in Shakespeare's sources, too, and may even be one reason for his attraction to them; Ovid, for instance, repeatedly stresses Lucrece's difficulty in speaking. But if the motif appears in Ovid and Livy, Shakespeare develops it more thoroughly and more systematically. The poem that opens and closes on references to publishing is packed with allusions to language. The characters praise and slander each other, they deliver declamations and orations, they swear oaths, they curse, they name and misname. And *The Rape of Lucrece*, like *Venus and Adonis*, repeatedly refers to various types of storytelling: ballads, nursery tales, and the stories of the historian. In light of this recurrent interest in language, it is not surprising that the ecphrasis of Troy includes no fewer than three stanzas on the orator Nestor, significantly more attention than any of the other figures, including even Hecuba, receives.

Many scenes in *The Rape of Lucrece* body forth the breakdown of language, and even where it succeeds in its functions we are often aware of its moral ambiguities, of the prices we pay for plundering our wordhoard. But, as I suggested earlier, critics need to be wary of the contemporary tendency to exaggerate Shakespeare's doubts about language, elevating what is one strand in his thought on the subject to a significance it does not deserve even, or perhaps especially, in reference to a work like *Love's Labour's Lost. The Rape of Lucrece* itself in fact includes positive as well as negative evaluations of language. But whether it is viewed positively or negatively, what is stressed above all is its relationship to social and political power.

Shakespeare explores the problematical nature of praise and flattery throughout his career—we may think especially of the flattering counselors in the history plays, of Lear and his daughters, and, of course, of the sonnets—but nowhere are the dangers of this type of speech more pronounced or more pernicious than in *The Rape of Lucrece*. It is by boasting of Lucrece that Collatine tempts his kinsman to rape her, and Shakespeare foregrounds that boast by omitting Tarquin's initial visit to Lucrece. I do not of course mean that praise is unimportant in the original version of the plot; after all, the compliments that the soldiers competitively lavish on their wives generate their fateful trip to see Lucrece. But by leaving out that trip Shakespeare puts more weight on the way Collatine's words affect Tarquin: her husband's tribute to Lucrece's virtue becomes not only an antecedent cause of the rapist's attack on her but one of the immediate and principal causes. This is, then, the first of many instances throughout *The Rape of Lucrece* in which we are forced to consider the potency—for good and ill—of language.

Moreover, Tarquin wins Lucrece's trust by praising Collatine:

> He stories to her ears her husband's fame,
> Won in the fields of fruitful Italy;
> And decks with praises Collatine's high name,
> Made glorious by his manly chivalry
> With bruised arms and wreaths of victory.
>   Her joy with heav'd-up hand she doth express,
>   And wordless so greets heaven for his success.
>
> Far from the purpose of his coming thither,
> He makes excuses for his being there;
>   (106–114)

It is telling that the assault on her ears shortly precedes the assault on her body. In defining lechery *The Cloud of Unknowing* links together "fleshly dalliance, glosing, flattery,"[85] and Shakespeare too is hinting at links between sexuality and flattery—links that become far more explicit in the sonnets. It is also telling that Tarquin apparently realizes that the way to please Lucrece is to compliment her husband, not herself: Shakespeare's heroine is innocent of the pride to which Augustine refers in describing Lucrece as "Romana mulier, laudis avida nimium" ("a Roman lady, too greedy of praise," p. 88), but her virtuous love for Collatine renders her greedy of his praise. When he praises her husband, Tarquin, like Iago, is again making a net of her own goodness.

Shakespeare's emphasis on the perils of praise foregrounds the unctuous compliments of the dedication. No doubt many readers, Renaissance and modern, initially peruse this conventional tribute rapidly and superficially. Troubled by the flattery described in the body of the poem, however, we may well come to review the flattery that preceded it in a new light. After reading *The Rape of Lucrece* we realize, for example, that the lines in question are at once a tribute to Southampton's power and also in a sense an attempt to gain power over him by praising him. Only in the sonnets does Shakespeare fully examine the issues about patronage that this dedication raises. But even the brief hints about such problems that we find in *The Rape of Lucrece* assume an important function in the poem: they intensify the parallels between our experience and Lucrece's. Our uneasy sense that we accepted the conventional compliments to Southampton cor-

[85]*The Cloud of Unknowing and The Book of Privy Counselling*, ed. Phyllis Hodgson, EETS, o.s. 218 (London: Humphrey Milford, 1944), p. 37.

responds to Lucrece's recognition that her assailant's praise is not to be trusted.

Slander is the reverse side of flattery, and it is no less dangerous. The most efficacious threat Tarquin makes is that if Lucrece does not yield to him he will kill her and one of her servants and announce that he caught her committing adultery with the murdered man. The potency of that threat testifies to the power of a lie and the vulnerability of the good when faced by one, issues to which we will return when considering the sonnets. We have already observed one reason slander is so effective: we are prone to misread signs and hence are easy targets for misleading ones. In short, slander is a kind of verbal equivalent of rape itself: the powerful overcome the weak, the evil turn the good into images of themselves.

But language provides power in another way as well; *The Rape of Lucrece* exemplifies the Renaissance fascination with the efficacy of oratory. We have noticed how skillfully Brutus sways his listeners. Despite the weakness and passivity with which she is associated in the final scenes of the poem, despite her initial difficulties in speaking, it is by oratory that Lucrece horrifies her listeners and ensures they will avenge her. "My tongue shall utter all" (1076), and in a poem loaded with images of darkness she brings the truth to light.

The description of Nestor, however, reminds us of the moral ambiguities inherent in rhetoric precisely when it is at its most successful.[86]

> There pleading might you see grave Nestor stand,
> As 'twere encouraging the Greeks to fight,
> Making such sober action with his hand
> That it beguil'd attention, charm'd the sight;
> In speech it seem'd his beard all silver white
>   Wagg'd up and down, and from his lips did fly
>   Thin winding breath which purl'd up to the sky.
>
> About him were a press of gaping faces,
> Which seem'd to swallow up his sound advice,
> All jointly list'ning, but with several graces,
> As if some mermaid did their ears entice.
>   (1401–1411)

We should not exaggerate the negative elements in what is in most ways an admiring portrait: the primary purpose of these lines is to

---

[86]For a different but not incompatible reading of this passage, see Donawerth, p. 17.

stress Nestor's oratorical skill. But the familiar notion of language as enchantment is no less troubling here than it was when we encountered it in *Venus and Adonis*. The image of "Thin winding breath" (1407) suggests the grace of "Nestor's golden words" (1420)—but also their insubstantiality. And as we read the second stanza we cannot be sure whether the listeners "swallow up" (1409) his advice in the sense of incorporating it into their very being or in the sense of losing it.

The process of storytelling is treated with similar ambivalence. Shortly after meeting Lucrece, Tarquin "*stories* to her ears" (106; italics added) her husband's fame, reminding us how easily storytelling may be conscripted into the service of flattery. Sinon offers his credulous listeners an "enchanting *story*" (1521; italics added). (This is but one of many instances in which the ecphrasis assumes in Shakespeare's narrative the roles a subplot plays in drama: its events mirror and hence comment on those in the main plot.) The adjective "enchanting" (1521) also encourages us to compare Nestor's mermaidlike enticements and think further about whether his stories are trustworthy. And Lucrece fears that slander will take the form of damaging narratives about her. On the other hand, storytelling serves more positive ends as well. By managing to recount the tale of the rape Lucrece secures revenge, and, however problematical his motives may be, Brutus rouses the people against the Tarquins by repeating her tale.

Behind Shakespeare's warnings about the dangers of storytelling may lie medieval theories about the sense of hearing. According to conventional analyses of evil, the five senses represent five gates through which the devil can enter the unwary Christian; thus the homily "Estote Fortes in Bello" ("Be Strong in War") warns us that the serpent may creep into our ears "if they are open to listen to slander, idle stories and lies."[87] Tarquin, Collatine, and Sinon are all guilty of telling idle stories and are forced to take the consequences. But, as we have seen, the poem offers us more central and more secular explanations of the reasons why boasting, slandering, flattering, and storytelling are all dangerous. Boasting, for example, is one of the counters in the competitiveness that warps Rome; in lieu of joining together to fight their external enemy in Ardea, Collatine and the king's son are using boasts to battle with each other.

The poem also focuses on a type of language very different from any we have examined so far, the oath. Vows figure in certain crucial

---

[87] "Estote Fortes in Bello," in *Old English Homilies and Homiletic Treatises . . . of the Twelfth and Thirteenth Centuries*, ed. Richard Morris, EETS, o.s. 29 and 34, p. 152.

moments of the poem: Lucrece, who views the rape as resulting in "an infringed oath" (1061), asks the lords who listen to her story to pledge to avenge her, and Brutus in turn then insists that they swear again. Power is relevant in these instances, as in other allusions to language: the speakers who elicit an oath from their followers are in a sense demonstrating their own power, and the oath itself is, as speech act theorists have shown, a tribute to both the efficacy of language and the efficacy of the social codes that make swearing a very significant act. In *The Rape of Lucrece*, then, as in so many of its author's plays, failures of language and its speakers are played against its potency as represented by the oath. And our suspicion that the solemn pledge is one of the props Brutus is using to manipulate his listeners reminds us again that it is that very potency of language that makes it so dangerous when used irresponsibly or maliciously.

The types of language we have examined so far are often successful—if successful in the service of ends of which we do not approve. But the poem is also very concerned with the failures of language and the inadequacies of its speakers. We have already examined this issue in relation to the set speeches in the poem. And throughout *The Rape of Lucrece* we find evidence that even the best of rhetoric is not always as persuasive as classical handbooks might lead us to believe.[88] In a tragic version of the scene in which Venus is aroused by Adonis' very attempts to cool her lust, Tarquin declares that Lucrece's words have had an effect precisely opposite from the one she intends:

> "Have done," quoth he, "my uncontrolled tide
> Turns not, but swells the higher by this let.
> Small lights are soon blown out, huge fires abide,
> And with the wind in greater fury fret;
> The petty streams that pay a daily debt
>   To their salt sovereign, with their fresh falls' haste
>   Add to his flow, but alter not his taste."
>
> (645–651)

Later the speaker himself develops a *paragone*, acknowledging that words do not express our emotions as effectively as we might hope:

> To see sad sights moves more than hear them told,
> For then the eye interprets to the ear
> The heavy motion that it doth behold,

[88]Compare Turner's observation that Lucrece is unable to persuade her audience (p. 86).

[140]

When every part a part of woe doth bear.
'Tis but a part of sorrow that we hear:
   Deep sounds make lesser noise than shallow fords,
   And sorrow ebbs, being blown with wind of words.
                                        (1324–1330)

The poem also focuses on its characters' recurrent inability to use language. Their lack of speech signals and symbolizes their lack of power. (Similarly, in a scene anticipating Lavinia's mutilation, Titus confronts his political impotence when he discovers no tribunes are present to listen to his pleas [III.i].)[89] Thus immediately before the rape Tarquin cuts off his victim's protests:

The wolf hath seiz'd his prey, the poor lamb cries,
   Till with her own white fleece her voice controll'd
Entombs her outcry in her lips' sweet fold.

For with the nightly linen that she wears
He pens her piteous clamours in her head.
                                        (677–681)

In using her own clothing against her, he is in a sense creating another internal division, much as he claims earlier that her own beauty invites him to rape her. More to our purposes here, however, is the fact that this act of violence anticipates and mirrors the more serious one he is about to commit. A metaphoric version of the mutilated Philomel, Lucrece lapses into a silence that aptly symbolizes the other kinds of powerlessness she endures.

As the poem progresses, a loss of speech continues to represent a loss of power. In an encounter that may be an ironic allusion to the highly verbal *domina-nutrix* scenes of the Senecan tradition, Lucrece and her maid confront each other speechlessly. And Lucrece initially finds it very difficult to tell Collatine and her other listeners about the rape: "Three times with sighs she gives her sorrow fire, / Ere once she can discharge one word of woe" (1604–1605). His "voice damm'd up with woe" (1661), Collatine in turn cannot express his grief. When it comes time to name her attacker Lucrece again is unable to speak:

---

[89]Lavinia's own silence is discussed, e.g., by Rudolf Stamm, "The Alphabet of Speechless Complaint: A Study of the Mangled Daughter in Shakespeare's *Titus Andronicus*," in *The Triple Bond: Plays, Mainly Shakespearean, in Performance*, ed. Joseph G. Price (University Park, Pa.: Pennsylvania State Univ. Press, 1975). The essay also appears under the same title in *ES*, 55 (1974), 325–339.

Here with a sigh as if her heart would break,
She throws forth Tarquin's name. "He, he," she says,
But more than "he" her poor tongue could not speak;
Till after many accents and delays,
Untimely breathings, sick and short assays,
   She utters this: "He, he, fair lords; 'tis he,
   That guides this hand to give this wound to me."

                       (1716–1722)

Similarly, shortly after her suicide Lucretius tries to talk, but he finds that "the deep vexation of his inward soul / Hath serv'd a dumb arrest upon his tongue" (1779–1780); he proves quite as inarticulate as his daughter and son-in-law. Finally, it is a measure of Brutus' power that he can speak in a situation in which others are speechless.

That speechlessness suggests yet another reason syneciosis is so apt a figure for Lucrece's Rome: committed to *eloquentia*, its citizens are frequently unable to utter a single word. The social significance of their inarticulateness emerges when we remember the Renaissance humanists' belief that language is not merely a system of symbols but rather also a means of communication between the members of a society. When they are deprived of language, the Romans endure yet another form of internal contradiction: though they revere familial and social bonds, they find themselves isolated from their families and their society by their silence.

VII

Shakespeare's generic decisions reflect the concern for the uses and abuses of language that I have been charting elsewhere in the poem. As many readers have observed, *The Rape of Lucrece* is very indebted to the complaint tradition.[90] When we look more closely at its relationship to that genre, however, we discover a central distinction: though Shakespeare borrows many motifs from the literary type in question, his narrative is also engaged in commenting on it and even undercutting it. Literary works regularly react against their generic parents and siblings, of course, but in this case the reaction is un-

[90]On that tradition, see "Introduction," Lily B. Campbell, ed., *The Mirror for Magistrates* (Cambridge: Cambridge Univ. Press, 1983); Farnham, chap. 7; Hallett Smith, pp. 118–130; E. M. W. Tillyard, "*A Mirror for Magistrates* Revisited," in *Elizabethan and Jacobean Studies Presented to Frank Percy Wilson* (Oxford: Clarendon, 1959).

usually extensive and intensive. In yet another version of syneciosis, the instances of the genre within this poem undermine themselves; indeed, *The Rape of Lucrece* might well be said to be a complaint against the complaint.

To trace this pattern, we need to define the generic context of his poem more precisely than we usually do. To begin with, Shakespeare's narrative evidently participates in that vast tradition of Tudor complaints that is rooted in the *Mirror* and ultimately in Ovid's *Heroides*. Hallett Smith has attempted to place *The Rape of Lucrece* in a narrower framework: the complaints written about inviolably chaste women in the 1590s.[91] Distinguishing these poems from their counterparts in the *Mirror*, he maintains that they substitute increased sentiment for the moral and political concerns of earlier works in the genre; the primary aim of these later complaints, he argues, is to move their readers, not to instruct them.

I would suggest, however, that both Shakespeare and his Elizabethan readers were more likely to interpret the poem in the context of a different but related kind of complaint. In some works of this type, the heroine does retain her chastity, but in others she loses it. And, significantly enough, she is threatened by a ruler, a situation that invites speculations on the uses and abuses of power; rather than neglecting the political questions threaded through the *Mirror*, these complaints simply approach them from a different perspective, that of the women who variously yield to the monarch's power or, alternatively, valiantly preserve their chastity in the face of it. No fewer than seven poems of this type appeared within the brief span of two years: Daniel's "The Complaint of Rosamond" (1592); Churchyard's "The Tragedy of Shore's Wife" (1593), a considerably expanded version of a poem in *A Mirror for Magistrates*; Chute's "Beawtie Dishonoured" (1593); Lodge's "The Complaint of Elstred" (1593); Barnfield's "The Complaint of Chastitie" (1594); Drayton's "Matilda" (1594); and of course *The Rape of Lucrece* (1594). Though these poems may deviate from the formula in small particulars (most obviously, Tarquin is not a king but the son of one), they follow it closely enough—and appear in close enough conjunction with each other—that contemporary readers would have sensed themselves in the presence of a subgenre.

In their preoccupation with the power of language the earlier poems in this tradition anticipate *Lucrece* itself. They typically expose the perils of praise, condemned in Drayton's "Matilda" as a "fond

[91]*Elizabethan Poetry*, pp. 116–130.

pratling Parrat" (153), and of praise's bastard brother, flattery. Chute's "Beawtie Dishonoured" includes a passage on the subject that could serve as a gloss to Collatine's tragically ill-considered boast:

> For till thou first with thine vnhappie storie,
> Ecchoing relations of my worth and me:
> Intitul'dst my name to my bewties glorie,
> Vnworthie knowne, of such a worth to be
> > Though not performed in so royall measure
> > Yet then I ioy'd a life of quyet pleasure.[92]

And these complaints repeatedly draw attention to the moral ambiguities involved in the process of persuasion, with Daniel actually bodying forth those dangers in his portrait of the woman who tempts Rosamond:

> Shee set vpon me with the smoothest speech,
> That Court and age could cunningly deuise:
> The one autentique made her fit to teach,
> The other learnt her how to subtelise:
> Both were enough to circumuent the wise.[93]

Wise, Rosamond is not, and she is easily circumvented by the wiles of rhetoric.

Another link between these poems and Shakespeare's narrative is their concern for the political implications of what Lucrece herself terms "private pleasure" (1478). Drayton renders explicit an implication in several other poems: the king's sexual aggression is a symptom of his tyranny. In "Matilda" we witness lust distorting the king's relationship not only with the title character but also with his other subjects: he actually banishes her father, a loyal follower, on trumped-up charges, lest Matilda be protected by her parent. And, as I have already suggested, the complaints in this group are very concerned with the nature of power, whether it be the sexual power of a woman or the political power of a monarch. One way Churchyard transforms the complaint of Jane Shore in the *Mirror* into the version he published in his *Churchyards Challenge* is by lengthening the heroine's

---

[92]Throughout my text Chute is quoted from [Anthony Chute], *Beawtie Dishonoured* (London, 1593); here I cite ll. 486–491.

[93]Samuel Daniel, *Poems and A Defence of Ryme*, ed. Arthur Colby Sprague (London: Routledge and Kegan Paul, 1950), ll. 218–222.

demonstration that she used her own power judiciously; this passage serves to increase our sympathy for her, but it also draws our attention to larger questions about power and the powerful. Similarly, Lucrece adduces Renaissance commonplaces on these issues when she pleads with Tarquin:

> This deed will make thee only lov'd for fear;
> But happy monarchs still are fear'd for love.
> With foul offenders thou perforce must bear,
> When they in thee the like offences prove.
> If but for fear of this, thy will remove,
>   For princes are the glass, the school, the book,
>   Where subjects' eyes do learn, do read, do look.
>   (610–616)

Despite these links between *The Rape of Lucrece* and the complaints in question, when we read Shakespeare's poem we are aware mainly of suggestive distinctions: *The Rape of Lucrece* includes the "notes of rufull plaint" that Joseph Hall mockingly ascribes to the complaint tradition (*Virgidemiarum*, I.v.2),[94] but this symphony is in a different key. And the difference is very like the one that separates *Venus and Adonis* from more typical contributions to its own genre: Shakespeare repeatedly renders the values and assumptions of the complaint problematical, generally by directing our attention to the psychological implications behind issues treated more straightforwardly in many of the complaints we are examining and in *A Mirror for Magistrates* itself. In certain cases in doing so he simply emphasizes an insight that is also present in the more sophisticated complaints composed by his contemporaries; in other instances, we can find no precedent at all for the questions he is raising.

What Chute terms "monster fame" (31, 493) plays as important a role in the 1590s complaints as in the *Mirror*. On the whole, however, it is a clear-cut role. Fame is dangerous, we are told, because it brings the king reports of his potential victim's beauty. At the same time, Fame encompasses a concern for reputation that is presented as at the very least understandable; thus these poems typically begin with their heroines lamenting the fact that their names have been forgotten and begrudging the reputations of women with similar or even less virtuous histories. Matilda implies that she has been mistreated not only

[94] *The Collected Poems of Joseph Hall*, ed. A. Davenport (Liverpool: Liverpool Univ. Press, 1949).

by the king who failed to seduce her but also by the poets who failed
to celebrate her:

> *Shores* wife is in her wanton humor sooth'd,
> And modern Poets, still applaud her praise,
> Our famous *Elstreds* wrinckled browes are smooth'd,
> Call'd from her grave to see these latter daies,
> And happy's hee, their glory high'st can raise.
>   "Thus looser wantons, still are praised of many,
>   "Vice oft findes friends, but vertue seldome any.
>
>   (43–49)

But the poem nowhere develops the subterranean implication of this
conventional passage: however pure she may be in other ways,
Matilda's desire for fame is suspect.

Shakespeare's scrutiny of such a desire is not, however, unique in
his subgenre: "The Complaint of Rosamond" also investigates the
dangers of an obsession with fame, as a few recent scholars have
pointed out. Because Rosamond is distinguished from other com
plaint heroines by certain psychological mannerisms, such as a marked
predilection for blaming others for her downfall, we are encouraged
to scrutinize many aspects of her self-portrayal more closely than
would otherwise seem appropriate. When we do so we see hints of her
characteristic vanity in her concern for fame—and we also observe, as
one reader has demonstrated,[95] that her tendency to transfer her
guilt to others is particularly manifest in her diatribes against fame.
Shakespeare, however, explores the moral and emotional consequences of a desire for fame even more thoroughly than Daniel. In
so doing he shows us how that desire is an important component of
the preoccupation with the public world that characterizes Rome's
shame culture. And he demonstrates that Lucrece's concern for fame
is at one and the same time laudable and pathological.

Similarly, the author of *The Rape of Lucrece* deviates from other
complaints by rendering the concept of guilt problematical. In the
Mirror and the 1590s imitations of it, virtuous figures like Matilda
experience no guilt. Its presence in former sinners such as Rosamond
is an important sign of repentance and hence a hint of their future
redemption. (Like their counterparts in the *Mirror*, they enjoy a guilt-

---

[95]Ronald Primeau, "Daniel and the *Mirror* Tradition: Dramatic Irony in *The Complaint of Rosamond*," *SEL*, 15 (1975), 25. Hulse also notes that the concept of fame is
problematical in the poem (p. 63).

edged security.) Lucrece's guilt, in contrast, is yet another pathological symptom, a key to the complexities of her character rather than
the state of her soul.

In addition, the role of sexuality in *The Rape of Lucrece* is very
different from that which it plays in the tradition of complaints that
we are scrutinizing. Impelled by lust and unencumbered by scruples,
their monarchs singlemindedly pursue their prey; their motives are
not anatomized in any detail. Shakespeare, in contrast, does dissect
the motivations behind the rape he portrays, concentrating especially
on the interplay between sexual desire and aggression. And his treatment of another aspect of sexuality, the concept of chastity, is equally
complex. The heroines in other complaints variously sinfully abandon and sedulously guard their chastity, but neither they nor their
readers experience any doubts as to the definition of that virtue. It
remains uncomplicated even in "The Complaint of Rosamond," in
many regards the most sophisticated poem of the subgenre save *The
Rape of Lucrece* itself. We simply recognize that, so to speak, nice girls
don't. In contrast, in scrutinizing Lucrece's guilt and the reactions of
other Romans to the rape, Shakespeare renders the idea of chastity
quite as complicated as it is in St. Augustine's meditation on the story,
though he arrives at very different conclusions from Augustine's.

The moral and psychological preoccupations that distinguish *The
Rape of Lucrece* from its counterparts help us to understand some of
the aesthetic distinctions between these works. The complaints we are
examining are nowhere closer to the *Mirror* than in their straightforward and sententious didacticism.[96] Admittedly, some moral points
are made more subtly—the obvious instance is our evaluation of Rosamond[97]—but by and large these poems are unashamedly direct in
pointing to ethical lessons. The dying Matilda, for instance, shares
with us her "pure thoughts" (918), which include a paean to chastity
and a critique of "fond preferments" (932). Though we can adduce
unambiguous morals from the perfidy of "Lust-breathed Tarquin"
(3), doing so is but a minor part of the way the poem educates us.
Here, as in *Venus and Adonis* and, of course, most of Shakespeare's
plays, the moral truisms that the characters deliver are more significant as symptoms of emotional tendencies in the speakers than as
sources of eternal truths. And here, again as in *Venus and Adonis* and
the plays, we learn from judging and rejudging—and often misjudg-

---

[96]Compare Campbell, esp. pp. 48–51.

[97]On Daniel's mode of didacticism, see Primeau; his thesis is that the poem's didacticism resides not in direct statement but rather in its ironic presentation of the heroine.

ing—the events before us, rather than from garnering the judgments of others. Indeed, not the least effect of our confusions about Brutus is to remind us how dangerous it is to rely on other people's judgments.

A comparison of the curse Jane Shore delivers in Churchyard's "The Tragedy of Shore's Wife" with the imprecations uttered by Lucrece under somewhat similar circumstances further demarcates Shakespeare's poem from the other 1590s complaints:

> I aske of God, a vengeance on thy bones,
> Thy stinking corps, corrupts the aire I knowe:
> Thy shamefull death no earthy wight bemones:
> For in thy life, thy workes were hated so,
> That everyman, did wish thy overthroe:
> Wherefore I may, though parciall nowe I am,
> Curse every cause, whereof thy body came.
>
> Woe worth the man, that fathered such a childe,
> Woe worth the howse, wherein thou wast begate:
> Woe worth the brests, that have the world begylde,
> To norish thee, that all the worlde did hate,
> Woe worth the Gods, that gave thee such a fate,
> To live so long, that death deserued so oft,
> Woe worth the chance, that let thee vp aloft.
>
> Woe worth the day, the time the howse and all,
> When subjects clapt the crowne on Richards head,
> Woe worth the Lordes, that sat in sumptuous hall,
> To honour him, that Princes blood to shead:
> Would God he had ben boyle in scalding lead.
> When he presumde, in brothers seat to sit,
> Whose wretched rage, ruld all with wicked wit.
>   ("The Tragedy of Shore's Wife")[98]
>
> Disturb his hours of rest with restless trances,
> Afflict him in his bed with bedrid groans;
> Let there bechance him pitiful mischances,
> To make him moan, but pity not his moans.

[98][Thomas Churchyard], *Churchyards Challenge* (London, 1593), p. 142. (In the book certain page numbers are repeated; page 142 should in fact be 152.)

Stone him with harden'd hearts harder than stones,
And let mild women to him lose their mildness,
Wilder to him than tigers in their wildness.

Let him have time to tear his curled hair,
Let him have time against himself to rave,
Let him have time of time's help to despair,
Let him have time to live a loathed slave,
Let him have time a beggar's orts to crave,
And time to see one that by alms doth live
Disdain to him disdained scraps to give.
(*The Rape of Lucrece*, 974–987)

First of all, as we have already observed, Shakespeare foregrounds the act of delivering a complaint, so that as we read these lines we evaluate Lucrece's very decision to deliver them: we interpret them not only as conventional literary rhetoric but also as unconventional human behavior. Like Venus, Lucrece gets carried away with her own speeches, and our sympathy and respect for her, though considerable, do not preclude dismay at that spectacle.

Moreover, just as the laments of the heroines in most epyllia are indistinguishable from each other, so Jane Shore's lines could be interchanged with comparable passages in many other complaints of the period: they reveal little about her situation or her sensibility. The same could certainly be said of a few of Lucrece's own statements, such as "Let him have time of time's help to despair" (983), but by and large as we go through the passage we see that it is far more precisely tailored than Churchyard's. To begin with, whereas antitheses are common in set speeches, we recognize that these instances of the figure reveal important truths about the speaker. Behind the allusion to Tarquin's bed may well lie an embittered sense of justice: it would be fitting that he suffer in the place in which he has brought her so much suffering. A few lines later, the allusion to hardened hearts recalls Lucrece's earlier description of his own pleas: "All which together, like a troubled ocean, / Beat at thy rocky and wrack-threat'ning heart" (589–590). In other words, the woman who believes she has assumed some of the worst qualities of her assailant is here wishing that that assailant in turn assume the role of his victim. There may be some reference, too, to the biblical punishment of stoning adulterers. The curious allusion to "mild women" (979) in the final lines of the stanza hints again, I think, at Lucrece's guilt that she herself was too mild, not fighting off the attack vigorously enough; she wishes other women to play the part that she herself failed to take on, so that the "rough beast" (545) who devised for her "a wilderness where are no laws" (544) himself becomes prey to a wild animal. In the next stanza, "Let him have time against himself to rave" (982) continues the preoccupation with self-destruction, with emotions turned inward, that characterizes the entire poem. And the stanza concludes on the references to beggars, part of a pattern of such allusions that foreshadow Tarquin's journey on Fortune's wheel from the highest to the lowest estate.

One distinction between *The Rape of Lucrece* and the complaints in question informs many of the other differences we have been enumerating: the playwright who composed *The Rape of Lucrece* alters his generic models to render his tale more dramatic in several senses of that dangerously protean term.[99] Most obviously, of course, he incorporates the passages that might have appeared as "The Complaint of Lucrece" within the larger framework of a narrative poem, thus ensuring that the main events of his heroine's life will be enacted before us, not recounted in retrospect as they would have been in a complaint. *The Rape of Lucrece* is dramatic, too, in that its declamations are a means toward subtle characterization, not an impediment to it; as we have seen, Shakespeare relates the conventional language of his set speeches to the situations of his personages in a way that a writer like Churchyard does not. And we have just observed that ethical problems like the dangers of fame are typically bodied forth in the behavior of characters, not set forth in a sententious couplet. In other words, moral issues are acted out rather than being confined to the discursive level of the poem. But perhaps the most striking instance of Shakespeare's dramatizing the complaint occurs when Lucrece gazes at the depiction of Troy. One of the most common conventions of set speeches is that their bereaved speakers express the wish to share their grief with others. Shakespeare, however, actually renders this idea as a dramatic episode: Lucrece's experience as she gazes at the tableau and, in particular, as she identifies with Hecuba.

In short, then, *The Rape of Lucrece* examines many of the values behind the subgenre it incorporates. The very act on which that literary type is based becomes problematical: the desire to intone a complaint rather than responding to experience in other ways is rendered

[99]For a different approach to the mode of the poem, see Walley, p. 480. Also cf. Smith, p. 113, who notes that it is dramatic in the sense that it incorporates multiple viewpoints.

as a psychological symptom the reader should evaluate carefully, not a literary convention he or she should accept unthinkingly. Engaged in examining the literary and social uses of language from so many other perspectives, Shakespeare's narrative also calls into question the moral predilections inherent in writing a complaint and the emotional predilections inherent in delivering one.

VIII

As she stares intently at the depiction of Troy, Lucrece provides an emblem for one of the most central preoccupations in *The Rape of Lucrece*: the problems of reading and writing history. Thomas M. Greene has distinguished simple imitation, in which the issues about history and time raised by literary imitation are unconnected to the central concerns of the work, and complex imitation, in which such issues are in fact treated thematically.[100] It would be hard to find a better example of the latter category than *The Rape of Lucrece*. If Shakespeare foregrounds the questions about chastity, fame, and so on that are obscured in most complaints, he also emphasizes the questions posed by imitation itself. His title character delivers a long declamation about time, while his repeated allusions to closure provide another perspective on temporal processes. And, above all, throughout *The Rape of Lucrece* he explores alternative ways of crafting histories. This interest in Clio is, of course, an extension of the poem's concern for other types of interpretation. It is an extension, too, of the preoccupation with identity that we have encountered throughout Shakespeare's narrative: a culture, like an individual, must know its past in order to know itself. And Shakespeare's historiography represents yet another version of syneciosis: seemingly similar historical narratives, like those in the Argument and the poem itself, though linked together prove very different.

Behind the treatment of history in this poem lie extensive and controversial Renaissance debates on the subject.[101] Central to these discussions is the question of whether historical accounts can be trusted. Following their classical predecessors, many Renaissance historians stress the reliability of such narratives: Amyot, for instance,

---

[100]Thomas M. Greene, *The Light in Troy: Imitation and Discovery in Renaissance Poetry* (New Haven: Yale Univ. Press, 1982), pp. 52–53.

[101]For a useful summary of the subject, see Herschel Baker, *The Race of Time: Three Lectures on Renaissance Historiography* (n.p.: Univ. of Toronto Press, 1967).

confidently declares that history "helpeth not itself with any other thing than with the plaine truth,"[102] and Camden observes that the historian can "recall home Veritie."[103] But this enthusiasm does not go unchallenged; indeed, the very texts that celebrate history with an assurance that anticipates Ranke's historicism may in other passages undermine the praises they are bestowing on Clio. Sir Walter Raleigh's confidence about history, for example, is undercut by his enumeration of the reasons it can be difficult to know the truth: "Informations are often false, records not alwaies true, and notorious actions commonly insufficient to discouer the passions, which did set them first on foote."[104]

As Raleigh's statement would suggest, Renaissance historians prove uncomfortably aware that a whole range of factors may prevent them from offering us that "plaine truth" that Amyot promises. Tracing the implications of the humanists' recurrent imagery of mining, Thomas Greene has charted their fear that recovering the past is a dangerous and difficult enterprise.[105] That fear is apparent even in Amyot, who, himself alluding to mines, admits that he may have missed some veins. One impediment to finding the truth is the unreliability of other historical accounts, a dilemma commonly deplored by students of history during the Renaissance. Playing on a pun that also appears in Shakespeare's sonnets, Sir Philip Sidney mocks the historian "authorising himself (for the most part) upon other histories, whose greatest authorities are built upon the notable foundation of hearsay."[106] But even historians more sympathetic to their own cause than the author of *An Apologie for Poetry* acknowledge the inadequacy of their sources. Jean Bodin, sophisticated on this as so many other issues, enumerates the questions we can adduce to test a historian's reliablility (he suggests, for example, we note whether he is writing about his own people or another nation) and proceeds to

---

[102]"Amyot to the Readers," in *Plutarch's Lives of the Noble Grecians and Romans Englished by Sir Thomas North*, ed. George Wyndham, 6 vols. (London: David Nutt, 1895–1896), I, 11. Future references to this edition will appear in the text.

[103]William Camden, *Britain*, trans. Philemon Holland (London, 1610), "To the Reader."

[104]*The History of the World*, ed. C. A. Patrides (London: Macmillan, 1971), p. 213. Page numbers in the text below refer to this edition.

[105]See *The Light in Troy*, esp. pp. 8–11, and his article, "Resurrecting Rome: The Double Task of the Humanist Imagination," in *Rome in the Renaissance*.

[106]*An Apology for Poetry, or, The Defence of Poesy*, ed. Geoffrey Shepherd (London: Nelson, 1965), p. 105.

evaluate his predecessors.[107]Another reason these historians themselves are prone to distrust their field is that they realize how frequently their colleagues prostitute Clio in the course of pandering to
their employers; Polydore Vergil, for instance, was widely known to
have been more interested in pleasing Henry VIII than in telling the
truth. Finally, several historians acknowledge the difficulty of writing
dispassionately about events, yet another issue on which contemporary historical thought echoes that of the Renaissance; Bodin discusses this problem at several points, while Raleigh admits the
problems of recording the historical events of one's own time.[108]

Another controversial issue in Renaissance historiography is the
nature of historical causality. Writers typically accept the conventional
wisdom about providentiality, even going so far as to see a new star as
a commemoration of the St. Bartholomew's Day massacre.[109] Thus
Raleigh, whose *History of the World* is crammed with allusions to the
wonder-working providence of God, declares that history allows us to
know "for what vertue and piety GOD made prosperous; and for
what vice and deformity he made wretched" (p. 48). But writers are,
of course, notoriously unwilling to hold consistently to the beliefs that
the Norton Anthology and its counterparts attribute to them, and the
providential interpretation of history is no exception. It is obviously
challenged by a Machiavellian model of political process; and
Herschel Baker among others has charted the underlying doubts
present even in the historians who seem most committed to the providential view.[110]

Also central to historiography during the Renaissance are discussions of the difference between history and poesy. These debates
were to culminate in the seventeenth century in a widespread insistence on separating the two fields, an insistence aptly symbolized by
Daniel's abandonment of his role as historian.[111] A related issue,
however, is more relevant to *The Rape of Lucrece*: most historians assert

---

[107]*Method for the Easy Comprehension of History*, trans. Beatrice Reynolds (New York:
Columbia Univ. Press, 1945), chap. 4.

[108]See, e.g., Bodin, p. 43, and Raleigh, p. 80.

[109]Baker, p. 68.

[110]Baker, pp. 68–70. Also see Henry Ansgar Kelly, *Divine Providence in the England of
Shakespeare's Histories* (Cambridge, Mass.: Harvard Univ. Press, 1970); he maintains that
the Tudors variously subscribed to not one but several different providential interpretations of history and that these interpretations are presented in Shakespeare's plays
as the attitudes of particular characters, not authorial judgments.

[111]See Hulse, chap. 5.

[153]

that texts in their field have no style, being unencumbered by rhetorical devices and principles. Thus Holinshed boasts in his dedicatory epistle, "I neuer made any choise of stile, or words . . . thinking it sufficient, truelie and plainelie to set forth such things as I minded to intreat of, rather than with vaine affection of eloquence to paint out a rotten sepulchre."[112] Similar assumptions lie behind Roger Ascham's advocacy of "playne and open" historical writing.[113] And in his *Britain* Camden takes pride in the fact that he has neglected the very issues that concern poets: "neither have I waied every word in Goldsmithes scales . . . neither purposed I to picke flowres out of the gardens of Eloquence," he writes in "To the Reader," quoting Cicero in support of his approach to historical prose.

Shakespeare's own experiences writing history in the years before he composed *The Rape of Lucrece* must have intensified his interest in the issues contemporary historians were debating. The process of comparing his sources repeatedly reminded him how much accounts of the same event can differ from each other—a concern that emerges in *Richard III* when the title character carefully plants reports of historical events like his wife's illness to further his own ends. Both the act of excerpting stories from the longer accounts he found in the chronicles and the process of shaping several plays into his first tetralogy demonstrated one reason historical accounts differ so much: where one opens a story and where one closes it in no small measure shapes how the events in between are viewed.[114] Thus even if one does not wholly accept the providential view of history, the events of the reign of Henry VI seem very different when one acknowledges that they culminate in the rise of Richard III. Similarly, selecting historical details from among the multitude in his sources must have made Shakespeare reflect on how what one omits affects a story. He was later to make this concern explicit in the Epilogue to *Henry V*, where the admission that the play was "mangling by starts" (4; that is, by omissions) the deeds of the heroes is not only a tribute to their glorious feats but also an acknowledgment of the difficulty of writing about those or any other historical happenings. It is likely, too, that during the early years of his career Shakespeare pondered the differences between the genres in which history can be told. Certainly he

[112]*Holinshed's Chronicles*, 3 vols. (London, 1587), I, "Epistle Dedicatorie."

[113]*A Report . . . of the affaires and state of Germany* (London: 1570?), sig. Aiv.

[114]Hayden White comments on the problems of turning a chronicle into history in *Metahistory: The Historical Imagination in Nineteenth-Century Europe* (Baltimore: Johns Hopkins Univ. Press, 1973), pp. 5–6.

must have mused on the distinctions between how the same stories are variously handled in the chronicles, in *A Mirror for Magistrates*, and in a play; and, like modern critics, he must have speculated on the distinctions between a tragedy and a history play about, say, Richard III.

In any event, it is evident that the act of writing *The Rape of Lucrece* raised these very issues for its author. Like Lucrece standing before the rendition of Troy, he studied others' accounts of historical events; unlike Lucrece, he confronted a number of different and even contradictory accounts. Thus Ovid and Livy disagree not only in their handling of a few minor facts but in their tone: Ovid's account is more emotional, offering more details about the characters' feelings and expressing more sympathy for them. In fact, the notes in the Ovid edition that Shakespeare apparently used draw attention repeatedly to the differences between the various retellings of Lucrece's story. In particular, a comparison of Livy's version with Ovid's foregrounds the issues about openings and closure that, as I have suggested, Shakespeare no doubt debated even before writing this poem. For Livy's account places Lucrece's tragedy in the broader historical context of the previous misdeeds of Tarquin's father and the subsequent political changes in Rome, while Ovid focuses on Lucrece herself, referring more briefly to the historical events that frame the story. In addition, comparing the prose historical narratives composed by Livy and Ovid with his own account (and with that of Chaucer, if he did indeed draw from that well of English undefiled) must have intensified Shakespeare's interest in how historical genres differ from each other.

Many of these suggestions about the creative biography of *The Rape of Lucrece* must remain speculative. It is, however, incontrovertible that the poem itself raises the very questions about the reporting of public events that engaged so many historians during the Renaissance: *The Rape of Lucrece* is a study in historiography as well as in history. If, as Robert Ornstein and others have shown, Shakespeare continues to experiment with historical form throughout his career, interpreting the genre in radically different ways each time he returns to it,[115] that same process of vision and revision is enacted synchronically within *The Rape of Lucrece*. For the poem plays several different ways of interpreting history against each other and in so

[115]*A Kingdom for a Stage: The Achievement of Shakespeare's History Plays* (Cambridge, Mass.: Harvard Univ. Press, 1972), p. 2. Simone compares the treatment of history in *The Rape of Lucrece* and its author's history plays taking a different perspective from mine; he argues, for example, that the view of history in the narrative poem is more pessimistic and closer to the tragic mode (see esp. pp. 118, 125).

doing invites us to speculate about what each of these ways reflects about the nature of history and the nature of its proponents.

The complaint is significant not only as a generic model for the narrative but also as one of the historical visions within it: the type of complaint that is found in *A Mirror for Magistrates* as well as in later imitations of that poem and is employed by Lucrece herself becomes a metaphor for Lucrece's characteristic approach to history. Such complaints are rooted in the events of the past, not those of the present or future. This temporal perspective reflects the role in history frequently assumed by those who deliver such poems: unlike their counterparts in the *Heroides*, the suffering (and often insufferable) protagonists of Elizabethan complaints cannot affect the present and future, except very indirectly, through their roles as moral exempla. The fact that most of the figures delivering such poems are ghosts not only explains but also symbolizes this powerlessness: however potent they have once been, at the point when they appear before us they are as insubstantial politically as they are physically.

Furthermore, by their very nature complaints focus on the suffering of their protagonists, referring only in passing to the larger historical backdrop. Thus Drayton's "Peirs Gaveston," unlike the Marlowe play in which that unlovely lover figures, concentrates primarily on the title character's own relationship to Edward II; the other problems of Edward's reign command comparatively brief attention. Similarly, though the complaints of women pursued by monarchs do raise important issues about the nature of tyranny, these poems devote less space to such problems than a prose tract or a historical drama might do.

It is evident, then, that the complaint typifies Lucrece's own approach to history. Unable to redeem or reshape the horrors of the past by achieving revenge in the present, unable to envision the long-term political results of the rape, she must depend on others to punish Tarquin. To the extent that we view her suicide as a pathetic gesture rather than a heroic one, it reflects her inability to function in the present; if the other characters who deliver complaints are ghosts, Lucrece chooses to become one.

The way she interprets the events of the Trojan war also exemplifies what I have termed the complaint's vision of history. As we have seen, rather than observing the episodes which hint that the suffering of Troy will be redeemed, she devotes most of her attention to Hecuba's grief. In so doing she demonstrates a concern with the horrors of the past rather than the hopes of the future and with the needs of the individual rather than with the broader historical and social issues of his or her culture.

In associating Lucrece with the complaint, then, Shakespeare is providing an image for the role of women in history.[116] This is not to say, of course, that he presents the complaint as an exclusively female approach to history: no reader of the *Mirror*, which included only male ghosts in its early editions, would be tempted to invoke the genre for that purpose. Shakespeare is, however, implicitly reminding us that the passivity of the complaint represents the role women typically assume in history: bemoaning events they cannot influence. His Lucrece takes her place among the wailing women in *Richard III*.

While bodying forth one vision of history in the person of Lucrece, Shakespeare also offers us a contrasting vision, the epic or heroic mode of reading writing history. *The Rape of Lucrece*, like many poems in the *Heroides*, implicitly contrasts the vision of its protagonist with the epic perspective of the men who normally dominate both historical texts and history itself. Brutus condenses many implications of this perspective when he exhorts Collatine,

> Courageous Roman, do not steep thy heart
> In such relenting dew of lamentations;
> But kneel with me and help to bear thy part
> To rouse our Roman gods with invocations,
> That they will suffer these abominations,—
>> Since Rome herself in them doth stand disgraced,—
>> By our strong arms from forth her fair streets chased.
>>> (1828–1834)

The epic approach to Clio invokes the sublimation or mitigation of suffering through "strong arms" (1834) rather than the expression of it in a "dew of lamentations" (1829). And it involves aggressively shaping historical happenings rather than being passively shaped by them, acting in the present and future rather than reacting to the past. Brutus plays Bolingbroke to Lucrece's Richard II.

The proponents of the epic viewpoint on history characteristically interpret causality providentially—and sometimes, as in the case of Brutus, conveniently see themselves as the agents of providence. Notice, for example, that he adheres to the most conservative notions

[116]On this issue, see esp. Linda Bamber, *Comic Women, Tragic Men: A Study of Gender and Genre in Shakespeare* (Stanford: Stanford Univ. Press, 1982), chap. 6; Madonne M. Miner, "'Neither mother, wife, nor England's queen': The Roles of Women in *Richard III*," in *The Woman's Part*. Bamber maintains that women are generally seen as supernumeraries in history; I am arguing, however, that Lucrece represents an alternative mode of participating in and interpreting history.

of how tyrants fall (and in so doing defuses the explosive issues about rebellion latent in the poem): he claims that in banishing Tarquin he will merely be an agent of the gods.

The epic perspective is in fact best represented by a character who is very important in *The Rape of Lucrece* even though it nowhere refers to him specifically: *pius* Aeneas.[117] It is possible that some of Shakespeare's readers were aware of the legend from *Metamorphoses* XIV to which the notes in many Renaissance editions of the *Fasti* refer: Aeneas, like Tarquin himself, is said to have attacked the city of Ardea. But whether or not they recalled this story, they would surely have realized that Lucrece's responses to the depiction of Troy mirror—and invite us to compare—Aeneas' reactions when he views the story of Troy on Dido's temple doors.[118] Throughout the *Aeneid* Aeneas dedicates himself, though at the cost of Dido and her values, to achievement. Thus, carrying his father and what that parent symbolizes on his back, he sets out to found a brave new world. In other words, like Brutus he is committed to the belief that the suffering of the past may be reshaped to yield a glorious future.

Unlike Brutus, however, he attempts to reshape it not only by committing glorious deeds but also by reading and recounting historical events so that they conform to the epic pattern: if his behavior before Dido's doors establishes him as a historian's audience, his performance at her feast, where he tells the story of Troy, establishes him as a historian.[119] Hence Aeneas' approach to history, so implicitly but so importantly present in *The Rape of Lucrece*, suggests the contours of an epic vision of Lucrece's story. To read or write history from this perspective, we come to realize, is to stress long-term gains rather than short-term griefs. This point is especially evident when the hero of the *Aeneid* reads the temple doors. While Lucrece found only sorrow in the fall of Troy, Aeneas finds *salus* (*Aeneid*, I.451, 463). By using that noun twice in the passage, Virgil encourages us to reflect on its varied meanings, from "physical safety" to "well-being" in a more general sense. And Aeneas reminds us, too, that an heroic ver-

---

[117]Several readers have noted parallels between *The Rape of Lucrece* and the *Aeneid* (e.g., see Miola, pp. 30–31, and Platt, pp. 1–3), but the issue demands far more attention than it has hitherto received.

[118]On this episode, see esp. W. R. Johnson, *Darkness Visible: A Study of Vergil's 'Aeneid'* (Berkeley: Univ. of California Press, 1976), pp. 102–107.

[119]Barbara J. Bono contrasts Aeneas' approach to history with that of Dido in *Literary Transvaluation: From Vergilian Epic to Shakespearean Tragicomedy* (Berkeley: Univ. of California Press, 1984), chap. 1. I wish to thank the author for making the manuscript available to me before publication.

sion of the rape of Lucrece would effect closure considerably after her suffering or death, encompassing the attempts to unseat the Tarquins and found a better society.

In addition to contrasting the historiography of the complaint with that of epic poetry, *The Rape of Lucrece* plays its Argument against the succeeding text. Though these versions are strikingly different from each other, most critics have ignored the distinctions between them. One reason for this neglect is the common tendency to overlook prefatory material. But the relationship between the Induction of *The Taming of the Shrew* and the play itself conclusively gives the lie to that habit. We have seen, too, that the dedication of *Venus and Adonis*, a document that rivals Venus' compliments to Adonis in its hyperbole if not in its humility, can and should contribute to our reading of the poem. Another reason scholars have neglected the differences between the Argument of *The Rape of Lucrece* and the poetic text is that they assume that the divergences between the two are inevitable and hence insignificant; any Argument, so this case goes, necessarily abbreviates the succeeding story, and therefore the resulting changes are not worthy of critical attention. But these assumptions ignore the complexities of a reader's reactions: knowing that such alterations have to occur often limits the intensity of our responses to them, but they may stimulate responses and reflections nonetheless and may hence function as an important part of our experience of the work. Moreover, a writer may heighten our reactions by emphasizing and, in particular, thematizing the inevitable distinctions between prefatory material and what ensues, as Shakespeare does when he weights the Prologue to *Troilus and Cressida* with polysyllabic, Latinate diction.

In the case of *The Rape of Lucrece*, the concern for different interpretations of history that we find throughout the narrative activates the potential significance of the contrasts between the Argument and the rest of the poem. But we are prepared for the significance of those differences even earlier in our experience of reading Shakespeare's narrative: the contrast between the formal rhetoric of the dedication and the simpler prose of the Argument makes us think more about the language of both of these texts:[120]

> The love I dedicate to your Lordship is without end; whereof this pamphlet without beginning is but a superfluous moiety. The warrant I have of your Honourable disposition, not the worth of my untutored

[120]On its style, cf. Tolbert, p. 77.

lines, makes it assured of acceptance. What I have done is yours, what I have to do is yours, being part in all I have, devoted yours.

Lucius Tarquinius (for his excessive pride surnamed Superbus), after he had caused his own father-in-law Servius Tullius to be cruelly murdered, and, contrary to the Roman laws and customs, not requiring or staying for the people's suffrages, had possessed himself of the kingdom, went, accompanied with his sons and other noblemen of Rome, to besiege Ardea.

Shakespeare crams instances of antithesis, alliteration, polyptoton, and epiphora into his dedication, as into the poem itself, while the clumsily long opening sentence of the Argument contains fewer rhetorical devices. This is not to say, however, that the Argument (or any prose passage) lacks a style. The passage exemplifies the Ciceronian habit of suspending meaning until the end of a clause or of an entire sentence, while the ablative absolute "Which done" also makes this passage sound Latinate. Recognizing the stylistic differences between the Argument and what precedes and follows it, we may begin to anticipate substantive differences as well between the poem and the Argument that purports simply to summarize it.

When, responding to such hints, we compare the Argument with the text itself, we discover a contrast quite as striking as that between the Prologue of *Troilus and Cressida* and the play. First, the time span of the Argument differs from that of the poem even more than the chronological boundaries of complaint and epic differ. As well as grounding Tarquin's actions in earlier ones by his father, the Argument devotes proportionately more space to the downfall of the Tarquins: in the poem the concluding allusion to the banishment of Lucrece's attacker seems so abrupt that one critic has speculated that Shakespeare is trying to skirt the politically tense issue of rebellion, while about one-fifth of the Argument discusses the events in question. A comparison of these two accounts reminds us, then, that the nature of our historical tracts depends in part on the questions they are attempting to answer: the time span of the Argument reflects the fact that it implicitly responds to the query, "Why were the Tarquins banished?" while the inquiry behind the poem might be phrased as "What happened to Lucrece?" In short, the concerns of the Argument are more political, those of the poem itself more personal.

These differing approaches to temporality reflect—and help to generate—differing approaches to historical causality. By playing up the tyranny of Tarquin's father, which is so clearly related to the son's sexual tyranny, and by stressing that the entire family is banished, the Argument hints at the providential view of history: the fall of the Tarquins is a just punishment for their misdeeds. In contrast, the abrupt opening and conclusion of the body of the poem mime on the narrative level the arbitrariness that characterizes Lucrece's own view of causality. We have less sense of the appropriateness of Tarquin's punishment, less sense of order being restored. At the same time, however, by linking the characters' behavior to the values of their society, the text suggests motivations more subtle than any indicated by the Argument: causality is traced to a network of human drives and assumptions and to the culture that breeds them. In a way, indeed, the difference between the Argument and poem corresponds to that between traditional political history and studies of *mentalité*:[121] the Argument traces historical change to the public actions of characters, such as besieging Ardea, while the poem uncovers the unspoken and even unconscious attitudes behind those actions, such as the image of the city besieged by barbarians.

But the most striking difference between the Argument and the poem that succeeds it lies in the way they treat emotion. The poem devotes considerably more attention to the feelings of its characters, while the Argument contents itself with obvious observations like "Lucrece, in this lamentable plight." In this respect the distinction between the two parallels that between Ovid and Livy. Similarly, the poetic version appeals to its readers' emotions, not only describing but also evoking "lacrimae rerum," while the Argument is in more senses than one very dry. The prose account of the events teaches us by appealing to our reason; as assured in its didacticism as the *Mirror*, it clearly demonstrates that tyrannous actions breed their own downfall. The succeeding poem, in contrast, performs its didactic function in no small part by engaging—and often confounding—our feelings.

As its detached tone would suggest, the Argument at first strikes us as an unimpeachable account of the facts: unswayed by the subtle political and moral judgments that lead the narrator of the poem to apply the judgmental verb "clothe" (1809) to Brutus' hypocritical behavior, the speaker in the Argument appears to be giving us, as it

---

[121]For a useful summary of distinctions between traditional and contemporary schools of history, see, e.g., Michael Kammen, "The Historian's Vocation and the State of the Discipline in the United States," in *The Past before Us*, ed. Michael Kammen (Ithaca: Cornell Univ. Press, 1980). For a typical example of the study of mentalité, see Robert Darnton, *The Great Cat Massacre and Other Episodes in French Cultural History* (New York: Basic Books, 1984).

were, all the truth that's fit to print. But this initial confidence in his trustworthiness in fact heightens our dismay when we discover unresolvable contradictions between the Argument and the text of the poem, such as their varying accounts of the events before the rape. And these doubts grow when we recognize the significance of some of the points that the Argument omits; leaving out both Brutus' earlier deceptions and his manipulations of his listeners, for example, casts a more positive light on his rise to power, avoiding the very facts that render the transition to republicanism morally problematic. As we read the Argument and contrast it with the text, then, our confidence in it wanes. We ourselves experience the loss of trust in seemingly objective sources that, as we have observed, characterizes Renaissance historians. And we ourselves are once again reminded of the ambiguities and multiplicities that the title character of the poem tries so hard to ignore.

In short, competition is not only a moral concern but also a structural device in *The Rape of Lucrece*: the poem repeatedly plays competing visions of the same historical event against each other. Shakespeare, like the modern historian Hayden White, is very conscious of the varying genres through which historical events can be told.[122] But if his concern with those genres anticipates many of the questions that White and other twentieth-century historians have been debating, it also contributes to the Renaissance discussions of history that we examined earlier. To begin with, in one regard Shakespeare's historiography is very conventional: the "graver labour" to which the dedication of *Venus and Adonis* refers, *The Rape of Lucrece* is an evidently didactic work, as histories were universally supposed to be. But Shakespeare's poem bears the same relationship to the pedagogical functions of history-writing as it does to those of the complaint: it teaches us by inviting us to participate in ambiguous moral experiences and judgments rather than to partake of unambiguous moral *sententiae*.

As my analysis of its conflicting genres would suggest, one of the principal truths Shakespeare's narrative offers us is that even historical accounts that seem totally reliable may exemplify the errors that Bodin charts. If the omissions in the Argument establish this point, the rest of the poem helps us to understand why history is so often

---

[122]Adapting the work of Frye, White argues that historical accounts may be categorized according to four "emplotments": romance, tragedy, comedy, satire (*Metahistory*, pp. 7–11). Also see his more recent work, *Tropics of Discourse: Essays in Cultural Criticism* (Baltimore: Johns Hopkins Univ. Press, 1978), chap. 2.

untrustworthy. For we witness both Lucrece and Brutus reshaping history, and we are reminded, too, of the ways Aeneas does so. Citing the instance of a general who attempts to report a battle which he has led, the modern historian Marc Bloch demonstrates the propensity for distortion inherent even in eyewitness reportage of history.[123] No literary work supports his observations more cogently than *The Rape of Lucrece*.

That poem demonstrates another issue that renders our understanding of history at best problematical: our decisions about where to begin a story and where to end it inevitably color our interpretations of the events in between those points. Established by the contrast between the competing views of history, this issue is echoed elsewhere in *The Rape of Lucrece* as well. In evaluating Brutus' behavior we confront our own dangerous drive for closure. Similarly, the *rime royal* stanza enacts on the prosodic level the points Shakespeare is making about closure in history.[124] For this stanzaic form incorporates three possible resting places within its seven-line structure of *ababbcc*: we may experience at least some sense of closure after line 4, line 5, and, of course, at the end of the stanza. In some verses enjambment undermines the potential closure after line 4, or, more often, line 5, but in others the tension between the various places we could stop provides an analogue to the tension between the various places we could terminate Lucrece's story itself:

> By this, starts Collatine as from a dream,
> And bids Lucretius give his sorrow place;
> And then in key-cold Lucrece' bleeding stream
> He falls, and bathes the pale fear in his face,
> And counterfeits to die with her a space;
>   Till manly shame bids him possess his breath,
>   And live to be revenged on her death.
>
>   (1772–1778)

Both the syntax and the rhyme tempt us to pause where Collatine does, at the end of line 5; the fact that the stanza does not end there but resumes to report his revenge mirrors the fact that Collatine himself rises up. Or, to put it another way, in lines 1 to 5 we find the

---

[123]*The Historian's Craft*, trans. Peter Putnam (New York: Knopf, 1953), pp. 48–50.

[124]It is possible that Shakespeare originally began to write the poem in sixains. For a statement of this theory, see Roland Mushat Frye, "Shakespeare's Composition of *Lucrece*: New Evidence," *SQ*, 16 (1965), 289–296.

response to history and the type of closure represented by the complaint, while the concluding lines move into the epic mode.

Shakespeare's narrative also implicitly participates in sixteenth-century discussions of historical causality. On one level, the story suggests itself as an exemplum of the providential interpretation. Tyrants are, conveniently enough, banished when and because that tyranny becomes manifest in a rape. We need not even worry about the unfairness of visiting the sins of the fathers on the sons, an issue that often troubles proponents of the providential view: in a sense here the sins of the son are visited on the father, but in fact both are guilty of the same type of wrongdoing. Yet, as I began to indicate earlier, the poem itself undercuts the providential viewpoint implicit in its Argument. The abrupt conclusion leaves us uneasy,[125] conscious that providence has chosen a morally dubious agent in the person of Brutus. Moreover, by focusing so much attention on Lucrece's pain, *The Rape of Lucrece* allows to surface what is often a troubling undercurrent in providential interpretations: the good must suffer so that the evil may be punished. For if Lucrece's rape is the necessary precondition to the change to republicanism, then she is being used by history much as she has been used by Tarquin and Brutus. Many have been able to accept that God's ways are mysterious, but we are hardly comfortable with the idea that they are also malicious. These problems, like so many others in the poem, are never resolved: they remain a disturbing reminder of the difficulties of interpreting history. Perhaps this early in his career Shakespeare found it easier to ponder such issues in relation to a culture other than his own. In any event, though, he was of course to raise the same troubled and troubling questions about providentiality in his later English history plays, perhaps most notably in *Henry VIII*.[126]

But the most original contributions to Renaissance historiography in *The Rape of Lucrece* concern those sibling rivals, history and poesy. Unlike Sidney, Shakespeare does not wholly discount the advantages of the former; the broader historical sweep of the Argument provides a perspective on the story that is clearly lacking in the poem itself. But as we read *The Rape of Lucrece* we are very aware that in omitting the subtle and shifting emotions of the actors in history, the Argument neglects a central component in their motivations. And in leaving out

---

[125]For a different but not incompatible explanation of that abruptness, see Platt, p. 1; he argues that Shakespeare is borrowing the epic convention of opening in medias res.

[126]Compare Frank V. Cespedes' arguments about the problems of a providential interpretation of *Henry VIII* ("'We are one in fortunes': The Sense of History in *Henry VIII*," ELR, 10 [1980], 413–438).

the moral questions that we discerned even—or especially—in the wordplay of the poem, the Argument ignores the ethical complexities that complicate seemingly straightforward events like Brutus' rise to power.

No doubt many of Shakespeare's contemporaries would have seconded his points about the advantages and limitations of these two modes of presenting the story. More original and more controversial is Shakespeare's implicit but unmistakable reminder that historical writing does indeed have a style. We have already observed that the contrast with the mellifluous rhetoric of the dedication draws attention to what is Latinate in the syntax of the Argument. Similarly, the contrast with the time span of the poem demonstrates that where the Argument opens and where it concludes are the result not of insignificant or arbitrary decisions but rather of a kind of artistic shaping that inevitably affects the whole meaning of the passage. Hence the historian too is inevitably, if at times unwittingly, a Second Maker. The differences between the Argument and the rest of *The Rape of Lucrece* do not reside in the fact that the former is more reliable because it is free of the colors of rhetoric; rather, each employs its own distinctive form of rhetoric. A number of twentieth-century historians have themselves recently become interested in the rhetoric of history-writing; Shakespeare would agree with J. H. Hexter when he observes, "Rhetoric is ordinarily deemed icing on the cake of history, but . . . it is mixed right into the batter."[127]

In short, Shakespeare's analysis of history and historiography extends and complicates his scrutiny of language itself. Having denied that the straightforward historical accounts represented by the Argument are privileged, having undercut the conventional wisdom that the absence of style guarantees the presence of truth, the poem questions the trustworthiness of any form of history, whether it be expressed as a prose narrative or as a type of poesy. It asks, in other words, whether all history-writing is but another example of the unreliability of narratives, like the flattering stories, the slanderous rumors, and the hypocritical lies with which the poem is so concerned. We may at first be tempted to answer in the affirmative, for *The Rape of Lucrece* alludes to no single instance of a historical mode we can trust. If Lucrece, like Renaissance historians, warns us that time will "blot old books and alter their contents" (948), newer history books may themselves prove no more reliable. On another level, however, Shakespeare's is not a counsel of despair. For the poem as a whole is evidently an attempt to write history more accurately than any of the

[127]*Doing History* (Bloomington: Indiana Univ. Press, 1971), p. 68.

accounts within it. And not the least of the skills *The Rape of Lucrece* teaches its readers is the ability to evaluate history and its sources better than the characters within the narrative are able to do. We come to acknowledge the limitations in both the complaint's and the epic's approach to history; we come to recognize the complex motivations of its actors. If Clio herself is raped by some of the personages in the poem and menaced by even the speaker in the Argument, Shakespeare's readers learn to treat her with more respect.

IX

Though syneciosis is the dominant figure in *The Rape of Lucrece*, its etymological sibling synecdoche also assumes an important role throughout the poem. Synecdoche appears at several key moments: Tarquin expresses the fear his posterity will curse his bones (209), Lucrece addresses to her hand remarks that refer to her entire body (1030–1033), alludes to an eye to represent a whole person (1143), and so on. By now we should not be surprised to discover that the presence of this trope signals Shakespeare's interest in the visions and viewpoints it may be said to represent. Indeed, so resonant are the implications of synecdoche that this figure can aptly serve to summarize many of the characteristics we have been observing in *The Rape of Lucrece*—and many of our own experiences in reading the poem.

The versions of history that we have just examined are partial in the sense of biased because they are partial in the sense of incomplete. All historians necessarily exclude certain facts, but the omissions in question in this poem are particularly troubling ones. By leaving out Brutus' manipulative rhetoric and the political ambitions that may lie behind it, the speaker in the Argument polishes away the moral dubiousness that stains the transition to republicanism. By ignoring the heroes who may promise some redress for Troy's sorrows, Lucrece avoids recognizing that the Trojans' suffering, like her own, may admit of solutions and resolutions. The gaps in such historical accounts exemplify a broader concern in *The Rape of Lucrece*: the human predilection for focusing on only part of a complex experience rather than seeing it steadily and seeing it whole. If syneciosis represents the tensions in the world and the characters that Shakespeare evokes, synecdoche in turn can symbolize what renders those characters' responses to their world so tragically inadequate.[128]

---

[128]Compare Danson's claim that synecdoche represents narrowness in *Coriolanus* (pp. 155–159).

In the ecphrasis of Troy, of course, synecdoche is a sign of artistic achievement:[129]

> For much imaginary work was there,—
> Conceit deceitful, so compact, so kind,
> That for Achilles' image stood his spear
> Gripp'd in an armed hand; himself behind
> Was left unseen, save to the eye of mind:
> A hand, a foot, a face, a leg, a head
> Stood for the whole to be imagined.
>
> (1422–1428)

Elsewhere in the poem, however, it is a sign of moral failure, a symptom of dangerously limited vision in a poem so deeply concerned throughout with types of seeing and blindness. Thus one way of diagnosing what is problematical in Lucrece's concept of chastity is to say that she takes the part for the whole: she assumes that not having sexual relations with anyone save one's husband is not one component of that complex concept but rather its entirety. Her husband and father allow grief, which should be part of their reaction to her death, to overwhelm all other responses. But it is of course Tarquin who most clearly exemplifies the dangers of synecdoche. Like Achilles in the depiction of Troy, he allows his spear to stand for his whole image: his crime results from the fact that he takes his falchion—and the phallic power and military values that it represents—as his total identity. In so doing he subsumes and subverts other vital parts of that identity, especially, as Lucrece points out, the moral principles befitting royal blood.

Synecdoche is also an apt metaphor for the experiences of a rape victim. Critics have observed how often this figure appears in *Titus Andronicus* and *Cymbeline*, connecting its presence with the preoccupation with dismemberment in those plays.[130] I would add that, in *The Rape of Lucrece*, as in the dramas in question, synecdoche and dismemberment are linked primarily because both symbolize one central experience of a woman who has been raped: the loss of integrity that we examined earlier. Moreover, in a sense rape represents the ultimate synecdochic treatment of a woman: her sexual parts are treated as her

---

[129]Bevington also notes the presence of synecdoche here (pp. 24–25).

[130]Ann Thomson notes that Posthumus mistakes the part for the whole and that synecdoche is a type of dismemberment ("Philomel in *Titus Andronicus* and *Cymbeline*," *Shakespeare Survey*, 31 [1978], 31); Tricomi observes that synecdoche is one of the most central figures in *Titus Andronicus* (p. 15).

whole being. Thus Tarquin behaves toward Lucrece as though she is nothing but the object of his lust; he ignores and in so doing destroys other aspects of her identity, such as her social role as a loyal wife and her sense of herself as a chaste woman. As an Elizabethan punster (or a twentieth-century critic who has spent too much time reading Elizabethan rhetoric) might put it, Tarquin acts as though Lucrece's thing is everything—and in so doing sets in train a process by which she is reduced to nothing. If, then, Lucrece suffers in part because of her own synecdochic vision, she is also the victim of that of her attacker.

Above all, however, synecdoche symbolizes our experiences reading *The Rape of Lucrece*. On one level we find we must acquire the positive values synecdoche expresses in the depiction of Troy; to judge people accurately we must learn what Tarquin's "parling looks" (100), say, tell us about his character as a whole. On another and more important level, though, synecdoche may be said to represent the mistakes in perception and interpretation that at times align us with the characters in the poem. To avoid miming the errors that Shakespeare is exposing, we come to realize, we must not confuse the partial account in the Argument with the historical vision of the poem as a whole. We must not allow our sympathy for Lucrece to blind us to the problems and the solutions that her own analysis of the rape omits. And we must not focus on what is heroic and noble in Roman values at the expense of observing the discordant notes in that culture.

But finally it is to synedosis itself that we should return when summarizing *The Rape of Lucrece*. Throughout the poem, as we have observed, instances of seeming antithesis collapse into examples of syneciosis. This trope represents the divisiveness in the Roman culture that Shakespeare evokes. It symbolizes the tension in the twinning that is effected between Lucrece and Tarquin, between Tarquin and Brutus, and between the readers of the poem and many of its characters. It is an apt description of Shakespeare's approach to the values of more traditional complaints and to the distinctions between the Argument and the body of his own text. And syneciosis, a figure grounded in conflict and contradiction, expresses the paradoxical nature of *The Rape of Lucrece* itself: this is a poem that proves most original in its insights even where it appears most conventional in its rhetoric. To adduce once more the definition of the rhetorician John Hoskyns, *The Rape of Lucrece* not only describes but also achieves "a strange harmony."

[3]

"Conceit deceitful":
The Sonnets

The frame through which I viewed the world changed too, with time. Greater than scene, I came to see, is situation. Greater than situation is implication. Greater than all of these is a single, entire human being, who will never be confined in any frame.

Eudora Welty

I

Though students of the Renaissance are currently questioning long-standing assumptions about the nature of Protestantism during the period, the role of the court, and even the very existence of the Renaissance itself, at least one truism from our textbooks remains unassailed and unassailable: the English sonnet rapidly degenerated into vapidity. *Astrophil and Stella* was seldom blessed with the heirs it deserved. Referring primarily to the heart as the site of the beloved's image but also to that organ as a symbol for emotion, Astrophil's Muse directs him to look in his heart and write. Sidney's successors, however, were prone to look only in the latest miscellany; while the 1590s did witness many good sonnets and some great ones, most works in the genre proved so derivative that it is actually hard to be sure whether a sequence like *Zepheria* is a seriously intended contribution to the tradition or a parody.[1]

In contrast, while Shakespeare's sonnets have been faulted on many grounds, few readers have claimed that they are just literary ex-

---

[1]On *Zepheria*, see Herbert J. C. Grierson, ed., *The Poems of John Donne*, 2 vols. (Oxford: Clarendon, 1912), II, 102–103.

ercises, totally removed from the emotions the sonnet customarily chronicles.[2] Indeed, as we read them we feel close—uncomfortably close—to the feelings they portray. While critics have noted this fact, they often ascribe it merely to the presence of autobiographical material, downplaying the mediation of formal conventions. Such interpretations implicitly establish the sonnets as diametrically opposed to *Venus and Adonis* and *The Rape of Lucrece*, at least according to conventional readings of those two works: thus in Shakespeare's lyric poems emotions are seen to subsume and perhaps even subvert an interest in literary strategies, while the reverse is true of the narratives. In fact, however, the sonnets resemble their author's narrative poems in a number of regards and above all in the ways they relate formal patterns to psychological ones.

The primary formal and psychological patterns that we will discern in the speaker of the sonnets are versions of paradox.[3] A consummately skillful rhetorician, he is repeatedly duped by his own words. He is most aggressive when he appears most humble, and vice versa. Though he is attracted to definitive closure in both rhetorical and emotional situations, he is also prone to undermine it. These and the many other paradoxes we will encounter largely stem from his responses to power, whether it be that of a lover in the usual sense or that of the patron who offers both an escape from and an intensification of the problems of romantic love.[4] In reacting to such pressures this speaker in turn determinedly asserts and even flaunts his own power, especially that deriving from language, and yet he is victimized as much by his attempts at mastery as by those of the Friend and Dark Lady.

As even this brief introduction to his temperament would suggest, many affinities link the speaker in the sonnets to the central characters in *Venus and Adonis* and *The Rape of Lucrece*. Like Venus and Lucrece he can delight, instruct, and move us through his skillful

---

[2]Katharine M. Wilson does argue, however, that the sonnets are a parody of other sequences (*Shakespeare's Sugared Sonnets* [New York: Barnes and Noble, 1974]).

[3]The relationship between that speaker and the author behind him is, of course, one of the more complex questions raised by the sonnets. This study assumes the two need not be precisely equated, though limitations of space prevent me from debating the issue at length. For two persuasive statements of that case, focusing especially on the question of Shakespeare's sexuality, see Booth, ed., *Shakespeare's Sonnets*, pp. 548–549; Barbara Herrnstein Smith, "Introduction," *William Shakespeare: Sonnets* (New York: New York University Press, 1969), pp. 23–25. The Booth edition will be cited hereafter as Booth, *Sonnets*.

[4]Compare Booth, *Sonnets*, pp. 431–432, on Shakespeare's play on the word "lover."

rhetoric. Yet he further recalls those heroines in that he is the principal victim of his own language: entrapped by the nets he has laid for others, he becomes further entangled the more he tries to free himself. And his reactions to the power invested in others—and to his own attempts to assert power—demonstrate his kinship to Lucrece in particular.

Above all, the sonnets resemble *Venus and Adonis* and *The Rape of Lucrece* in the extent to which they use formal strategies to explore psychological ones. Despite the assumptions of virtually all critics, the sonnets are in fact grounded in a nondramatic mode, which both reveals and symbolizes their speaker's temperament. Within that mode they deploy a number of the rhetorical patterns and devices that we find in other sequences, including the five on which this chapter will focus: equivocation, excusing, closure, flattery, and what has been termed the ugly beauty conceit. Though these patterns are so common, in Shakespeare's sonnets they serve to illuminate the idiosyncrasies and complexities of the speaker's sensibility: undramatic in their mode, these poems nonetheless prove intensely dramatic in their evocation of their central personage. Hence it is by examining both the mode of the sequence and these five formal strategies that we can come to understand this paradoxical character. And in so doing we will also recognize our own affinities to him. To read Shakespeare's sonnets is to become lost in the "hertes forrest"—and to realize that in many ways that heart is our own.

II

We assume that the nondramatic poetry of a great playwright will in fact be dramatic in many senses of that complex term. And we assume that when a writer who among his manifold gifts is a skilled storyteller chooses to write sonnets, at least some of them will be narrative. Though *Venus and Adonis* and *The Rape of Lucrece* challenge the conventional wisdom about their author in many other ways, they do implicitly support such presuppositions about his sonnets: because he renders the epyllion tradition so dramatic and reinterprets Senecan conventions as a way of characterizing Lucrece, we anticipate a similar approach to the mode of the sonnets. Such expectations help to explain why, despite all the other controversies about these lyrics, certain concepts are so repeatedly and so uncritically brought to bear on interpretations of them. We are regularly informed, for example, that they are "dramas" or "stories," a view reflected in the frequency with which critics of the sonnets include the word "dramatic" in the titles of their studies and then proceed to comment on the "plots" and the "characters" that they find in the sequence.[5] But in literary criticism, as in so many other human activities, we are prone to see what we expect to see, and nothing else. While Shakespeare's sonnets evidently do include certain dramatic and narrative elements, in focusing on that aspect of them we have overlooked a more revealing and more surprising fact: several of the characteristics central to other dramatic and narrative poetry, including other Renaissance sonnet sequences, are signally absent from Shakespeare's contributions to the genre. And, more to our purposes here, it is through that very absence that these poems reveal many of the subtleties of their speaker's temperament.

A comparison of Shakespeare's Sonnet 87 with two other works that also concern a leavetaking demonstrates the mode of his sonnets. The famous lines of Drayton's *Idea* 61 remind us how a poem in what is essentially a lyric mode can in fact become dramatic:

> Since ther's no helpe, Come let us kisse and part.
> Nay, I have done: you get no more of Me,
> And I am glad, yea glad with all my heart,
> That thus so cleanly, I my Selfe can free.
> Shake hands for ever, Cancell all our Vowes,
> And when We meet at any time againe,
> Be it not seene in either of our Browes,
> That We one jot of former Love reteyne;
> Now at the last gaspe, of Loves latest Breath,
> When his Pulse fayling, Passion speechlesse lies,
> When Faith is kneeling by his bed of Death,
> And Innocence is closing up his Eyes,

---

[5]See, e.g., Giorgio Melchiori, *Shakespeare's Dramatic Meditations: An Experiment in Criticism* (Oxford: Oxford Univ. Press, 1976); G. K. Hunter, "The Dramatic Technique of Shakespeare's Sonnets," *EIC*, 3 (1953), 152–164; Robert Berkelman, "The Drama in Shakespeare's Sonnets," *CE*, 10 (1948), 138–141. Philip Martin maintains that Shakespeare's sonnets are less dramatic than Donne's lyrics in that the speaker is less fully realized, but far more dramatic than the sequences of other Elizabethan sonneteers (*Shakespeare's Sonnets: Self, Love, and Art* [Cambridge: Cambridge Univ. Press, 1972], pp. 138, 142–143). T. Walter Herbert suggests that we read the sonnets as statements by characters in their author's plays ("Dramatic Personae in Shakespeare's Sonnets," in *Shakespeare's "More Than Words Can Witness": Essays on Visual and Nonverbal Enactment in the Plays*, ed. Sidney Homan [Lewisburg, Pa., and London: Bucknell Univ. Press and Associated University Presses, 1980]).

The Sonnets

Now if thou would'st, when all have given him over,
From Death to Life, thou might'st him yet recover.

Rather than describing the episode in which the lovers part, Drayton enacts it. We are asked to believe (and thanks to his skill the illusion is persuasive) that we are actually witnessing the speaker bidding farewell to his lady. We are as conscious of her implicit but powerful presence as that speaker is himself. And we are conscious, too, that what the poem claims to enact is a specified and unique moment in time. To be sure, Drayton briefly uses allegory to distance us from that moment—but his main reason for establishing such a distance is to create a foil against which his final appeal to the woman will seem all the more immediate.

Though Petrarch's *Canzonière* 190 is primarily concerned with rendering certain states of mind—the poet's joy at the beauty of Laura and his intense sorrow at her loss—he evokes those states by telling a story:

> Una candida cerva sopra l'erba
> verde m'apparve con duo corna d'oro,
> fra due riviere all'ombra d'un alloro,
> levando 'l sole, a la stagione acerba.
>
> Era sua vista sì dolce superba
> ch'i'lasciai per seguirla ogni lavoro,
> come l'avaro che 'n cercar tesoro
> con diletto l'affanno disacerba.
>
> "Nessun me tocchi," al bel collo d'intorno
> scritto avea di diamanti e di topazi.
> "Libera farmi al mio Cesare parve."
>
> Et era'l sol già vòlto al mezzo giorno,
> gli occhi miei stanchi di mirar, non sazi,
> quand'io caddi ne l'acqua et ella sparve.

A white doe on the green grass appeared to me, with two golden horns, between two rivers, in the shade of a laurel, when the sun was rising in the unripe season.

Her look was so sweet and proud that to follow her I left every task, like the miser who as he seeks treasure sweetens his trouble with delight.

[173]

"Let no one touch me," she bore written with diamonds and topazes around her lovely neck. "It has pleased my Caesar to make me free."

And the sun had already turned at midday; my eyes were tired by looking but not sated, when I fell into the water, and she disappeared.[6]

Petrarch's poem may be visionary and mystical, but like other narratives it is firmly anchored in time. It has a clear beginning, middle, and end: at the opening of the poem the speaker sees the deer, then he admires her, and then he loses her.

Shakespeare interprets a leavetaking very differently in Sonnet 87:

> Farewell, thou art too dear for my possessing,
> And like enough thou know'st thy estimate.
> The charter of thy worth gives thee releasing;
> My bonds in thee are all determinate.
> For how do I hold thee but by thy granting,
> And for that riches where is my deserving?
> The cause of this fair gift in me is wanting,
> And so my patent back again is swerving.
> Thyself thou gav'st, thy own worth then not knowing,
> Or me, to whom thou gav'st, else mistaking;
> So thy great gift, upon misprision growing,
> Comes home again, on better judgment making.
>   Thus have I had thee as a dream doth flatter,
>   In sleep a king, but waking no such matter.

The opening word, "Farewell" (1), suggests that this sonnet is going to enact a parting in much the same way that Drayton's does; and the third quatrain does in a sense tell a story. Yet Shakespeare's poem is not necessarily a rendition of a particular event that takes place at a particular moment: one cannot tell whether the parting is in the process of happening or has already occurred. His primary concern is not to imitate an incident in which a lover says farewell but rather to evoke the lover's reflections on the process of parting. And Shakespeare's sonnet differs from Drayton's in another and no less significant way: while most of the assertions in Drayton's sonnet are addressed to the beloved, most of those in Shakespeare's are not. In

---

[6]*Petrarch's Lyric Poems: The "Rime Sparse" and Other Lyrics*, ed. Robert M. Durling (Cambridge, Mass.: Harvard Univ. Press, 1976).

the couplet, for example, Shakespeare's speaker seems to be brooding on his experiences rather than either enacting them or announcing their significance to the person he has loved.

The characteristics of that couplet and of the sonnet in which it figures recur throughout Shakespeare's sonnet sequence. The narrative, dramatic, and lyrical modes are not, of course, necessarily exclusive of each other, either in general or in Shakespeare's sonnets in particular.[7] In his sequence as a whole, and not infrequently within a single sonnet, we do encounter instances of all three modes. Sonnets 153 and 154, for example, are certainly narrative according to virtually any definition of that term; and, as I have already indicated, the entire sequence is indubitably dramatic in the important sense that it bodies forth the speaker himself. Nonetheless, it is not the presence of some narrative and dramatic elements but rather the absence of others that is most striking when we read Shakespeare's sequence and most telling when we compare it with the sonnets composed by other Renaissance poets. And that absence reflects central patterns in his speaker's temperament.

One of the clearest indications that the majority of Shakespeare's sonnets are in certain senses neither narrative nor dramatic is that they do not include a temporal sequence of events, as does, for example, Petrarch's "Una candida cerva sopra l'erba."[8] As we read Shakespeare's sonnets, we witness tortuous shifts in the speaker's emotions and judgments, but very seldom do we encounter a chronological progression of occurrences. Instead, his monologues take place in the

---

[7]The definition of "lyric," "dramatic," and "narrative" has, of course, long been one of the most complex and most controversial problems in literary theory. The three modes have been differentiated through their "radicals of presentation," analyzed in terms of linguistic models, compared to three stages in the life of a human being or the development of a society, and so on. A useful summary of the various theories may be found in Paul Hernadi, *Beyond Genre: New Directions in Literary Classification* (Ithaca: Cornell Univ. Press, 1972), especially chaps. 2 and 3. This essay adopts the traditional and widely accepted contrast between the emphasis on the subjective and introspective in the lyric and the enactment of an external situation in the dramatic. For an influential encapsulation and expansion of that position, see Northrop Frye, *Anatomy of Criticism* (Princeton: Princeton Univ. Press, 1957), esp. pp. 243–337. (A few recent critics have attempted to refine or undercut the customary interpretation of the lyric as a subjective form. See, e.g., Käte Hamburger, *The Logic of Literature*, 2d ed., trans. Marilynn J. Rose [Bloomington: Indiana Univ. Press, 1973].)

[8]On the role of the temporal in drama, as opposed to lyric poetry, see, e.g., Jackson G. Barry, *Dramatic Structure: The Shaping of Experience* (Berkeley: Univ. of California Press, 1970), esp. pp. 110–125.

kind of eternal present that is usually a mark of lyric poetry.[9] Characteristically, they generalize about an event that recurs frequently
rather than focusing on one instance of it: "When I consider everything that grows" (15.1); "When to the sessions of sweet silent thought
/ I summon up remembrance of things past" (30.1–2). Even a poem
like Sonnet 48, which at first appears to be launching a chronological
story ("How careful was I, when I took my way, / Each trifle under
truest bars to thrust" [1–2]), soon switches to the sort of atemporal
generalizations that are in fact more typical of the sequence ("Thee
have I not locked up in any chest" [9]).

In another sense, too, the sonnet sequence that so vividly evokes the
horrors of time is not itself rooted in time: Shakespeare's poems seldom refer to datable real incidents or even to incidents that occur at a
specific, though symbolic, moment. Petrarch alludes to the date of his
meeting with the real woman who was transformed into Laura and
the date of her death, and his sequence may also have complex symbolic relationships to the calendar.[10] Spenser's sonnets are apparently
keyed to the seasons. One of Daniel's refers to a trip to Italy. But in
Shakespeare we find very few such references. To be sure, in one
poem the speaker does suggest that he met his beloved three years
before; but nowhere else does he allude to time in so specific a way.[11]
And Shakespeare is no more specific about place. We know that
Sidney's Stella takes a ride on the Thames, while Shakespeare's sonnets never mention a particular locale.

The omission of such allusions to place and time is all the more
suggestive in light of Shakespeare's repeated—one is almost tempted
to say frenetic—puns on "will." Like Sidney's play on "rich" or his
adoption of the pseudonym "Astrophil," these puns are evidently
intended to remind us that the poems in question are linked to autobiographical experience.[12] One would presume that the same atti-

[9]Anne Ferry comments acutely on the role of the lyric present in the poems about
time (All in War with Time: Love Poetry of Shakespeare, Donne, Jonson, Marvell [Cambridge,
Mass.: Harvard Univ. Press, 1975], pp. 3–63).
[10]See Thomas P. Roche, Jr., "The Calendrical Structure of Petrarch's Canzonière," SP,
71 (1974), 152–172, for a summary of previous work on the temporal structure of
Petrarch's sequence and a thought-provoking new theory.
[11]Sonnet 107 is sometimes used by scholars in their attempts to date the sequence;
but its allusions to events are vague and ambiguous, as is suggested by the contradictory
theories about dating that they have engendered. For a summary of these hypotheses,
see Hyder Edward Rollins, ed., The Variorum Shakespeare: The Sonnets (Philadelphia: J. P.
Lippincott, 1944), I, 263–268.
[12]John Burrows makes a similar point about Langland's puns on "will" in Piers
Plowman in an unpublished paper delivered at the University of Sussex Renaissance
Colloquium, February 1975; I am indebted to his remarks.

tudes that lead a poet to pun on, and hence draw attention to, his own name might well encourage him to refer to specific dates and places. But this Shakespeare chooses not to do.

The lack of a temporal perspective in most of his sonnets reflects the absence of anecdotal sonnets.[13] With only a handful of exceptions, Shakespeare's sequence omits not only the mythological stories that so frequently grace the sequences of other sonnet writers but also nonmythological allegories such as Spenser's *Amoretti* 75 ("One day I wrote her name vpon the strand, / But came the waues and washed it away" [1–2]). Moreover, Shakespeare seldom chooses to narrate an incident that happens to the lovers. Compare, for example, his ninety-first sonnet with *Astrophil and Stella* 41:

91

Some glory in their birth, some in their skill,
Some in their wealth, some in their body's force,
Some in their garments, though new-fangled ill,
Some in their hawks and hounds, some in their horse;
And every humor hath his adjunct pleasure,
Wherein it finds a joy above the rest.
But these particulars are not my measure;
All these I better in one general best.
Thy love is better than high birth to me,
Richer than wealth, prouder than garments' cost,
Of more delight than hawks or horses be;
And having thee, of all men's pride I boast;
    Wretched in this alone, that thou mayst take
    All this away, and me most wretched make.

41

HAVING this day my horse, my hand, my launce
    Guided so well, that I obtain'd the prize,
    Both by the judgement of the English eyes,
And of some sent from that sweet enemie *Fraunce*;
Horsemen my skill in horsmanship advaunce;
    Towne-folkes my strength; a daintier judge applies

---

[13]The absence of anecdotes is briefly noted by Anton M. Prikhofter ("The Beauty of Truth," in *New Essays on Shakespeare's Sonnets*, ed. Hilton Landry [New York: AMS Press, 1976], pp. 113–114); Prikhofter goes on to argue, however, that the poems are characterized by intense "situational visualization" (p. 122). James Winny also observes the absence but attributes it to the lack of events from Shakespeare's life (*The Master-Mistress: A Study of Shakespeare's Sonnets* [London: Chatto and Windus, 1968], chap. 1).

His praise to sleight, which from good use doth rise;
Some luckie wits impute it but to chaunce;
    Others, because of both sides I do take
My bloud from them, who did excell in this,
Thinke Nature me a man of armes did make.
How farre they shoote awrie! the true cause is,
    Stella lookt on, and from her heavenly face
    Sent forth the beames, which made so faire my race.[14]

While both poems play the values of the court against those of love, Sidney does so by telling a story. (It is significant, too, that Shakespeare's speaker is more alienated from that court than Astrophil is; his psychological distance from it parallels the distancing effected by Shakespeare's mode.) Or, to put it another way, it is as uncharacteristic of Shakespeare to begin a sonnet with "One day" as it is characteristic of many other sonneteers to do so.

A sonnet that does not narrate an anecdote may, of course, be anchored in a specific event or situation nonetheless: it can be the outgrowth of an occurrence which, though not recounted systematically, is mentioned frequently and specifically in the course of the poem. Most readers have assumed that the vast majority of Shakespeare's sonnets are "situational" in this sense. But in point of fact comparatively few of them are. In some of Shakespeare's monologues the reflections are inspired not by a particular situation but by a general problem: thus in Sonnet 94 the speaker evokes a certain kind of personality, and Sonnet 129 is an anguished consideration of the nature of lust. Because poems like these rely so heavily on generalizations, critics regularly describe them as interesting exceptions to Shakespeare's approach elsewhere in the sequence. They are, however, merely extreme instances of their author's tendency to detach the speaker's emotions and speculations from an immediate situation.[15]

Similarly, some poems in the sequence suggest that a specific incident lies behind the speaker's reactions but omit any discussion of

---

[14]*The Poems of Sir Philip Sidney*, ed. W. A. Ringler (Oxford: Oxford Univ. Press, 1962).

[15]For the conventional argument that such poems are atypical in the sequence, see, e.g., Carol Thomas Neely, "Detachment and Engagement in Shakespeare's Sonnets: 94, 116, 129," *PMLA*, 92 (1977), 83–95. Attempting to distinguish those three poems from the others in the sequence, she writes, "Not actions themselves, they are about inaction. . . . The three sonnets are deliberately detached from the particulars of the relationship" (p. 83).

details. We learn little about the "forsaking" to which Sonnet 89 alludes, for example, or about the reasons for the parting described in the absence sonnets. As we read Sonnet 35 we do not know what the "sensual fault" (9) to which it refers may be or even whether "fault" indicates a particular lapse or a general character trait. While Sonnet 122 is indubitably based on an episode, the gift of a notebook, it specifies no further information about that event; instead the poem turns at once to broader observations about the relationship between giver and receiver, such as "Nor need I tallies thy dear love to score" (10). In contrast, when Sidney describes Stella's journey on the Thames in *Astrophil and Stella* 103, he devotes the poem to details about the episode itself, such as the behavior of the winds and her own blushes.

In other words, if we try to enumerate the situations on which Shakespeare's sonnets are based, we find that our list is short and the events on it vague. The poet encourages the Friend to marry; there is a period of separation, and there are one or more quarrels; they exchange one or more notebooks; the Friend betrays the speaker with the Dark Lady. In *Astrophil and Stella*, in contrast, a sequence about two-thirds the length of Shakespeare's, the situations include a stolen kiss, Stella's illness, that ride on the Thames, an absence, a quarrel, Astrophil's triumph in a tournament, and many more. As these lists would suggest, the image of a footprint, so potent and so revealing a metaphor in the *Canzonière*, might also serve as an emblem for Shakespeare's approach to the genre: he bases his sonnets on mere traces of events.

If most of Shakespeare's sonnets do not tell stories, neither do they enact dramas in the way that Drayton's *Idea* 61 does. One Shakespearean has observed, "By setting up a system of tensions between forces presented as persons, Shakespeare's sonnets engage the reader's interest in a manner akin to the dramatic,"[16] and it is true that some of these works, notably the poems addressed to Time, do operate this way. But most do not: Shakespeare's sonnets embody the tensions of conflicting forces, but those forces are more often internalized within the speaker than dramatized as characters.

Though the Friend and the Dark Lady dominate the speaker's thoughts, in some important respects they do not function as active participants within the sonnets. The problems engendered by their behavior are frighteningly immediate, but the characters themselves are not. Except for the fact that the young man is attractive and the

[16]Hunter, p. 154.

[179]

lady is dark, we do not know how they look.[17] Unlike the main characters in most sonnet sequences, they are never assigned names, even fictional ones, even in those poems that refer to them in the third person rather than in the second. The epithets by which they are addressed serve, if anything, to distance us further from them. When, for example, Shakespeare opens Sonnet 56 on the command, "Sweet love, renew your force" (1), he establishes an unresolved ambiguity about whether the poem concerns his beloved or the abstract quality of love or both.[18] When he directs an apostrophe to "Lascivious grace" (40.13), he initially seems as much to be brooding on the abstraction that the epithet expresses as to be talking to a person who has been reduced (or who has willingly reduced himself) to the state expressed by that oxymoron. Similarly, only once (34.13) in 154 sonnets does Shakespeare allude to the movements or gestures of the beloved in a way that suggests that he is physically present and actually listening to the speaker. Contrast *Astrophil and Stella* 31, which so unequivocally sets up the fiction that Astrophil is in the presence of the moon, or *Astrophil and Stella* 47, whose "Soft, but here she comes" (13) so effectively signals Stella's arrival.

It is a truth as significant as it is neglected that the Friend and the Dark Lady are not quoted directly within the poems. Despite all his experience in writing plays, Shakespeare chooses not to create the kind of dialogue on which such sonnets as *Astrophil and Stella* 54 or *Idea* 24 or even *Amoretti* 75 are based. On those rare occasions when the words of the beloved are recorded, they are presented in a form that distances us from the statements and their speakers: the poet either uses indirect discourse to report what the beloved has said ("When my love swears that she is made of truth" [138.1]) or predicts what he or she is likely to say rather than what has actually been said ("O then vouchsafe me but this loving thought: / Had my friend's muse grown with this growing age" [32.9–10]).

Similarly, Cupid makes only the briefest of appearances in the sonnets, and when he is present, Shakespeare, unlike most of his contemporaries, does not attempt to render him as a dramatic character. Whereas *Astrophil and Stella* 8, for instance, describes the behavior of the god of love at some length, Shakespeare's Sonnet 137 turns imme-

[17]Hunter also notes this fact but interprets it very differently, arguing that, despite the paucity of visual description in the sequence, "the brilliance of the language makes the context of [the speaker's] emotions so vivid that the reader naturally supplies from his imagination a complete dramatic situation" (p. 155).

[18]The ambiguity in Sonnet 56 is also noted in Booth, *Sonnets*, p. 230.

diately from its brief apostrophe to him ("Thou blind fool love" [1]) to a direct, unallegorical anatomy of the speaker's feelings. It is revealing, moreover, that the kinds of human characters who populate other sequences and create miniature dramas by arguing with the speaker are totally absent from Shakespeare's poems. The ladies who are Laura's companions, the cynical friend who berates Drayton, the court nymphs who criticize Astrophil—no figures like these appear in Shakespeare's sonnets.

Nor is Shakespeare prone to replace them with internalized characters. Though the morality tradition influences his sequence in other ways, only rarely does he depict the conflicts within his speaker as allegorical personages engaged in a confrontation. Many of his sonnets concern a debate between opposing forces such as reason and passion; but very few evoke that debate through allegorical characters like those that figure so prominently in *Astrophil and Stella*.

Most of Shakespeare's sonnets are not narrative, then, in the sense that the speaker is not recounting a story to the reader or to any other implied audience. And they are not dramatic in the sense that we are not witnessing a confrontation that occurs at a specific place and time between a speaker and a particular listener or even between two clearly distinguished personages within the speaker. Instead, the lyric mode predominates. Some of the poems resemble an internalized meditation, others a letter, others a monologue that the beloved hears but apparently does not respond to. The soliloquy immediately presents itself as a parallel to and an inspiration for Shakespeare's unusual approach to the sonnet, and in certain respects the comparison is illuminating.[19] The speaker in Shakespeare's sonnets often seems to be thinking aloud, to be at once speaking audibly and meditating.

---

[19]Other narrative forms also provide partial parallels. Thus the absence of other characters and hence other viewpoints in the sonnets links them to the dramatic monologue. Robert Langbaum argues that that form reflects a belief in the insubstantiality of truth (*The Poetry of Experience: The Dramatic Monologue in Modern Literary Tradition* [London: Chatto and Windus, 1957], pp. 107ff.); this preoccupation also characterizes the sonnets. They differ from most dramatic monologues in several important respects, however; in particular, most of these lyrics are not, as we have seen, rooted in a specific situation. Writing about the interior monologue, Seymour Chatman notes that in it there is "no deference to the ignorance or expository needs of a reader or another character" (see "The Structure of Narrative Transmission," in *Style and Structure in Literature: Essays in the New Stylistics*, ed. Roger Fowler [Ithaca: Cornell Univ. Press, 1975], p. 250). In this respect, as in many others, the sonnets are closer to the interior monologue than most other narrative forms; they do not conform completely, however, to this or any of the other categories that Chatman and other students of narrative have established.

[181]

But, as the passages that I have cited suggest, in one crucial way the sonnets differ from the soliloquies that are so frequently embedded in their author's plays: the soliloquy normally takes place at a unique moment and is often provoked by a clearly defined event that has preceded it, whereas most of the sonnets are signally lacking in those types of particularization.

That lack is manifest in Shakespeare's deictics: he typically chooses distal ones for any event outside the speaker's consciousness. Thus even Sonnet 34, one of the few poems in the sequence clearly to imply the listener's presence, also implies a distance between the speaker and that listener by using "those" rather than "these": "Ah, but those tears are pearl which thy love sheeds" (13). Similarly, Sonnet 35, a poem in which the speaker slips into an uneasy affinity with the Friend and his values, nonetheless also concludes on a hint of their separation: "To *that* sweet thief which sourly robs from me" (14; italics added). Proximal deictics, in contrast, appear when the speaker is talking about his own actions, especially that of writing a poem. Thus earlier in Sonnet 35 he uses "this" for his excusing of the Friend and, in particular, for the sonnet at hand in which that unsavoury operation is performed: "All men make faults, and even I in this" (5). And Sonnet 39, an explicit statement of the Friend's absence, reinforces that statement in its final line by contrasting the "here" that refers in part to the sonnet with the "hence" that refers to the Friend's departure ("By praising him here who doth hence remain" [14]). Throughout the sequence, in other words, what is immediate is the speaker's own mind and heart.

While a lengthy discussion of the order of the sonnets is outside the scope of this book, the nondramatic mode that I am describing does carry with it certain implications about that controversial issue.[20] The subject is complicated by the fact that English sonnet sequences vary

[20]For a useful summary of the issue, see Rollins, *Sonnets*, appendix 4. The many thought-provoking twentieth-century comments on it include Michael J. B. Allen, "Shakespeare's Man Descending a Staircase: Sonnets 126 to 154," *Shakespeare Survey*, 31 (1978), 127–138; C. L. Barber, "Shakespeare in His Sonnets," *Massachusetts Review*, 1 (1960), 651 (another version of this essay appears as the Introduction to *William Shakespeare: The Sonnets*, Laurel Shakespeare [New York: Dell, 1960]); R. P. Blackmur, "A Poetics for Infatuation," in *The Riddle of Shakespeare's Sonnets*, ed. Edward Hubler (1962; rpt. New York: Octagon Books, 1982), p. 131; Hilton Landry, *Interpretations in Shakespeare's Sonnets* (Berkeley: Univ. of California Press, 1963), pp. 3–5; J. W. Lever, *The Elizabethan Love Sonnet* (London: Methuen, 1956), pp. 169–173; Kenneth Muir, *Shakespeare's Sonnets* (London: George Allen and Unwin, 1979), pp. 6–13. The most thorough case for reordering is made by Brents Stirling in *The Shakespeare Sonnet Order: Poems and Groups* (Berkeley: Univ. of California Press, 1968).

The Sonnets

considerably in their structure; *Astrophil and Stella*, say, is significantly more unified than *Delia*, and even the cycles that do manifest a calendrical structure may include large sections of poems that are not arranged in any discernible order.[21] On the whole, though, C. S. Lewis' caveat is very salient; he points out that we often encounter merely "an island, or . . . an archipelago, of narrative in the lyrical sea"[22] and suggests therefore that focusing on these sections of narrative is rather like appreciating a Mozart opera mainly because of its plot.

Any reader of Shakespeare's sonnets can at least understand why many scholars have devoted so much time to rearranging them. The poems do clearly form groups (though, as Stephen Booth has demonstrated, those groups often overlap confusingly).[23] And the sonnets are more unified in their themes and their images than even their most fervent admirers sometimes admit. Ultimately, however, the undramatic mode of the sonnets should lead us to abandon our attempts to reorder them. It is unlikely that Shakespeare himself envisioned a coherent and sequential order for these poems; the most sensitive of the rearrangements as well as the most unlikely ones are predicated on fundamental misunderstandings about this sequence and the experiences it charts.

The nondramatic mode that I have ascribed to the sonnets raises doubts about whether a narrative order for the poems was ever intended. The sequence is, as we have observed, far more concerned with how the speaker views experience than with the events that generate his reflections. And the poet behind that speaker surely would not even try to arrange those reflections to correspond to the order of the happenings that provoke them. In many cases doing so would be impossible, since the poems allude not to a specific incident but to recurrent events or states of mind. And even when a sonnet does stem from a particular incident, such as the gift of the notebook, we cannot suppose the speaker is brooding on it immediately after it occurs or, indeed, that his repeated reflections on it occur at roughly the same time as each other; there are no poems in the language more acute on the way the mind obsessively returns to past events. Perhaps the best analogues in the visual arts are the repeated visions and revisions of

[21]See Roche, "The Calendrical Structure of Petrarch's *Canzonière*."

[22]*English Literature in the Sixteenth Century Excluding Drama* (Oxford: Clarendon Press, 1954), p. 327.

[23]Stephen Booth, *An Essay on Shakespeare's Sonnets* (New Haven: Yale Univ. Press, 1969), pp. 116–118; hereafter cited as Booth, *Essay*.

Monet's haystacks or Stieglitz's "Equivalents." Hence to assume that the sonnets describe a chronological sequence of external incidents is to ignore the psychological patterns that in fact shape them. Eudora Welty again offers an observation that can illuminate Shakespeare's sonnets: "The events in our life happen in a sequence in time, but in their significance to ourselves they find their own order, a timetable not necessarily—perhaps not possibly—chronological. The time as we know it subjectively is often the chronology that stories and novels follow: it is the continuous thread of revelation."[24]

Yet even a reader with reservations about my emphasis on the internalized nature of the sonnets should have doubts on other grounds about reshaping them into a chronological pattern, for that process implies a very different notion of love from that conveyed by these poems. Those who reorder the sequence typically assume that, say, the speaker's recognition of the Friend's faults would preclude his continuing to write poems of joyous praise, while in fact the sonnets repeatedly document his attempts to discredit or ignore the painful truths he has discovered. Similarly, it is more than possible that the speaker would affirm his sense of oneness with the Friend after discovering the liaison with the Dark Lady as well as before: these would not be the only poems in which he protests too much.

The primary significance of the mode of the sonnets—and the primary relevance to this chapter—lies in how Shakespeare's rejection of many narrative and dramatic elements affects the characterization of his speaker. It is possible that the playwright who composed the sonnets rendered them undramatic in the senses we have defined partly because he wanted to experiment with a mode different from that of his plays and partly because, writing in the shadow of Sidney's immensely successful and influential sequence, he wished to do something different with the genre, to "make it new" in the sense of avoiding the kinds of incidents that Sidney presents so skillfully. But probably another reason Shakespeare reshaped the genre as he did is that he aimed to body forth the speaker's own emotions as immediately and intensely as possible. Certainly that is the effect of his approach to the genre.

In this sequence, unlike most of its counterparts in the 1590s, the reader need channel little or none of his or her attention to an exposition of a situation or an exploration of the beloved's reactions to it: we focus instead on the poet-lover himself. For example, the impact of

---

[24]Eudora Welty, *One Writer's Beginnings* (Cambridge, Mass.: Harvard Univ. Press, 1984), pp. 68–69.

Sonnet 12, at first glance a comparatively impersonal poem, in fact stems not merely from its vivid depiction of time's ravages but also from its moving evocation of its speaker's sensibility:

> When I do count the clock that tells the time,
> And see the brave day sunk in hideous night,
> When I behold the violet past prime,
> And sable curls all silvered o'er with white,
> When lofty trees I see barren of leaves,
> Which erst from heat did canopy the herd,
> And summer's green all girded up in sheaves
> Borne on the bier with white and bristly beard;
> Then of thy beauty do I question make
> That thou among the wastes of time must go,
> Since sweets and beauties do themselves forsake,
> And die as fast as they see others grow.

In one sense this sonnet is a carefully documented argument. The quatrains, which present a series of facts marshaled to support the thesis in the sestet, function as part of a syllogism (all sweets and beauties die; you yourself are a sweet and beauty; therefore you will die). But in presenting this case the poem repeatedly directs our attention to the mind brooding on it: this lyric is as much concerned with the speaker's thoughts about death as with ways of combating that inevitable but unendurable fact. The first five lines contain no fewer than four verbs referring to the speaker's processes of cognition ("do count" . . . "see" . . . "behold" . . . "see"), three of which are preceded by the personal pronoun "I." The anaphora in lines 1 and 3 ("When I") further heightens the emphasis on the speaker's sensibility. "Then of thy beauty do I question make" (9), which follows the opening two quatrains, contains in microcosm the characteristics that we have been noting, for one may gloss those words in two ways: (1) I ask you a question ("thy beauty" functioning as synecdoche in this interpretation) or (2) in my own mind I raise a question about your beauty. Even while communicating with the beloved, then, the speaker also seems to be communing with himself.

Shakespeare's rejection of many of the dramatic and narrative potentials of his genre not only directs our attention to the speaker but also defines certain characteristics of his experience to which we will return throughout this chapter. By presenting not a linear progression of events but rather the circularity of repeated internal meditations, the sequence enacts in its very structure the sense of stasis that this poet-lover so frequently feels. On many occasions this stasis is positive: a number of the sonnets celebrate a relationship "to constancy confined" (105.7). More often, however, the lack of linearity reflects the darker side of the speaker's sensibility. Trapped in brooding rather than acting or even being acted on, he cannot escape his own worries and uncertainties any more than he can escape the relationships that engendered them.[25] His mind is tormented with calamities that the future may bring (his beloved will betray him, Time will destroy even this most precious of mortals) or that the present, unbeknownst to him, may already hold (his two friends may have already been unfaithful to him, the beloved may be morally stained). And these calamities are rendered more painful because the speaker is powerless to prevent future disasters or even to be certain that such calamities have not in fact come to pass:

> Yet eyes this cunning want to grace their art;
> They draw but what they see, know not the heart.
> (24.13–14)

> And even thence thou wilt be stol'n, I fear.
> (48.13)

In dramas, including the miniature version of drama that a sonnet can embody, characters often commit definite actions; in narratives, even fourteen-line narratives, usually definite events occur. But, as the passages above suggest, the dominant mood of Shakespeare's sonnets is fearful anticipation and troubling suspicion, not clear-cut events.

The speaker is unsure not only about what has happened but also about how to evaluate it. If presented within the intense and concentrated form of the sonnet, both the narrative and the dramatic modes tend to suggest moral and epistemological certainties. When sonnet writers use mythological allegories, for example, they generally do so in order to make some simple but significant point about love; Cupid's tricks may remind us that love is deceptive, and Venus' fickleness that women are untrustworthy. Similarly, in narrating an event

[25]For an analysis of the speaker's lack of resolution in relation to time, see L. C. Knights, "Revaluations (V): Shakespeare's Sonnets," *Scrutiny*, 3 (1934), 158–160, reprinted in *Explorations: Essays in Criticism Mainly on the Literature of the Seventeenth Century* (1947; rpt. New York: New York University Press, 1964) and in *Elizabethan Poetry: Modern Essays in Criticism*, ed. Paul J. Alpers (New York: Oxford Univ. Press, 1967).

involving a lover and his mistress, sonneteers usually establish some important facts about the participants, such as the lady's unremitting and unremorseful chastity. And when sonnets imitate a dialogue between opponents, the two figures generally argue neatly antithetical positions. A victory for one position or the other, or possibly a synthesis of both, is achieved by the end of the sonnet. Even if the poet-lover himself remains trapped in his moral dilemma, a sequence relying extensively on narrative and dramatic modes can establish important verities. Thus *Astrophil and Stella* as a whole documents truths about Neo-Platonism that Astrophil can only imperfectly grasp. In so frequently avoiding the narrative and dramatic, Shakespeare's sonnets decline to attribute to their willful Will the kinds of ethical truths and moral assurances that those modes can generate. Hence these poems create in formal terms the types of moral confusion they are also exploring thematically.

As is so often the case in the sonnets, rhetorical figures mirror other formal patterns. If the absence of linearity in their structure reflects the fact that the speaker is condemned to return with only small variations to the same thoughts and problems, types of repetition also establish that point. These figures range from the repetition of the same word ("Sweet thief, whence didst thou steal thy sweet that smells" [99.2]) to anaphora ("So long as men can breathe or eyes can see, / So long lives this, and this gives life to thee" [18.13–14]), traductio ("Thou truly fair wert truly sympathized / In true plain words by thy true-telling friend" [82.11–12]), and anadiplosis (". . . to make the taker mad; / Mad in pursuit" [129.8–9]).[26]

The mode of the sonnets also shapes the contours of the portrait of the speaker in another way: it expresses his unusual isolation. His counterparts in most English sonnet sequences are actively engaged in dialogues, frequently implicit but nonetheless evident, with a whole range of other characters. While stylistic analyses of sonnet sequences customarily study their pronouns only in terms of what is revealed about the relationship between the poet and his mistress, those same parts of speech often also reflect the relationship between the poet and a larger audience: if the use of "she" suggests a distance between

[26]The question of whether "Made" (9) should in fact be emended to "Mad" has been the source of considerable critical controversy. For a summary of the debate, see Booth, *Sonnets*, pp. 445–446, and Thomas M. Greene, "Anti-hermeneutics: The Case of Shakespeare's Sonnet 129," in *Poetic Traditions of the English Renaissance*, ed. Maynard Mack and George deForest Lord (New Haven: Yale Univ. Press, 1982). In any event, the sequence does include other instances of anadiplosis.

the lover and his lady, it may also imply that he is sharing his feelings with a group of sympathetic courtiers or even with more intimate friends.[27] And, of course, adapting a convention of Continental sonnets, some English sonneteers do address their reflections on love to a particular friend; in *Amoretti* 33, for example, the speaker shares his thoughts with a historical personage, Spenser's friend Ludovic Bryskett. Addressees may also range from allegorical figures like Cupid to other women at court. Though claiming to be "most alone in greatest companie" (27.2), in fact Astrophil, like most of his counterparts, generally speaks to a broad and varied audience. This multiplicity of internal audiences aptly reflects the actual conditions of sonnet writing, in which a poem might be variously published, circulated in manuscript among friends or, presumably, sent to an actual woman.

In the direction of address, as in so many other respects, Shakespeare's sequence differs strikingly from those of his contemporaries. As we have observed, the Friend and Dark Lady often do not appear to be listening to the speaker and even more often if they listen they do not seem to respond in any way. Like many of the characters in *Antony and Cleopatra*, he spends more time talking about those he cares for than talking to them. Moreover, the approach to narrative and dramatic elements that we have been tracing suggests his extraordinary isolation from others as well. Directing his poems neither to companions (save the Friend, who is in the relevant senses not friendly at all) nor to allegorical figures, he stands in particularly sharp contrast to Astrophil, who regularly opens poems with lines such as "Alas have I not paine enough my friend" (14.1) and "Flie, fly, my friends, I have my death wound; fly" (20.1). These implications about the isolation of Shakespeare's speaker are supported as well by direct statements: Sonnet 29 bemoans a lack of friends, while Sonnet 31 refers to dead ones.

Equally significant is the absence of a larger, if less intimate, audience. Speaking as he does primarily to himself and secondarily to an unresponsive Friend and Dark Lady, Shakespeare's poet-lover is robbed of the role that provides some comfort and dignity to even his most self-pitying counterparts in other sequences; that is, he very seldom attempts to instruct or persuade the community. Thus, for example, in Sonnet 132 he promises he will "swear beauty herself is black" (13), and in Sonnet 137 he criticizes the aesthetic and moral

[27] For a discussion of Shakespeare's pronouns from a perspective very different from my own, see Melchiori, chap. 1.

judgment behind that promise—but none of these poems is devoted to attempting to convince others that, as it were, black is beautiful.

Similarly, compare *Amoretti* 86 with Sonnet 69:

86

Venemous toung tipt with vile adders sting,
    Of that selfe kynd with which the Furies fell
      theyr snaky heads doe combe, from which a spring
      of poysoned words and spitefull speeches well.
Let all the plagues and horrid paines of hell,
    vpon thee fall for thine accursed hyre:
      that with false forged lyes, which thou didst tel,
      in my true loue did stirre vp coles of yre,
The sparkes whereof let kindle thine own fyre,
    and catching hold on thine owne wicked hed
      consume thee quite, that didst with guile conspire
      in my sweet peace such breaches to haue bred.
Shame be thy meed, and mischiefe thy reward,
    dew to thy selfe that it for me prepard.[28]

69

Those parts of thee that the world's eye doth view
Want nothing that the thought of hearts can mend.
All tongues, the voice of souls, give thee that due,
Utt'ring bare truth, ev'n so as foes commend.
Thy outward thus with outward praise is crowned;
But those same tongues that give thee so thine own,
In other accents do this praise confound
By seeing farther than the eye hath shown.
They look into the beauty of thy mind,
And that in guess they measure by thy deeds;
Then, churls, their thoughts—although their eyes were kind—
To thy fair flow'r add the rank smell of weeds;
    But why thy odor matcheth not thy show,
    The soil is this, that thou dost common grow.

Both poems play the speaker's judgments against those of the world. But whereas Spenser's speaker addresses and attempts to still or at

---

[28]All citations from Spenser are to *The Works of Edmund Spenser: A Variorum Edition*, ed. Edwin Greenlaw, Charles Grosvenor Osgood, Frederick Morgan Padelford, and Ray Heffner, 11 vols. (Baltimore: Johns Hopkins Univ. Press, 1943–1957).

least requite those critical tongues, Shakespeare's is apparently as incapable of affecting his opponents as Venus is of moving Adonis or Lucrece of dissuading Tarquin. Here, as in the narrative poems, one possible implication is that rhetoric is not always as powerful as the schoolmasters of Shakespeare's England—and the classical texts they propounded—would claim. But it is not really clear whether rhetoric is lacking or whether the speaker himself at times lacks the self-respect and self-confidence to flourish its colors. What is clear is that the speaker is as alienated from the larger community as from the unfriendly Friend and the Dark Lady. Once again, in other words, the mode of the sonnets, the result of curtailing the narrative and dramatic elements in them, serves to express the modality of their principal character; once again Shakespeare's approach to generic conventions is intimately related to his approach to human experience.

But the fact that he cannot influence the world around him hardly guarantees that the speaker is not himself influenced by it.[29] As concerned with reputation as Shakespeare's Roman characters, he recalls Lucrece in particular in his preoccupation with gossip and slander. Playing out his adulterous liaison under the "false adulterate eyes" (121.5) of others, he is, again like Lucrece, the victim of the very judgments that he is powerless to affect. For observers repeatedly gossip about the Friend's behavior ("Some say thy fault is youth" [96.1]) and castigate his own (in Sonnet 112, for example, he is hurt by "vulgar scandal" [2]). The world is too much with him, and it is a source of censure rather than solace, a wilderness populated by a whole pride of Blatant Beasts.

III

The nondramatic mode of the sonnets, then, functions dramatically in that it directs our attention to their speaker's temperament. The principal way the sequence reveals his character, however, is by associating it with the five rhetorical strategies enumerated above: equivocation, especially in the service of assigning praise and blame; excusing; unsatisfactory closure; praise; and the ugly beauty motif.

---

[29]Several critics have commented on the speaker's consciousness of the world around him. See, e.g., Joan Grundy, "Shakespeare's Sonnets and the Elizabethan Sonneteers," *Shakespeare Survey*, 15 (1962), 45–46; Hallett Smith, *The Tension of the Lyre: Poetry in Shakespeare's Sonnets* (San Marino: Huntington Library, 1981), p. 68.

Many other sonnet cycles incorporate these patterns, but none explores their psychological dimensions as thoroughly or as thoughtfully as Shakespeare's sonnets. In this sequence, as in *Venus and Adonis* and *The Rape of Lucrece,* rhetorical configurations manifest and mime psychological ones.

As their affinity for the oxymoron would suggest, sonnets are rooted in contradictions and equivocations. One instance of both of those patterns is obvious—though often not very significant—in the behavior of their speakers: these characters are prone at times to say one thing while meaning or doing another. On one level, of course, seemingly disinterested praise is really a self-interested bid for the lady's favor and favors; controlling and sublimating sexuality as they generally do, however, English sequences direct less attention to this form of deceit than do many of their French predecessors. Similarly, the direction of address in these poems is often equivocal: poems that ostensibly speak to someone other than the lady are, one suspects, frequently intended to be overheard by her. Prepared by that suspicion, we may see *Delia* 4 as a skillful enactment of occupatio: the speaker declares to some unspecified audience that he does not wish to tell Delia how unhappy she is making him and hence in a sense does precisely that. And Astrophil hopes, one imagines, that not only the moon that he is directly addressing but also his own starry lady will hear the laments in *Astrophil and Stella* 31.

Such deceits and conceits are common in the English sonnet, but only Sidney and Shakespeare himself anatomize their effects on their speakers with any subtlety, and each of them does so very differently. Sidney focuses in particular on the contrast between Astrophil's aesthetic pronouncements and his actual performance, offering that contrast as an analogue to his behavior as a lover. Thus the sequence opens on lengthy and detailed expressions of anti-Petrarchism. The mooning, self-pitying Petrarchan style is explicitly criticized when Astrophil mocks those who "give each speech a full point of a grone" (54.4), and it is implicitly criticized by contrast with the physical energy Astrophil manifests in courtly tournaments and the verbal energy he manifests in his intellectual jousts with Stella. Similarly, he carefully distinguishes his own concern with real emotions and a real woman from the clichés composed by those "that do search for everie purling spring, / Which from the ribs of old *Parnassus* flowes" (15.1–2).

As the sequence progresses, however, it becomes increasingly clear that Astrophil is not following his own advice; indeed, his sonnets might serve as exempla of the very faults he earlier charts. One scholar unpersuasively attempts to explain away the disparity by hypothesizing that the sonnets on aesthetic issues were composed earlier and merely slotted into a sequence they only imperfectly fit;[30] another claims that no contradiction exists, for what Astrophil is rejecting is not ornamented language per se but rather the abuse of ornament.[31] Yet we cannot really deny that Stella's lover does not write with the unadorned simplicity that he so often praises. Nor should we attempt to deny it, for it is part of the point of the sequence: it is one instance of the many conflicts between theory and practice that characterize— and torment—Astrophil. His erected wit teaches him valid artistic principles, but his infected will prevents him from realizing them, much as his rational perceptions about love and himself as a lover seldom guide his behavior. Astrophil is, in other words, portrayed in terms of his unwillingness or inability to practice what he preaches, and Sidney explores the defenses and rationalizations that repeatedly produce that situation.

The contradiction between pronouncement and praxis is also evident in Shakespeare's sonnets: their speaker is a living oxymoron. Critics have, of course, noted this contradiction in particular poems, but they have been prone to overlook the fact that it reflects one of the most important configurations in the speaker's temperament.[32] For Shakespeare's sonnets, like *Astrophil and Stella,* show the psychological cost of equivocating. Thus in Sonnet 58 Shakespeare's speaker blames the Friend even while composing a couplet that declares he will not do so. As one critic points out, Sonnet 94 uses irony, a form of dissimulation, in the process of criticizing dissimulation.[33] Sonnet 99

---

[30]Ann Romyne Howe, "*Astrophil and Stella*: 'Why and How,'" *SP*, 61 (1964), 159–161.

[31]Neil L. Rudenstine, *Sidney's Poetic Development* (Cambridge, Mass.: Harvard Univ. Press, 1967), pp. 198–205. For an argument closer to mine though different, see David Kalstone, *Sidney's Poetry: Contexts and Interpretations* (Cambridge, Mass.: Harvard Univ. Press, 1965); this study maintains that Astrophil's protestations of sincerity should be read as "a series of rather troubled and self-conscious gestures" (p. 130).

[32]For discussions of his self-contradictions from perspectives different from mine, see Michael Cameron Andrews, "Sincerity and Subterfuge in Three Shakespearean Sonnet Groups," *SQ*, 33 (1982), esp. 314–319; Margreta de Grazia, "Shakespeare's View of Language: An Historical Perspective," *SQ*, 29 (1978), 386–388, and "Babbling Will in *Shake-speare's Sonnets* 127–154," *Spenser Studies*, 1 (1980), esp. 126–127; Muir, p. 81. Though Gerald Hammond makes a number of trenchant points about the ways the sonnets undercut their ostensible purposes, his observations are limited by his thesis that the primary purpose of these subterranean reversals is to bolster the poet's ego and undercut the Friend (*The Reader and Shakespeare's Young Man Sonnets* [Totowa, N. J.: Barnes and Noble, 1981]).

[33]Landry, *Interpretations*, p. 20.

may be, as Stephen Booth suggests, parodic.[34] Proudly proclaiming his independence from courtly praise, in Sonnet 125 he proceeds to declare, "No, let me be obsequious in thy heart" (9). The adjective he chooses may mean either "dutiful" or, more ominously, "servile":[35] the conflict between the two denotations enacts the conflict between the freedom and self-respect that the poem ostensibly and ostentatiously celebrates—and the subservience that its central figure still on some level suffers. In all these instances, what we are witnessing is not a subtle movement from one attitude to another (though that pattern recurs many times in the sonnets, demonstrating one of the senses in which they are in fact dramatic) but rather an uneasy coexistence that may well remind us of the syneciosis in *The Rape of Lucrece*.

The most frequent form these tensions assume, however, is a conflict between one of the poles of epideictic oratory, praise or blame, and a sentiment that contradicts it.[36] Sometimes praise and blame themselves jar against each other; sometimes blaming clashes with excusing or defending. Renaissance readers must have found these tensions quite as troubling as the speaker himself does, for they were schooled in the significance of—and the obvious differences between—praise and blame. Aristotle, after explaining that epideictic oratory is based on praise and blame, enumerates in detail the qualities worthy of praise and the most effective ways of celebrating them. His lengthy anatomy of these epideictic types evidently interested Latin rhetoricians, who devote considerable attention to the subject of praise and blame; for example, the anonymous author of the *Rhetorica ad Herennium* in III.vi himself lists what should be praised, while in the *Institutio Oratoriae* (II.iv) Quintilian commends praise and blame as fit exercises for schoolchildren. Nor did Renaissance rhetoricians ignore the subject; indeed, Aristotle's commentators give disproportionate attention to his strictures on it, and Renaissance literary theorists frequently categorize genres in terms of the epideictic dichotomy.[37]

Many Renaissance poets acknowledge and emphasize the distinction between praise and blame—witness, for instance, the unam-

[34]Booth, *Sonnets*, p. 324.

[35]*Oxford English Dictionary*, s.v. "obsequious."

[36]Though the existence of this pattern in the sequence as a whole has never received the attention it merits, critics have commented illuminatingly on its presence in particular poems or groups of poems. See, e.g., William Empson, "They That Have Power," *Studies in English Literature* (Tokyo), 13 (1933), 459–460; Jane Roessner, "Double Exposure: Shakespeare's Sonnets 100–114," *ELH*, 46 (1979), 357–378.

[37]See O. B. Hardison, Jr., *The Enduring Monument*, pp. 40–42 and chap. 4.

biguous division between satirical and laudatory poems in Jonson's *Epigrammes*. Alternatively, praise and blame are often conjoined in Renaissance poesy—but conjoined in the service of clear and consistent ends. Thus the monitory epistle, and especially those instances of it by Donne, demonstrates that skillfully proferred praise can make blame more palatable. And *Astrophil and Stella* 44 is a particularly clever version of a balancing act performed by so many sonnets of the period: the poet wittily plays his criticisms of Stella for hurting him against his tributes to the positive qualities that enable her to cause that pain.

In Shakespeare's sonnets, in contrast, the metamorphoses of praise into blame and vice versa occur more frequently and more troublingly than in other poetry of the period. Sometimes it is impossible for the reader—and apparently even for the speaker—to distinguish praise or blame from its opposite. The siblings become Siamese twins. Or, to borrow the dichotomy that Rosalie Colie so fruitfully establishes when charting the generic coordinates of the sonnet tradition, the poems commingle the flavors of *mel* and *sal*, of sweet tributes and satiric rebukes.[38]

Sonnet 96 exemplifies the complexities of this process. A poem that describes the contradictory impressions that the Friend produces in onlookers, it also actually enacts the contradictions, locating them within the speaker as well as within the people he is describing. In so doing it raises two closely related and unresolved questions: does the Friend really turn evil into good, or does he just create an illusion of doing so? and is the speaker subtly blaming his subject for deceit, or is he too persuaded of the Friend's virtue?

> Some say thy fault is youth, some wantonness,
> Some say thy grace is youth and gentle sport;
> Both grace and faults are loved of more and less;
> Thou mak'st faults graces that to thee resort.
> As on the finger of a thronèd queen
> The basest jewel will be well esteemed,
> So are those errors that in thee are seen,
> To truths translated, and for true things deemed.
> How many lambs might the stern wolf betray,
> If like a lamb he could his looks translate;
> How many gazers mightst thou lead away,

[38]See *Shakespeare's Living Art*, pp. 80–96; *The Resources of Kind: Genre-Theory in the Renaissance* (Berkeley: Univ. of California Press, 1973), pp. 67–75.

> If thou wouldst use the strength of all thy state!
> But do not so; I love thee in such sort,
> As thou being mine, mine is thy good report.

The vagueness of the repeated word "Some" (1, 2) has the same effect as the synecdochic allusion to "That tongue" (95.5): the judgmental world is bodied forth only vaguely and, as it were, partially, a situation that makes it harder to evaluate and respond to its charges. (This description of the Friend's critics deepens, then, the speaker's inability to reach and influence them.) The neat dichotomy apparently established in the first two lines is in fact undercut by the repetition of "youth" (1, 2)—an undercutting, one might add, that proleptically introduces the confounding of another distinction, the one between praise and blame, that is enacted throughout the poem.[39] Line 4 is the first of many examples of the ambiguity behind that blurring: does it mean that the Friend turns faults into graces or merely that he makes faults seem graces?

This concern with deception is then intensified in the second quatrain by the word "basest" (6), which can signify not only "mean" but also "counterfeit." The final lines of the second quatrain pose similar questions about whether or not the Friend is deceiving his admirers: though editors have assumed that "translated" (8) should simply be glossed "transformed,"[40] here, as in line 10, surely the word would also carry with it connotations of literary translations. That resonance in turn raises the possibility of a faulty interpretation, an association especially active for Renaissance readers acutely aware of the problems of translation so often discussed by the humanists. A translation may in fact be a traduction and hence a seduction. In other words, is the speaker praising the Friend for his ability to wipe out errors or blaming him for a far more dangerous ability merely to cover them over? The literary connotations of "translate" foreground, too, what has been another question throughout the poem: if the Friend is in fact guilty of deception, is the speaker one of its victims or merely one of its chroniclers, and is this poem an instance of the pretense that foul is fair or simply a warning that some have found it so?

---

[39]Compare Booth, *Sonnets*, pp. 312–313, on patterns of what he terms "simultaneous equation and distinction" (p. 312) in the poem; the patterns he identifies are, however, different from the ones analyzed here.

[40]See Booth, *Sonnets*, p. 312, and W. G. Ingram and Theodore Redpath, ed., *Shakespeare's Sonnets* (1964; rpt. New York: Holmes and Meier, 1978), p. 220.

The third quatrain supports our suspicions about the Friend by comparing him to a wolf, and the allusion to "gazers" (11) invokes and reminds us of the dangers in both Petrarchan adoration and courtly flattery. And if "the strength of all thy state" (12) is praise for the Friend's powers, on another level the speaker may be blaming him for misusing those powers.

The multiple readings to which the couplet lends itself return us again to the questions of whether the Friend is behaving dishonorably and whether this poem itself exemplifies how he deceives his "gazers" (11). It may, for example, be interpreted, "I love you so much that my reputation benefits from your good name"—or, alternatively, "I love you so much that I will deliver good reports of you (like the report in this poem), even if that praise is not deserved." Hence these lines refer to the possibility that the speaker may praise when he should instead blame, and, appropriately, they are so ambiguous themselves that we are not sure whether they represent a compliment or a rebuke. We are, however, all the more conscious of their sinister meanings because those significances are not present in the same couplet when it appears in the context of Sonnet 36.[41] In short, then, the unresolved tensions of the poem suggest the reasons the speaker so often confounds praise and blame: the Friend's behavior is ambiguous, and he himself is so torn by the ambiguities that he cannot or will not reach clear judgments.

He confronts similar problems in a similar way throughout the sequence. Sonnet 40 raises a question very like the ones posed in Sonnet 96: does the phrase "in whom all ill well shows" (13) mean that ill has become good or that it merely seems to be? The first meaning would be a product of the love expressed earlier in the sequence, the second a result of the condemnation that is poisoning—but not, apparently, totally destroying—that love. The opening of Sonnet 95, "How sweet and lovely dost thou make the shame / Which . . . Doth spot the beauty of thy budding name" (1–3), again asks whether the Friend is transforming or merely concealing evil. As the poem progresses we witness the speaker's attempt to call a spade a spade, a sin a sin, but we do not lose our awareness that in many sonnets it is the speaker himself who attempts to make the Friend's guilt "sweet and lovely" (1). Sonnet 69 exemplifies another form of indirection. After

---

[41]Critics are divided on whether the repetition of the couplet was a mere mistake. For explanations of its function different from mine, see, e.g., Jean Fuzier, "Mine is thy good report. A Note on Shakespeare's Sonnets 36 and 96," *Cahiers Elisabéthains*, 9 (1976), 55–58; Klause, p. 320.

enumerating the judgments of "the world's eye" (1), the poem concludes, "But why thy odor matcheth not thy show, / The soil is this,
that thou dost common grow" (13–14)—leaving us uncertain about
whether the speaker is again reporting the verdicts of others or offering a climactic opinion of his own.

Most readers have assumed that, rather than offering us a volatile
admixture of praise and blame throughout, Sonnet 84 devotes its
quatrains to celebrating the Friend's achievement—only to turn
abruptly to the criticism of the couplet, "You to your beauteous blessings add a curse, / Being fond on praise, which makes your praises
worse" (13–14). In fact, however, the metaphors in the quatrains call
into question the validity of the praise. For "this rich praise" (2) and
"Lean penury within that pen doth dwell" (5), like the many other
metaphoric allusions to riches in the sequence, remind us that a poet
is customarily attracted to a patron by the wealth of his purse as well
as that of his soul. And that reminder inevitably leads us to distrust
the motives for which this poet is complimenting his Friend and
hence to wonder whether he does in fact deserve the praise bestowed
upon him.

In Sonnet 35, a poem as complex as it is neglected, the imagery
again equivocates, undermining what is being said overtly:[42]

> No more be grieved at that which thou hast done:
> Roses have thorns, and silver fountains mud,
> Clouds and eclipses stain both moon and sun,
> And loathsome canker lives in sweetest bud.
>
> (1–4)

After an opening line that sounds authoritative, even magisterial, the
speaker proceeds to adduce exempla that will excuse the Friend. He is
in fact praising, not just excusing: to be compared to a rose, to celestial bodies, and to a "sweetest bud" (4) is surely to be and to feel
complimented. Yet he is condemning as well, for lines 2, 3, and 4
move on a crescendo of increasing criticism. In line 2 the corrupting
agent is merely the grammatical object, while in the subsequent lines it
assumes the more prominent position of the subject. This grammatical shift is mirrored by the increase in the degree of corruption suggested by the verbs: they change from "have" (2) to "stain" (3), which

---

[42]One of the few critics to comment on this quatrain is William Bowman Piper, in
"Evaluating Shakespeare's Sonnets," *Rice University Studies*, 69 (1979); he notes shifts in
the lines but interprets them differently from the way I do (pp. 14–16).

in the context of clouds and eclipses need not imply a permanent discoloration, to "lives in" (4). "Loathsome" (4) confirms the intensity of the implicit criticism in line 4. We may also, however, discern a countervailing pattern, if a faint one: as the criticisms grow increasingly intense, the metaphors also elevate the subject of corruption, so that we move from roses and fountains to the grandeur of moon and sun and thence to the superlative adjective "sweetest" (4). What we are witnessing, in brief, is a pattern that is intensely dramatic in precisely the sense these poems usually are: the speaker's position is shifting in the course of the sonnet. Unable or unwilling to sustain the detached forgiveness of the opening line, he becomes more and more critical. Yet, uncomfortable with the rebukes he is implicitly offering, he attempts to counterbalance them with compliments like "sweetest" (4), disguising the taste of salt with sugar. It is suggestive, too, that this quatrain, like Sonnet 35 as a whole, moves from apparent certainty to confusion and ambivalence—a pattern that anticipates the formal problems with closure that are so characteristic of these poems.

One of the most central questions about the sequence is why its speaker shifts between criticism and compliment in Sonnet 35 and so many poems like it. I previously merely suggested that he is "unable or unwilling" to maintain a particular stance, but the distinction between those adjectives is a significant one, carrying with it many implications about the central subject of this chapter: the character of the speaker and how it is revealed through formal devices. Is he, in other words, skillfully manipulating rhetoric, or is he the unwilling victim of his own words? Calling into question many critical assumptions about the sonnets, the answer to that interpretive problem reveals the speaker to be as subtly realized as the personages in Shakespeare's major plays—or, indeed, Venus and Lucrece.

A few scholars have maintained that he exemplifies the type of deliberate, even cunning use of rhetoric that alarms Kent and other plain speakers. As the best proponent of this reading puts it, "He is a manipulator of lies, not their victim."[43] Thus the conflict between the discursive and the metaphorical levels of the opening quatrain of Sonnet 35 stems not from an uncontrolled emotional tide but rather from a well controlled rhetorical strategy: the speaker is introducing his criticisms subtly, in a form that, like Sidney's sweetened medicine,

---

[43]Klause, p. 312. Similarly, De Grazia, "Shakespeare's View of Language," pp. 386–388, argues that the speaker misuses language in order to satisfy his lust; in "Some Features of Form and Style in Sonnets 97–126," Winifred Nowottny discusses the speaker's "tact as a friend" (in Landry, New Essays, p. 73).

will prove more palatable to the powerful hearer whom he fears to offend.

The evidence sometimes cited for this position is strong. The procreation sonnets, for example, evidently exemplify the same strategy such readers have found elsewhere in the sequence, strengthening the case that it is prevalent throughout. One might add, too, that the sonnets offer an additional type of testimony which, though neglected by critics, would seem to prove that the poet-lover is deliberately and skillfully using rhetoric. For these poems repeatedly incorporate rhetorical and logical devices advocated for deceiving others, and Renaissance readers were schooled to associate these techniques with a cunning use of language. Thus Puttenham, like many of his counterparts, includes ironia as a figure of dissembling.[44] Noting the potential dangers of this trope, Henry Peacham warns us that it should not be used by an inferior to a superior.[45] Sonnet 94 does precisely that. Hence, according to such readings, that labyrinthine sonnet violates the social norms that Peacham establishes for a reason necessitated by the same social system that generates those norms: the proud, aristocratic youth who is at least one of the targets and one of the subjects of the poem would not accept more overt criticism. Antiphrasis, which some rhetoricians distinguish from irony, involves saying one thing when one means the opposite; the sonnets in which the poet complains of the Friend's behavior in the course of declaring that he will not complain might serve as textbook examples of this figure of deception.

Especially relevant to the sonnets, however, is one of Aristotle's topoi: in II.xxiii.24 of the *Rhetoric*, he advises the orator to respond to instances of slander by explaining the reason for the false opinion. That is, of course, precisely the procedure followed in a line like "For still temptation follows where thou art" (41.4) and in many others in the sequence. And it is also the procedure to which one couplet alludes ironically: "In nothing art thou black save in thy deeds,/ And thence this slander as I think proceeds" (131.13–14). Given the widespread influence of the *Rhetoric*, many Renaissance readers would instantly recognize the topos and assume the speaker to be knowingly and artfully invoking a familiar formula for explaining away apparent faults.

The work of Renaissance logicians also provides a number of glos-

---

[44]Page 189.

[45]*The Garden of Eloquence*, ed. William G. Crane (Gainesville, Fla.: Scholars' Facsimiles and Reprints, 1954), p. 36.

ses for the apparent methods of Shakespeare's speaker. Adapting the list in Aristotle's *Of Sophistical Refutations*, they enumerate what they term "sophistical fallacies," many of which are familiar to any reader of the sonnets. Thus Thomas Blundeville's *The Arte of Logike*, whose title page proclaims its usefulness to ministers defending the faith "against all subtill Sophisters," lists equivocation, the playing on double meanings of a word, as one of the principal fallacies.[46] This caveat highlights, of course, the ideological distinction between most Renaissance rhetoricians and logicians, for what Blundeville is condemning might also be seen as the figure of antanaclasis, which Puttenham among others admires.[47] But what is relevant for our purposes is that, given the Renaissance interest in sophistical fallacies, no doubt many of Shakespeare's original readers associated wordplay like the puns on "will" in Sonnets 135 and 136 not only with the cleverness of antanaclasis but also with the knowing deceptiveness of equivocation. Similarly, among the sophistical fallacies is amphibology, the syntactical equivalent of logical equivocation, in which a grammatical construction may be read more than one way. As editors and readers have often discovered to their chagrin, the sonnets are packed with examples; in "O let me true in love but truly write" (21.9), for instance, is "true in love" in apposition to "me," or does it instead refer to the person being addressed? This ambiguity enacts syntactically one of the most troubling questions that the speaker explores elsewhere in the sequence: is his Friend indeed faithful to him? And, more to our purposes now, it also exemplifies the sort of ambiguity that might well be produced by a speaker deliberately dabbling in the sophistical fallacies in order to persuade a listener unresponsive to more direct forms of entreaty.

And yet, as Herbert reminds us in "The Church-porch," "Wit's an unruly engine, wildly striking . . . sometimes the engineer" (241–242).[48] Despite all the evidence to the contrary that we have amassed, one could instead make a strong case that Shakespeare's speaker is not using rhetorical devices but instead being used by them. According to this reading, rather than equivocally confounding praise and blame as a subtle means of making points to the Friend, he does so because he is so confused he cannot decide which his subject merits or which he himself wants to bestow; rather than filling poems that claim

[46]*The Art of Logike* (London, 1599), sig.Y2ᵛ.

[47]On this disagreement between the logicians and the rhetoricians, see Donawerth, *Shakespeare and the Sixteenth-Century Study of Language*, pp. 113–114.

[48]*The Works of George Herbert*, ed. F. E. Hutchinson (Oxford: Clarendon, 1941).

not to complain with unmistakable complaints in an attempt to change the Friend's inconsiderate behavior, he does so because he is torn between anger and admiration. His rhetorical equivocations stem from psychological ones. The sequence also offers considerable evidence for this interpretation. Its frequent references to civil war, its repeated allusions to a loss of identity, all suggest a character who is losing touch with his own emotions and with the language intended to express them. He has "Gored [his] own thoughts" (110.3); in other words, he has both wounded them and made them multicolored.[49] This wordplay on "Gored" implies, then, that we harm ourselves in the process of achieving multiple perspectives, such as the notion that the Friend is worthy of both praise and blame. It is possible to see much of the rhetoric in the sonnets as a symptom of that harm, the product not of a skilled sophister but of a mind diseased. As the speaker himself puts it, "My thoughts and my discourse as madmen's are, / At random from the truth vainly expressed" (147.11–12).

Not only can we adduce internal support for this interpretation of the sonnets, we might also cite many episodes in their author's plays to testify to his fascination with self-deception. Thus Malvolio's reactions to the tricks played on him—reactions which demonstrate that he is the victim as well of the trick he plays on himself when he persuades himself that Olivia loves him—constitute one of the most emotionally and morally significant episodes in *Twelfth Night*. The conventions of comedy rub against the complexities of human emotion, blistering the mood of the play: for all his ridiculousness, we feel Malvolio's pain, and we cannot avoid emotional involvement simply by rejoicing in or even accepting the banishment of the "refuser of festivities" figure. Here and elsewhere Shakespeare forces us to recognize behind literary conventions one of the most fundamental facts about human emotion: lovers are notoriously prone to be deceived in and by their own "thoughts and . . . discourse" (147.11), to attempt to praise someone worthy only of blame or to proffer courtly praise in the very act of rejecting that mode of speech.

If, then, it seems likely that the speaker in the sonnets is knowingly employing rhetorical strategies, very much in control of his thoughts, his feelings, and his discourse, we could make a persuasive alternative case that he is instead taken in by his own lies. As we weigh the evidence and ponder these alternatives, we are likely to become increasingly confused. And that confusion is, I would suggest, the very point: our difficulty in separating the deception of others from the

---

[49]See Ingram and Redpath, p. 254; Booth, *Sonnets*, pp. 354–355.

deception of oneself, manipulating language and emotions from being manipulated by them, mimes the speaker's own experience. He is in fact captive and victor, and he is both at once. Hence it is not surprising that we could marshal so much evidence for both positions. Very much as Hamlet's feigned emotional imbalance slips imperceptibly into the real thing, so the games this poet-lover plays on and with his audience become games played on himself. In a sense his is a world of antimetabole, the figure Puttenham dubs the "Counterchange"[50] ("Applying fears to hopes, and hopes to fears" [119.3]). For Shakespeare recognizes that if we tell lies often enough and persuasively enough we begin to believe them.[51]

At many points in the sequence there is another reason as well why we cannot finally separate the witty use of rhetoric from the unwitting victimization by it. The practical demands of the patronage system (one does not directly criticize one's benefactor) accord to the psychological demands of love (one does not express or perhaps even acknowledge too many flaws in the beloved). The speaker has a stake in beginning to believe his own fabrications. Shakespeare is showing us how many motivations may lie behind a single speech or even a single word, including a number that the person who is talking may not recognize.

Sonnet 138 demonstrates these patterns more clearly than any poem in the sequence:[52]

> When my love swears that she is made of truth,
> I do believe her though I know she lies,
> That she might think me some untutored youth,
> Unlearnèd in the world's false subtleties.
> Thus vainly thinking that she thinks me young,
> Although she knows my days are past the best,
> Simply I credit her false-speaking tongue:
> On both sides thus is simple truth suppressed.

[50]Page 208.

[51]For a different analysis of these issues, see Lanham, chap. 5, who finds a clash between what he terms the "rhetorical" and the "serious" approaches to languages. One of the several problems with his thesis is that many Elizabethan rhetoricians would not have supported his dichotomy.

[52]Many critics have commented perceptively on this poem. See, e.g., the debate between Richard Helgerson ("Shakespeare's Sonnet CXXXVIII," *Expl.*, 28 [1970], Item 48) and Richard Levin ("Shakespeare's Sonnet 138," *Expl.*, 36 [1978], 28–29); the issue on which they disagree, whether Shakespeare is in control of his emotions and his rhetoric throughout, is salient to my argument.

But wherefore says she not she is unjust?
And wherefore say not I that I am old?
O love's best habit is in seeming trust,
And age in love loves not to have years told.
  Therefore I lie with her, and she with me,
  And in our faults by lies we flattered be.

To begin with, the first line establishes that this sonnet, like so many in the collection, describes a repeated process and hence one that we may assume reflects a common pattern in the speaker's approach to experience. In line 2 he admits to making the same mistake over and over, noticing it but not avoiding it. This line also reveals what is most peculiar and most important about that mistake: he writes not, "I do pretend to believe her" but rather "I do believe her." In other words, the line reports the combination of knowingness and naiveté, victimizer and victimized, that, as I have suggested, is so characteristic of this personage. The very act of writing the poem, too, suggests the inseparability of the states we are describing: to compose this sonnet is to detach oneself from the process, to report it with some objectivity and some wryness—and yet the poem moves from its earlier implicit criticisms of the process it describes to a defense of it ("O love's best habit is in seeming trust" [11]) and even an acknowledgment that the speaker has no intention of abandoning it ("Therefore I lie with her, and she with me, / And in our faults by lies we flattered be" [13–14]).

Other sonnets in the sequence, too, deepen in meaning when we realize that the speaker may be both a powerful rhetorician and a powerless victim. Take, for instance, the two poems that I have cited as examples of the difficulties of interpreting the speaker's behavior, Sonnet 35 and Sonnet 96. Sonnet 35 actually moves from a implicit assertion that the speaker is in control of the situation, able to judge and to forgive ("No more be grieved at that which thou hast done" [1]) to the admission that he has lost control ("I an áccessary needs must be / To that sweet thief which sourly robs from me" [13–14]). But within the poem we witness the confusion of the two roles—and the confusion caused by them. Thus "All men make faults" (5) is on one level an authoritative and emotionally detached attempt to place the Friend's sins in a broader context—but on another level, of course, it is an admission that the speaker too has made faults, and that this poem in particular represents not a judicious use of rhetoric but an abuse of it. That implication becomes explicit immediately afterward: "and even I in this, / Authórizing thy trespass with compare" (5–6). Similarly, the opening of Sonnet 96—"Some say thy fault is youth, some wantonness, / Some say thy grace is youth and gentle sport" (1–2)—may be seen in part as an externalization of the speaker's own divided feelings on the subject, with the faulty parallelism created by the repetition of "youth" signaling the fact that the distinction between the two positions is not as clear-cut as one might think. In other words, within these opening lines we find both the sort of generalization we associate with the speaker's role as skilled rhetorician and an acknowledgment of the feelings that interfere with that role.

Shakespeare's plays, too, often remind us that it is common for lovers to be at once victor and captive, deer and hunter. He demonstrates how the kin of madmen and poets vainly flourish their wit as a deflection of tension, sexual and otherwise, and an assertion of power; witness the extraordinary first encounter of Anne and Richard III or the quarrels between Benedick and his distinctly unbeatific Beatrice. And he repeatedly shows us how easy it is to begin to believe the praise we shower on the beloved, especially since doing so purifies the motives for which we have bestowed our compliments. Perhaps even that plainspeaker Enobarbus is carried away in the barge speech not only by his vision of Cleopatra but also by his own words.

But the self-deception of the speaker in the sonnets, like that of the dramatic characters I have named, is by no means wholly negative. What we are witnessing, after all, is an intensity of devotion that on some level we respect even as we wish its objects were more worthy of it. His commitment to love and to the language that celebrates it are deep enough for him to continue to fight for those values against all the odds. If we respect him for the wit and cleverness that lead him knowingly to commingle praise and blame in the service of instructing and persuading the Friend and Dark Lady, on some level we even admire the loyalty, and the sheer energy that in turn generate that commingling in the service of his own illusions. This is not to deny that our primary reactions to his self-deception are, in both senses of the word, critical. But it is important to remember that just as he joins compliments and rebukes when evaluating the behavior of the Friend and Dark Lady, so our reactions to him are divided along similar lines.

In showing how the speaker combines self-control and its loss, freedom through and entrapment in rhetoric, Shakespeare continues the exploration of sexual politics that we found in *Venus and Adonis* and *The Rape of Lucrece*. The speaker in the sonnets is as preoccupied with power as Venus herself. Like her, he characteristically defines his relationships with the Friend and Dark Lady in terms of mastery.

Exaggerating a Petrarchan cliché, he rings the changes on the idea of slavery throughout Sonnets 57 and 58. But the concern is also apparent in poems ostensibly on subjects other than power. We encounter it even—or especially—in the sexual badinage of Sonnet 151:

> My soul doth tell my body that he may
> *Triumph* in love; flesh stays no farther reason,
> But rising at thy name doth point out thee,
> As *his triumphant prize*—proud of this pride,
> He is contented *thy poor drudge* to be.
>
> (7–11; italics added)

Not only the frequency but also the variety of the allusions to power here is striking: within a few lines Will's will moves from master to servant, a translation of the physiological facts of sexuality into the imperatives of power.

A similar movement is enacted repeatedly in the sonnets as the speaker shifts back and forth between his roles as victim and manipulator of the beloved and of the language of love. We need to beware of our tendency to comment on power in Renaissance literature as though it were monolithic: in fact, many literary works evoke situations in which it changes hands as rapidly as it did in the court itself. Even more to the point, in sonnet sequences in particular it is all too possible to be at once very powerful and very powerless. Thus in Shakespeare's sonnets the fact that his verse can challenge "Devouring time" (19.1) gives the speaker real power over the beloved, a strength that is if anything intensified by the fact that his subject is "fond on praise" (84.14). Yet we can never forget that he bestows these compliments in part because he is dependent on the Friend's patronage, a situation of which we are subtly reminded by the financial imagery, and in part because he is desperately dependent on the Friend's opinion of him. And, to return to the issue we have been exploring here, his ability to lace praise with blame is a testament to the speaker's rhetorical and hence political power; yet his inability to maintain moral distinctions, to distinguish meriting praise from deserving condemnation, demonstrates his powerlessness.

Shakespeare's preoccupation with equivocation and its consequences is also expressed through a series of recurrent tropes. Throughout the sequence images of civil war like those in Sonnet 35 express the divisions in the speaker; one sign of the extraordinary unity of this sequence is that those images develop from a darker and more psychological perspective the concern with self-destruction introduced in the procreation sonnets. Images of testifying falsely in a court of law remind us of this poet-lover's own predilection for perjury; thus in Sonnet 125 he angrily dismisses a "suborned informer" (13), and, as one editor has reminded us, he also implicitly alludes to suborning in Sonnet 152 ("Or made them swear against the thing they see" [12]).[53] Conscious of how heavily their court system depended on informers, whether honest or suborned, Renaissance readers no doubt would have found these references especially striking.[54]

Other figures of speech also relate to the duplicity that is so central to the speaker's world and to his own behavior. Occupatio, the figure in which one declares that one does not wish to say something and hence in fact says it, is very common in this sequence: it is one of the principal devices that the speaker uses to undercut whatever he is ostensibly doing. Thus he accuses the Friend of injury by declaring, "And patience tame to suff'rance bide each check, / Without accusing you of injury" (58.7–8), and in Sonnet 85 he writes a poem about the fact that he cannot write poems. If on one level amphibology, that equivocal syntax that can be read in more than one way, could be cited to demonstrate that the speaker is deliberately employing rhetorical and logical tricks, on another level it enacts the uncontrolled divisions within him. Sonnet 87, for example, concludes, "Thus have I had thee as a dream doth flatter: / In sleep a king, but waking no such matter" (13–14). The fact that "In sleep a king" (14) could modify either "I" or "thee" reflects the divided feelings about praising the Friend that we have encountered throughout the poem: is he indeed kinglike, or does he only entrap others into a false sense of their own grandeur? In the same poem we also encounter an example of how puns with divided meanings can reflect the speaker's divided feelings: is the addressee "dear" (1) in the sense of "precious" or merely of "expensive"?

IV

Hallett Smith notes that paradiastole, the figure that Puttenham terms the "Curry-favel,"[55] is very common in Shakespeare's sonnets, though he does not explore the point at any length.[56] We should not

[53]Booth, *Sonnets*, p. 532.

[54]On the fear of informers in the period, see Stephen D. White, *Sir Edward Coke and 'The Grievances of the Commonwealth,' 1621–1628* (Chapel Hill: Univ. of North Carolina Press, 1979), esp. pp. 67–69.

[55]Page 184.

[56]Smith, *The Tension of the Lyre*, pp. 19–20.

be surprised to find that the trope devoted to excusing something by giving it a more favorable name plays so central a part in this sequence: as we have seen, naming interests Shakespeare throughout his nondramatic—and dramatic—works. But nowhere in the canon is excusing more significant than it is in the sonnets. This act, like that of equivocation, results from and reveals the most central patterns in the speaker's temperament.[57]

Excusing is, of course, a common pastime in more conventional Petrarchan sequences, whose poet-lovers variously engage in justifying the lady's stony disregard by praising her chastity and justifying their own desires by blaming the slings and arrows of outrageous Cupid. Shakespeare's sonnets, however, approach this process of excusing much as they do that of equivocally undermining one's ostensible purpose: packed as they are with instances of and variations on the act of offering excuses, they devote more attention to that activity than we find in most other sonnets, and in so doing they show us how it relates to the speaker's sensibility.

We have already observed that Sonnet 35 describes and demonstrates the dangers of offering excuses. Sonnet 41 does so too, though in different ways:

> Those pretty wrongs that liberty commits,
> When I am sometime absent from thy heart,
> Thy beauty and thy years full well befits,
> For still temptation follows where thou art.
> Gentle thou art, and therefore to be won,
> Beauteous thou art, therefore to be assailed;
> And when a woman woos, what woman's son
> Will sourly leave her till he have prevailed?
> Ay me, but yet thou might'st my seat forbear,
> And chide thy beauty and thy straying youth,
> Who lead thee in their riot even there
> Where thou art forced to break a twofold truth:
>   Hers, by thy beauty tempting her to thee,
>   Thine, by thy beauty being false to me.

[57]For different perspectives on the issue of excusing, see, e.g., G. P. V. Akrigg, "The Shakespeare of the Sonnets," *Queen's Quarterly*, 72 (1965), 86–87; John D. Bernard, "'To Constancie Confin'de': The Poetics of Shakespeare's Sonnets," *PMLA*, 94 (1979), 81. The latter attributes the acts of praising and excusing not to psychological pressures in the speaker but rather to the development of a sacramental theory of the poetry of praise; one could, however, reconcile this thesis with my argument by examining the reasons the speaker wishes to develop that theory and noting the tensions within it.

The oxymoron that opens the poem may indirectly prepare us for the internalized oxymoron in the speaker: to describe wrongs as "pretty" (1) can be the result of an attraction to loving hate or even, to return to our earlier analyses, of a tendency toward another oxymoron, praising blame. But at this stage the phrase mainly focuses our attention on the subject of the poem, and "pretty" (1) not only excuses his faults but also suggests their insignificance in a way that a seemingly more positive modifier such as "handsome" would not. That act of excusing continues in the second half of the line; in a sequence that relies comparatively seldom on personifications, it is particularly striking that the abstract force of liberty, not the Friend himself, is blamed. Then the process of shifting the blame from the Friend to liberty, a force that is related to him, yields to a more extreme attempt to attribute his mistakes to others: he is, line 4 tells us, a helpless victim of temptation, and the fact that it "follows" (4) implies that, rather than being part of him like liberty, it is in fact separate.

Having suggested in this way that the Friend is the passive victim of external forces, the speaker proceeds in the next quatrain to express that passivity grammatically: "therefore *to be won* . . . therefore *to be assailed*" (5,6; italics added). Meanwhile, the wordplay on "gentle" (5) may make us a little uneasy, reminding us as it does that the subject of this poem is gentle in the sense of aristocratic and that, as Sonnet 94 and others hint, he may have misused the privileges of his social status. But this undercurrent is itself gentle: it does not noticeably ruffle the smooth surface of excuses. Lines 7 and 8 continue the process of shifting the blame, this time locating it not in an allegorized force but rather in woman, that root of all evil. (At the same time, however, "woman's son" [7] hints at a more positive image of the female.) In "till he have prevailed?" (8), however, the undertow of criticism of the Friend becomes a little stronger. First of all, the phrase may mean not "have won (i.e., seduced) her" but rather "have resisted her assault";[58] the conflict in those meanings, I would suggest, reflects the conflict in the speaker's evaluations. In any event, the reference to prevailing jars against all of the other implications of passivity and in so doing reminds us that the praise expressed earlier in the sonnet may well merely be the product of the speaker's desire to justify the behavior of the Friend. But the sonnet demonstrates yet another type of civil war: at the very moment when we begin to see the earlier comments in the poem as dangerously subjective, the speaker implies they are not by proffering a rhetorical question and hence appealing

[58]See, e.g., Ingram and Redpath, p. 96.

to common consent: "And when a woman woos, what woman's son / Will sourly leave her till he have prevailed?" (7–8).

We see, then, that the octet subtly anticipates the reproaches offered in the sestet, much as in actual speech we may signal our antagonism by particular turns of phrase before we openly express it. But even in the final six lines of the poem, the process of excusing continues: the speaker invokes allegorical figures from a medieval morality to avoid criticizing the immorality of the Friend directly, again deflecting his blame. That same deflection is in evidence in another passive construction that, like the previous ones, itself describes passivity ("thou art forced" [12]) and in the repeated reproaches directed toward the woman. And once again the speaker tempers any criticism by bestowing a compliment: he who commits "pretty wrongs" (1) is himself graced by beauty. Here, as earlier in the poem, we see how the process of excusing is closely related to the activity we analyzed earlier, confounding praise and blame.

Sonnet 129 has been explicated often and well, but readers have neglected one particular perspective on it: for all its guilt and bitterness, the poem is also a study in the process of offering excuses:

> Th' expense of spirit in a waste of shame
> Is lust in action, and till action lust
> Is perjured, murd'rous, bloody, full of blame,
> Savage, extreme, rude, cruel, not to trust,
> Enjoyed no sooner but despisèd straight,
> Past reason hunted, and no sooner had,
> Past reason hated as a swallowed bait,
> On purpose laid to make the taker mad;
> Mad in pursuit, and in possession so,
> Had, having, and in quest to have, extreme,
> A bliss in proof, and proved, a very woe,
> Before, a joy proposed, behind, a dream.
>   All this the world well knows, yet none knows well
>   To shun the heav'n that leads men to this hell.

While the context in which it appears encourages us to read this poem as on some level an excuse for the speaker's lust, for much of the sonnet he distances himself—and, indeed, all of mankind—from that passion. It is striking that the subject of the poem is "lust" and only indirectly the lustful. Though, as one critic has maintained, "lust" may be read as a personification of the human beings stricken with that passion,[59] this is not its primary meaning: the poem deflects attention from those victims and onto the personification. This sonnet is, in other words, impersonal in a sense different from that in which the adjective is normally applied to it: people figure only indirectly in the first seven lines. And this deflection of attention is even mirrored in a syntactical pattern: just as these lines emphasize not the subject experiencing the lust but rather that emotion itself, so the opening two lines reverse subject and predicate and in so doing emphasize the latter. As the poem progresses, of course, it does allude to someone in the grip of passion, "the taker" mentioned in line 8. But it does so only to excuse him in another way: he is, like the figure in Sonnet 41, a victim and, again like that figure, a victim of women.[60]

The couplet, however, complicates the kinds of distancing that the speaker has attempted to achieve earlier in the poem. Its antimetabole establishes an impression of order and control, but in another sense the figure also signals a change in the speaker's own stance, for he is now admitting that he and others must assume some of the blame for not resisting "Th'expense of spirit in a waste of shame" (1). He supports that admission, too, with an indirect hint of his guilt: by writing "this hell" (14) rather than "that hell," especially in a sequence that normally uses distal deictics, he may be implying his proximity to temptation.

Yet the poem does not abandon the process of excusing even now. For once again there is a scapegoat: "the heav'n that leads men to this hell" (14). Previous hints that woman lays—and is—the bait, as well as some of the sexual connotations of "heav'n" and "hell" (14) relevant in this context, indicate that the scapegoat is in fact, as it were, a she-goat—a realization that activates the ambiguity in "men" (14), reminding us that on one level it refers to mankind but that at this moment the speaker wishes instead to limit it to a particular gender. The tensions between the broader meaning of the word and the narrower one it may assume here may lead us to reflect on the tensions in the speaker that generate this usage and especially on his drive to pardon some people even if the price is blaming others.

The patterns of excusing that we have traced at some length in Sonnets 41 and 129 reappear frequently throughout the sequence. Indeed, the sonnets provide us with a virtual compendium of the

[59]Helen Vendler, "Jakobson, Richards, and Shakespeare's Sonnet CXXIX," in *I. A. Richards: Essays in His Honor*, ed. Reuben Brower, Helen Vendler, and John Hollander (New York: Oxford Univ. Press, 1973), esp. p. 189.

[60]Compare Vendler, pp. 186, 191.

processes by which we can justify faults. One of the most common we have already examined: one may shift the blame. It is, for example, possible to externalize and allegorize the mistake; in Sonnet 95 the speaker blames the Friend's vices in the telling phrase, "those vices . . . Which for their habitation chose thee out" (9–10), and in Sonnet 101 he attributes his silence to his "truant muse" (1) rather than to himself. Such allusions to one's muse were, of course, commonplaces, but we are tempted to see this personification as an instance of deflecting blame: in many other cases the speaker does just that, and our suspicions are further intensified by his suggestion that his muse give the very excuse he himself has offered in other sonnets, that true beauty does not require praise. Similarly, though neither mythological gods nor the Christian one normally assumes a prominent role in this sequence, Sonnet 58 opens, "That god forbid, that made me first your slave" (1); blaming his servitude neither on the Friend's insistence nor on his own passivity but rather on a deity's design, the speaker implies that it is virtually inevitable.

Elsewhere, as we have already seen, he does shift the blame from the Friend's shoulders to his own, assuming a role rather like that of the evil counselors in the history plays, whom courtiers can conveniently blame for the monarch's misdeeds. (Shakespeare, like many of his contemporaries, realizes that not the least perquisite of kingship is that whipping boys are provided even when kings grow up—and especially if they do not grow up enough.) In certain of the sonnets, though, guilt is transferred not to another human being but to a force of nature; in the lines "Anon permit the basest clouds to ride / With ugly rack on his celestial face" (33.5–6), for instance, the speaker is evidently divided between castigating the clouds and assigning the responsibility to the person who will "permit" (5) the damage they cause. Sonnet 58 is again revealing: by writing "I am to wait" (13) rather than "You make me wait" or "I choose to wait," the speaker at least temporarily avoids direct criticism.

The anthology of excuses includes other types as well. Rather than reassigning the fault to a different agent, one can reinterpret the error itself. Thus, as we have already observed, a grammatical modifier may, as its name suggests, modify and modulate: "Those *pretty* wrongs that liberty commits" (41.1; italics added). Or, employing the rhetorical device euphemismos, the speaker may claim that the fault was not merely pretty but also *felix*: "But that your trespass now becomes a fee; / Mine ransoms yours, and yours must ransom me" (120, 13–14). The sense of logical strain we feel in such instances reflects the emotional strain on the speaker of offering unlikely excuses.

The preoccupation with justifying others or oneself that we find in the sonnets extends throughout their author's career. It is, however, perhaps most central in the *Henry IV* plays. The renowned monologue in which Hal excuses himself for spending so much time in the tavern proves (if further proof were needed) that in a sense he is indeed the son of both that master of excuses Falstaff and of his biological father, who is also given to attempts to justify his own behavior. Another suggestive instance is the conclusion of *Measure for Measure*, which attempts to draw distinctions between the sanative process of forgiving and the dangerous one of merely excusing.

In the sonnets themselves excusing occupies so central a role that many other issues may be seen as radiating from it, like the scratches on the mirror that George Eliot describes. Shakespeare is concerned that an aristocrat's propensity for offering excuses and being excused by others symptomizes the arrogance of power: "As on the finger of a thronèd queen / The basest jewel will be well esteemed" (96.5–6). And the issue of excusing raises the questions about language itself that we explored in earlier chapters: excusing is a form of renaming—vices become "pretty wrongs" (41.1)—and it can be as self-serving and as dangerous as Venus' many attempts to call the world around her by the names she would prefer. Condemning the use of metaphor to couple a mismatched signifier and signified ("My mistress' eyes are nothing like the sun" [130.1]), Shakespeare also traces the way the poet presides at an equally unfortunate union when he mislabels deeds in the process of apologizing for them. The appearance of metonymy in other contexts—"O lest *the world* should task you to recite" (72.1; italics added), "Lean penury within *that pen* doth dwell, / That to his subject lends not some small glory" (84.5–6; italics added)—echoes that misnaming by the speaker.

The primary reason the sonnets catalogue types of excusing so exhaustively, however, is that in so doing they can explore their speaker's psyche. In particular, the poems document the way the speaker's very identity slips away when he attempts to excuse the Friend,[61] a process mirrored rhetorically in the instances of metonymy that we just noted and in another figure that involves a related type of switching, antimetabole ("But day by night and night by day oppressed?" [28.4]). Like the dyer's hand to which he himself refers in Sonnet 111, he takes on the faults of those he loves—"Myself corrupting salving thy amiss" (35.7)—an analogue to the way he may

---

[61]Many scholars have noted the speaker's loss of identity. See, e.g., Barber, "Shakespeare in His Sonnets," pp. 662–663; Winny, pp. 116–117.

contract a venereal disease from the Dark Lady. Sonnet 35 and many of the Dark Lady poems comment directly on this loss of identity, and it is also implicit in the many sonnets, such as 109 and 110, in which he accuses himself of immoralities and infidelities strikingly like those for which he has criticized the Friend. The ambiguous syntax of Sonnet 142 enacts the process of identification, for it is impossible to be sure which of the participants is responsible for the "sinful loving" (2): "Love is my sin, and thy dear virtue hate, / Hate of my sin, grounded on sinful loving" (1–2).[62] But perhaps the deepest and most troubling similarity between the speaker on the one hand and the Friend and the Dark Lady on the other is that all three have an extraordinary propensity for making the foul seem fair, whether it be through the "conceits deceitful" of poetic language or simply through the charms of an appearance that can turn faults into graces or darkness into brightness.

If his propensity for offering excuses suggests that the speaker is subjugating himself to those he excuses, it also reminds us again of other facets of his temperament. The threats offered by impersonal forces like time he can challenge directly, if not always persuasively: "No! Time, thou shalt not boast that I do change" (123.1). But the threats from those he loves he cannot always face: in particular, he denies the very existence of their faults. This is, of course, a common human activity, but he does it to an unusual extent. It is part of his characteristic tendency to react indirectly to tensions, to undercut praise with blame rather than blaming openly. Another reason he offers excuses so frequently also harks back to the earlier part of this section: just as his deliberate strategy of, say, lacing compliments with reproofs turns into an uncontrolled propensity for behaving that way, so the process of excusing enjoined on him by a poet's relationship to his patron and a lover's to his mistress seems to become a mannerism, a habit of mind. In short, Shakespeare is again charting the ways we may be affected, morally and emotionally, by our own rhetoric.

V

For Shakespeare, to paraphrase a contemporary slogan, the personal is poetical. Not only is the speaker's character revealed through his participation in the two rhetorical patterns we have examined, equivocating and offering excuses; it is also disclosed through his

[62]Compare Booth, *Sonnets*, p. 491.

reactions to two of the rhetorical problems that commonly appear in other sonnet cycles, closure and flattery. It is obvious that the sonnets comment on certain aesthetic dilemmas associated with their genre, such as the conflict between simple and ornate poesy. What is not so obvious is that Shakespeare's sequence also explores its genre's problematical approaches to closure and to flattery and does so by embodying them in the behavior of his speaker. Hence the sonnets turn certain aesthetic dilemmas that dogged and often defeated other sequences to their advantage: those dilemmas come to seem not faults in the sequence per se but rather patterns in the psyche of its speaker.

The first of these aesthetic challenges is closure, which often proves particularly problematical in the sonnet. It is, as Barbara Herrnstein Smith has shown us, especially difficult to achieve when the poem represents an interior speech.[63] Our meditations do not customarily terminate as neatly as an epigrammatic statement does. These difficulties may be intensified in the form termed the "Shakespearean sonnet," for, as Paul Fussell, another student of poetic technique, has suggested, the relationship between quatrains and couplet can suggest disproportion and imbalance.[64]

Renaissance sonnet writers develop a range of strategies for coping with prosodic problems like these. Thus Daniel at several points redresses the imbalance through concatenation, which reminds us that the end of one sonnet is also the beginning of another and thus effects a graceful progress from one to the next:

> If this be loue, to liue a liuing death;
> O then loue I, and drawe this weary breath.

>   Sonnet X.
> O then I loue, and drawe this weary breath,
> For her the cruell faire.

Like its rhetorical equivalent anadiplosis, concatenation suggests both stasis and change (an impression intensified in this instance by the fact that, while most of the line is the same, the third and fourth words are in fact reversed). The effect of stasis is appropriate to the subject of undying love. But concatenation is also appropriate to the comparatively serene mood of this sequence in another way as well: it renders the closing of one sonnet and the opening of another as an

---

[63]Smith, *Poetic Closure*, pp. 139–150.
[64]*Poetic Meter and Poetic Form* (New York: Random House, 1965), pp. 119–120.

orderly, controlled process. (This may explain why Donne employs concatenation in "La Corona" but not in the more emotionally chaotic *Holy Sonnets*.) In short, Daniel here solves the problem of closure by dissolving it: if one reads the poems sequentially, the chains of concatenation unchain the couplet from the pretense of finality.

Though Sidney employs a sonnet structure very different from those of Shakespeare or Daniel, one of the several ways he approaches closure is particularly relevant to Shakespeare's sequence: the author of *Astrophil and Stella* characteristically concludes his sonnets with an abrupt "turn." The famous ending of Sonnet 71, "'But ah,' Desire still cries, 'give me some food'" (14) is the most obvious instance, but the sequence offers a number of other examples as well:

> True, that on earth we are but pilgrims made,
>   And should in soule up to our countrey move:
>   True, and yet true that I must *Stella* love.
>
>   (5.12–14)

> Sure you say well, your wisdome's golden mine
>   Dig deepe with learning's spade, now tell me this,
>   Hath this world ought so faire as *Stella* is?
>
>   (21.12–14)

What is striking about these endings and the many like them in *Astrophil and Stella* is that Sidney renders thematic an imbalance like the one of which Paul Fussell writes; that is, because the solid if dull reasoning of all the preceding lines can be overturned by the briefest allusion to Stella, the poem becomes a tribute to her powers. Poems like these use prosody to make the point that is acted out dramatically in Sonnet 47: "O me, that eye / Doth make my heart give to my tongue the lie" (13–14). In other words, a mere thought or sight of her is an unanswerable rebuttal to all the arguments against loving her. The discussion of that subject, like the sonnet itself, is irrefutably closed.

Most readers would agree that in many poems Shakespeare employs his final couplets effectively, if unoriginally, to summarize or bring to a climax his preceding arguments.[65] "This were to be new made when thou art old, / And see thy blood warm when thou feel'st it cold," (2.13–14) refers back to the imagery earlier in the sonnet and neatly encapsulates the case the poem has been making. And it is important to remember that a large number of Shakespeare's sonnets

[65]Compare Piper, pp. 6–8.

do have endings of this type: critics who are interested in the problematical couplets tend to overlook the poems that conclude more straightforwardly, just as those whose primary concern is the embittered sonnets are prone to ignore or misread the many lyrics in the sequence that express a very different mood. Nonetheless, the fact remains that many of the poems do terminate in lines that strike us as feeble or unpersuasive, manifesting an emotional or logical weakness that is at times reflected in a prosodic one.

Thus some couplets seem to fail because they offer pat solutions to difficult problems; we are uneasy with their tidiness, an impression intensified by the balance inherent in the couplet form. When the jealousy displayed in Sonnet 42 ends on "But here's the joy, my friend and I are one; / Sweet flatt'ry, then she loves but me alone" (13–14), we are conscious that the phrase "Sweet flatt'ry" (14) could well gloss the couplet itself, with all the negative connotations of flattery very much in play. Similarly, "Pity me, then, dear friend, and I assure ye, / Ev'n that your pity is enough to cure me" (111.13–14) does not persuade the reader that the diseases of the heart chronicled in the previous twelve lines can be cured as readily as the speaker hopes. The jingly rhyme increases our sense that the speaker is whistling in the dark, our sense that the couplet is merely another vain attempt to solve his dilemmas.

Other couplets offer responses that seem inappropriate reactions to what has come before. Once again we are more aware of the stresses that make the speaker seek reassurance than of the reassurance that the couplet claims to provide. The quatrains of Sonnet 33, for example, draw attention to the wrongs that the poet has suffered at the hands of his beloved:

Full many a glorious morning have I seen
Flatter the mountain tops with sovereign eye,
Kissing with golden face the meadows green,
Gilding pale streams with heav'nly alchemy,
Anon permit the basest clouds to ride
With ugly rack on his celestial face,
And from the forlorn world his visage hide,
Stealing unseen to west with this disgrace.
Ev'n so my sun one early morn did shine,
With all triumphant splendor on my brow;
But out alack, he was but one hour mine,
The region cloud hath masked him from me now.

(1–12)

Here Shakespeare develops the metaphor of the sun in a way that emphasizes its guilt and hence by implication that of the Friend. Thus "Flatter" (2) and "Gilding" (4) have connotations that are at the very least ambiguous: flattery can be sycophantic, and gilding can be deceptive. The sort of couplet that these quatrains lead us to expect is something like "I thought our love an everlasting day / And yet my trust thou didst, my love, betray." If we try to read the poem through with this couplet tacked on the end, we find that the uncanonical lines fit the spirit of the poem. If, on the other hand, we read the sonnet through with the couplet that Shakespeare did in fact write—"Yet him for this my love no wit disdaineth; / Suns of the world may stain when heav'n's sun staineth" (13–14)—we become uneasy. Shakespeare's speaker is trying to fool himself; he takes one conceivable moral from the metaphor (the Friend's betrayal is justified by that of the sun) and neglects the more central one that the reader has been observing (the Friend, like the sun, has been culpably deceptive).

As we have already noticed, Sonnet 95 ends on a threat and hence exemplifies perclusio, a mode of concluding a discourse recommended by many rhetoricians: "Take heed, dear heart, of this large privilege; / The hardest knife ill used doth lose his edge" (13–14). More often, though, the abrupt threats on which the sonnets terminate function differently from those advocated by the rhetoricians: the speaker himself is not menacing but menaced, not victor but captive. Such couplets act out the impingement of new thoughts— especially new apprehensions and doubts—on the speaker's troubled consciousness.[66] Sonnet 92, for example, ends, "But what's so blessèd-fair that fears no blot? / Thou mayst be false, and yet I know it not" (13–14). The couplet of Sonnet 52 indicates that the speaker's possession of his beloved Friend is in fact far less secure than he has implied earlier in the poem: "Blessèd are you whose worthiness gives scope, / Being had to triumph, *being lacked to hope*" (13–14; italics added). Just as an unexpected fear enters the speaker's mind and disturbs the peace he has been attempting to achieve, so an unexpected idea enters the couplet and disturbs its potential function as a neat summary of the preceding quatrains.

---

[66]Compare Joel B. Altman's statement that schoolchildren were trained in destructio or subversio, which involved overturning a previously established argument (*The Tudor Play of Mind: Rhetorical Inquiry and the Development of Elizabethan Drama* [Berkeley: Univ. of California Press, 1978], pp. 46–47). On Shakespeare's use of couplets that overturn the previous arguments, also see M. M. Mahood, *Shakespeare's Wordplay* (London: Methuen, 1957), pp. 103–104.

The couplet of Sonnet 34, which we touched on in a different context earlier, would at first glance seem to be the opposite of the ones we have just been examining: "Ah, but those tears are pearl which thy love sheeds, / And they are rich, and ransom all ill deeds" (13–14). The speaker appears to be substituting forgiveness for bitterness, peace for turmoil. And yet not so. Modern readers of these lines have neglected the resonance they would have had for Shakespeare's own readers: contemporary theological debates included the conflict between the Counter-Reformation position that tears can indeed "ransom" (14) sins and help to bring grace and the Reformers' contention that, though they could be a sign that grace had been achieved, they could not help to effect it.[67] Behind this controversy lies the central doctrinal difference between seeing contrition as a cause of the forgiveness of sins on the one hand and viewing it merely as a result of forgiveness on the other. The Catholic position produced an extensive "literature of tears," in which the precious droplets were often celebrated as a sign of the pain the repentant sinner must endure. Though we do not know enough about Shakespeare's own religious convictions to predict his position on the issue, we can be sure that the debate was central enough theologically to make it likely that he and many of his readers knew of it. This is not, of course, to say that Shakespeare's audience would have seen the sonnet as a serious contribution to the controversy, but nonetheless their reading of the couplet in question is likely to have been affected by their awareness of that conflict. To those members of his audience who held the Protestant position, the speaker's assurance might seem yet another instance of his fooling himself, whistling in his theological darkness. And those who maintained that tears could bring redemption would realize that the issue was problematical: even if they accepted the assurance offered on the discursive level of the couplet, the mood it evoked might well be tinged with some anxiety and tension. If we cannot say of this couplet, as of several others, that it "calls all in doubt," neither can we claim that it puts our minds to rest.[68]

In short, many of the sonnets end on a "turn" that radically reverses what has come before, the same structure that we encountered in *Astrophil and Stella.* Yet in fact the conclusions in these two sequences are significantly different. Sidney typically substitutes true certainty for seeming certainty; thus Stella's beauty is a definitive argument for

[67]See Richard Strier, "Herbert and Tears," *ELH*, 46 (1979), 221–247.

[68]Landry, *Interpretations*, p. 59, arrives at the same position on this couplet from another perspective, arguing that its abruptness makes it unpersuasive.

loving her, while Neo-Platonic generalizations only seemed to prove that one should not do so. Shakespeare's sonnets, in contrast, often move from assurance and assurances (however tainted they may be by our sense that the gentleman protests too much) to doubt. When Sidney's conclusions surprise us, they illuminate the rest of the poem with the clarity and force of a flash of lightning; in contrast, Shakespeare's couplets are typically threatening but indeterminate in their results, like storm clouds sliding into a sunny sky.

Why, then, does Shakespeare so often compose unconventional couplets?[69] Assuming that most of those that do not persuasively summarize the quatrains are failures, many readers have attributed them to the difficulties of achieving closure inherent in the sonnet form, while others have blamed the poet's conflicting purposes or the intractability of the material he is trying to summarize. In fact, however, most of the couplets in the sonnets represent not a symptom of the aesthetic problems Shakespeare was confronting but rather a response to them—and one that further illuminates the speaker's character.

That response is all the more impressive when one acknowledges that the problems of closure that we touched on earlier were especially severe for Shakespeare himself. For the so-called Shakespearean sonnet is, as so many of its readers have remarked, one of the most orderly of literary forms; it is tightly structured and compact. Its couplet is the most orderly and ordering of its elements. No matter what ideas are presented in the couplet, in contrast to the syntactical and metrical complexities of the preceding quatrains it is prone to sound pat. Frequently, too, the convictions expressed in the concluding lines of a sonnet will be so epigrammatic that they mirror and intensify the impression of assurance that the couplet intrinsically conveys.

The experiences evoked by Shakespeare's sonnets are, however, unusually tumultuous even in a genre that specializes in psychological torment. Moreover, in a number of ways his sonnets focus our attention on the speaker's chaotic reactions. We would no more expect a man who is wrestling with the kinds of unresolved contradictions plaguing Shakespeare's speaker to express them in the carefully structured and epigrammatically decisive lines of a couplet than the Elizabethans would have expected a madman in a play to speak in

---

[69]For explanations of the couplets different from mine, see esp. Smith, *Poetic Closure*, pp. 142–145, 214–220. I am indebted to Stephen Booth for several useful suggestions about this section of the chapter.

verse. Like the poet in Donne's "The Triple Fool," we assume that grief brought to numbers cannot be so fierce.

Rather than ignoring these characteristics of his form, Shakespeare dramatizes them in more than one sense of that verb: they serve to illuminate the disturbing ethical dilemmas he is investigating and the disturbed speaker he is evoking. The reader comes to view the sentiments in many of the couplets not as objective summaries of the problems that the quatrains have been exploring but rather as yet another symptom of the anguish and confusion those problems have caused for the speaker and yet another sign of his ways of responding to tension.

To understand the nature of those failures—and the nature of the character responsible for them—we need to place the couplets in a broader context: they are but one instance of a preoccupation with closure that runs throughout the sequence. One effect of the syntactical complexity that we have noted several times is that often we cannot be sure where a thought ends; thus, as William Empson has shown, the seemingly neat pattern of paired alternatives that opens Sonnet 81 shifts to a greater syntactical ambiguity when we recognize that the lines could in fact be combined in any number of ways:[70]

> Or I shall live your epitaph to make,
> Or you survive when I in earth am rotten,
> From hence your memory death cannot take,
> Although in me each part will be forgotten.
> Your name from hence immortal life shall have,
> Though I, once gone, to all the world must die.
> The earth can yield me but a common grave,
> When you entombèd in men's eyes shall lie.
>
> (1–8)

On another level, the feminine endings in Sonnet 87 create an impression that the lines are trailing off indeterminately, an effect that parallels the speaker's depression and difficulty at ending the relationship:

> Farewell, thou art too dear for my possessing,
> And like enough thou know'st thy estimate.
> The charter of thy worth gives thee releasing;
> My bonds in thee are all determinate.

[70] *Seven Types of Ambiguity* (New York: Harcourt, Brace, 1931), pp. 69–70.

For how do I hold thee but by thy granting,
And for that riches where is my deserving?
The cause of this fair gift in me is wanting,
And so my patent back again is swerving.

(1–8)

The conclusion of the sequence as a whole is also problematical. This is, of course, a difficulty that other sonnet writers of the period faced as well. It is complicated by both the conditions of transmission, which meant that many sonnets circulated individually or in groups as well as being published in a sequence, and by the conditions of love itself, which is prone to end not with a bang but a whimper. Several poets of the English Renaissance, however, meet these challenges with a similar solution: they in effect conclude their sonnet sequences on a poem that is not a sonnet. Thus it is no accident that anacreontic poetry and the "Epithalamion" appear at the end of the *Amoretti* or that the "Complaint of Rosamond" follows *Delia*.[71] On one level this solution is merely the equivalent of ending a stanza by varying a prosodic pattern that has been established earlier, switching, for example, from iambic pentameter to an Alexandrine. But the generic shifts in the sequences in question also imply a significant shift in vision. Both Spenser and Daniel are looking at the problems explored in their sequences from a different perspective, which is represented by the change to a different genre. Behind that shift lies the implication that the values inherent in and symbolized by the sonnet, notably the emphasis on obsessive and undying passion, virtually preclude closure: to end the sequence and the emotions it details, one must, literally and metaphorically, move to a different genre.

Shakespeare, however, does not terminate his sequence in quite this way. It is very possible that, as some readers have claimed, he intended his two anacreontic poems, Sonnets 153 and 154, to be the final sonnets in the sequence. They do assume a function rather like that of the "Epithalamion" or the "Complaint of Rosamond," providing a different generic perspective on love, and it is also suggestive that in this case, as in Spenser's anacreontics and Daniel's complaint, the perspective is more detached. Yet their detachment does not in fact generate a satisfactory sense of closure. For the subject of these sonnets is the very impossibility of achieving distance from love and the

---

[71]Thomas Roche also notes that sequences sometimes end on poems in a different genre ("Shakespeare and the Sonnet Sequence," in *English Poetry and Prose, 1540–1674*, ed. Christopher Ricks [London: Barrie and Jenkins, 1970], pp. 105–106).

inaccessibility of any finality, any cure:

> For men diseased; but I, my mistress' thrall,
>   Came there for cure, and this by that I prove:
>   Love's fire heats water, water cools not love.
>
> (154.12–14)

Hence the poems undercut their ostensible purpose. And if the two sonnets are indeed different versions of each other, as seems likely in light of their close similarity,[72] by a happy accident that very fact also reflects the difficulty of, as it were, saying it once and for all. In other words, Sonnet 153 and 154 document the speaker's unsuccessful attempts to detach himself from his emotions and hence experience a sense of finality. (Compare the way Sonnets 94 and 129 represent not the objective stance that some readers have claimed to find in them but rather, as we saw in the case of 129, a failed essay at such a stance.) Suggesting that the Dark Lady sonnets destroy the equilibrium achieved in the poems addressed to the Friend, one critic observes, "There is never a last word."[73] While one might well question his assumptions about how much equilibrium we find even in the sonnets about the Friend, that observation could stand as an epigraph to the whole sequence.

Why, then, does Shakespeare refuse to speak—or allow his poet-lover to speak—that last word? Why do the sonnets avoid closure on so many levels, ranging from the single line to the individual sonnet to the group of poems as a whole? The answer, as I briefly suggested earlier, is that this sequence transforms an aesthetic problem in its genre into an emotional problem in its speaker: both his frenetic attempts to achieve closure and his repeated failures to do so are as central to his character as Hamlet's recurrent decisions not to kill Claudius are to his.

First of all, the couplets that seem deliberately to oversimplify experience effectively mirror the speaker's vain attempts to resolve the conflicts in his own mind, to transform syneciosis into antithesis. He finds in the couplet's straightforward verities (and the straightforward syntax in which these apparent truths are expressed) a welcome alternative to the torturing ambivalences with which he has been wrestling (and the tortuous syntax in which he has expressed them).

---

[72]See Nowottny, "Some Features of Form and Style," pp. 88–89; she argues that many paired sonnets in fact represent different versions of the same poem.
[73]Philip Edwards, *Shakespeare and the Confines of Art* (London: Methuen, 1968), p. 29.

The Sonnets

Like the Duke proposing marriage at the end of *Measure for Measure*, he attempts to resolve a tangled complex of emotional and moral problems through the formal mode of resolution normally associated with his genre. And he fails precisely in the way the Duke does: the issues are more complicated and more indeterminate than either character wishes to face, a complexity aptly reflected in the fact that both works concern experiences that are normally not associated with comedy and the sonnet respectively and hence do not lend themselves to the forms of closure those literary types customarily provide. The search for easy answers—and easy outs—is one of the frailties that flesh is heir to, and it interests Shakespeare throughout his career. In the sonnets, as in *The Rape of Lucrece*, we can see a link between the characters' grasping at overly neat solutions and the ways they assess people: attracted to absolutes even while he is overwhelmingly conscious of ambiguities, the speaker in the sonnets at times yields to the temptation to portray the Friend as an abstract idealization, much as he yields to the temptation to end certain sonnets on grand generalizations.

But this poet-lover's attempts to achieve the ethical and emotional certainties associated with closure so often fail, whether because those grand generalizations are unconvincing or because he acknowledges fear and threats. One reason for this failure reflects a central if often subterranean concern of the sonnets: what comes later may change our view of what has come before, so every conclusion is necessarily inconclusive. The "plot" of the sonnets, however skeletal we have seen it to be, reinforces this point: most obviously, the speaker's recognition of the Friend's "sensual fault" (35.9) discredits or at least calls into question descriptions of his perfections, raising the issue of whether the Friend has changed or whether the speaker's initial impressions of him were faulty. And the reader experiences a series of reinterpretations that mime those of the speaker; the feudal language that we may have been tempted to categorize as a merely light-hearted adoption of a convention, for instance, becomes more ominous when we encounter the exaggeration of that convention in lines like, "But like a sad slave stay and think of nought / Save where you are how happy you make those" (57.11–12).

Shakespeare also draws our attention to an important truism about syntax: what is to come often changes our tentative conclusions about what we have already read. Thus when we interpret "Sweet love, renew thy force, be it not said / Thy edge should blunter be than appetite" (56.1–2), we do not at first realize that the poem is addressing the force of love rather than the beloved. Sonnet 145 is often dismissed as an unfortunate and unsuccessful game, with even the most sensitive of editors asserting that it is hardly worth reprinting.[74] In truth, however, this poem is not unimportant, for it enacts a version of the issue we are considering, the way the future can change the past:

> Those lips that love's own hand did make
> Breathed forth the sound that said, I hate,
> To me that languished for her sake.
> But when she saw my woeful state
> Straight in her heart did mercy come,
> Chiding that tongue that ever sweet
> Was used in giving gentle doom;
> And taught it thus anew to greet:
> I hate she altered with an end,
> That followed it as gentle day
> Doth follow night, who like a fiend
> From heav'n to hell is flown away.
>> I hate from hate away she threw,
>> And saved my life saying, not you.

In this case what is suggested is the insubstantiality of lovers' words and of the relationship within which these particular words are spoken.

But if the nature of experience renders closure problematical, the character of this particular speaker renders it virtually impossible. Attracted though he may be to absolutes, he is, as we have observed, involved to the point of obsession with doubts and fears about what is to come. The concern with time manifest in the procreation sonnets is often described primarily as a rhetorical ploy designed to convince the addressee to be fruitful and multiply, yet that concern evidently also reflects the speaker's own preoccupation with the changes the future may hold. Once again we cannot separate the dancer from the dance, habits of mind from rhetorical strategies.

Other emotional patterns intensify the speaker's difficulties with closure. If the poet-patron relationship makes it hard for him to express criticisms directly, his own character makes it impossible: he is far more prone to sandwich reproaches in between compliments. In certain circumstances, of course, this may be a more effective way of

---

[74]Ingram and Redpath, p. 334. Stephen Booth is more appreciative of the poem, but he defends it from an angle different from mine (*Sonnets*, p. 500).

delivering rebukes, but in a poem such as Sonnet 35 we may well wonder to what extent those rebukes would even be heard by the person to whom they apply. Because of his inability to confront his feelings fully and openly, it is particularly difficult for the speaker to resolve them; sometimes he himself is too confused to think through his divided emotions, and sometimes—to the limited extent that these poems involve some communication with the Friend and Dark Lady—he cannot frankly express his criticisms to the people they concern. As Blake reminds us,

> I was angry with my friend:
> I told my wrath, my wrath did end.
> I was angry with my foe:
> I told it not, my wrath did grow.
> ("A Poison Tree," 1–4)[75]

But we should not be too intolerant of Shakespeare's speaker. Though his problems with closure, like those of Venus, draw attention to certain idiosyncratic emotional limitations, they also exemplify the most familiar forms of human behavior. He is not the first lover nor the last who "in a nett [seeks] to hold the wynde." Others have reached for reassurances in the face of doubt, achieving a dubious certainty by seeing and hearing only what they wanted to see and hear. Others have attempted to misread the beloved's face and words, to suppress doubts, only to find them rising to the surface. The tension between the sense of order and stability implied by the couplet and the anarchic sentiments that Shakespeare's couplets so often express is ultimately the tension defined in other sequences and in Shakespeare's own Sonnet 147 as the conflict between Reason and Will, or, to put it another way, a conflict between form on the one hand and the reforming and deforming force of love on the other.

Shakespeare's couplets, then, embody both the all-too-human desire to seek finality and certainty and the all-too-human difficulties of doing so. Hence they trouble us—and teach us—more through what they do (or fail to do) than through what they say, in much the same way that Polonius' urge to inflict maxims on his son or Ulysses' attempt to educate his fellow warriors are far more instructive per se than the actual content of their speeches. And if, as Stephen Booth suggests, the couplets establish order at the end of the sonnets in

[75] *The Complete Writings of William Blake*, ed. Geoffrey Keynes (London: Oxford Univ. Press, 1966).

much the same way it is established at the end of the plays,[76] we must qualify his observation with the reminder that what is achieved when many of these poems conclude is closer to the insensitively imposed type of closure that a Fortinbras brings than to that of an Albany or a Malcolm.

VI

Shakespeare, like other Renaissance sonneteers, faced a rhetorical dilemma even more difficult than that of closure: the slippage of praise into flattery. We have discussed praise from another perspective earlier in this chapter, but it is also relevant here: like closure, it is an aesthetic problem that the sonnets confront by presenting it as a moral and psychological dilemma for their speaker.

"What may words say . . . where truth it selfe must speake like flatterie?" (35.1–2), Astrophil demands and in so doing summarizes one of the principal challenges faced by the author of the sequence, his own "brother *Philip*" (83.1), as well as by the other sonneteers of the period. On the one hand, praising the beloved is central to the mission of the sonneteer, a point Petrarch enforces by his repeated puns on "Laura" and "laudo." And, as we have seen, classical theories of epideictic poetry justify that role and even urge it on the writer. Yet the sonneteer's compliments can easily seem mechanical or, worse, suspect—does his praise reflect disinterested admiration or a desire to ingratiate himself? Many sonneteers respond to these concerns merely by denying them. Thus Daniel, for example, protests,

> None other fame myne vnambitious Muse,
> Affected euer but t'eternize thee:
> . . . . .
> For God forbid I should my papers blot,
> With mercynary lines, with seruile pen.
> (*Delia* 48.1–2, 5–6)

Sidney, in contrast, acknowledges the validity of the problem: though Astrophil himself asserts, "Not thou by praise, but praise in thee is raisde" (35.13), the reader comes to suspect that praise in Astrophil himself is in fact lowered: in a sequence that discusses the pressures of sexuality far more openly than most of its English counterparts, we

---

[76]Booth, *Essay*, p. 131.

see his compliments as yet another weapon in his campaign against Stella's virtue.

It is hardly surprising that Shakespeare's sequence devotes even more attention to the issue of praise than do the sonnets by his contemporaries, for we encounter similar questions throughout his dramatic works as well. If his monarchs are threatened by the civil wars of the barons, they are no less threatened by the all-too-civil tongues of their courtiers. Thus early in the play Richard II is able to observe to Bolingbroke and Mowbray, "I thank you both. Yet one but flatters us" (I.i.25), but later on he is, as Gaunt points out, the victim of flatterers. The monarch who flaunts his power over language and his power through language is himself subject to the deceptive words of others. Hence it is wholly fitting that toward the end of the play he addresses a "flattering glass" (IV.i.279): the image of his looking into that mirror is an emblem of the fact that his identity has been shaped by the flattering visions of himself that his courtiers provide. Described in *King John* as "sweet . . . poison for the age's tooth" (I.i.213), flattery becomes a dangerous temptation in many of the comedies as well; in *Love's Labour's Lost*, for instance, Berowne reminds us, "To things of sale a seller's praise belongs" (IV.iii.235). And, of course, the problem reaches a climax in *King Lear*, which asks whether one can deliver the compliments demanded at court while still retaining one's integrity—and still maintaining that of the king who demands those compliments. Kent and Cordelia say no in thunder.

In the sonnets Shakespeare explores such dilemmas in much the same way Sidney does, relating them to the behavior of his speaker.[77] But he broadens the subject more than Sidney,[78] encompassing in his lyrics not only the problems of a poet praising his mistress but also those of his praising his patron. And he devotes far more attention to the moral dilemmas created by praise than either Sidney or any other English sonneteer. On this as on many other issues in Shakespeare's

---

[77]Though the problem of praise in the sequence has never received as much attention as it deserves, some critics have in fact considered it briefly. See Booth, *Sonnets*, pp. 191–192, for a discussion of "damning with fulsome praise" (p. 191); A. J. Gilbert argues that changes in style make praise seem suspect ("Techniques of Focus in Shakespeare's Sonnets," *Language and Style*, 12 [1979], 260); Rodney Poisson notes the tension engendered by flattery ("Unequal Friendship: Shakespeare's Sonnets 18–26," in Landry, *New Essays*, pp. 11–13; also in *English Studies in Canada*, 1 [1975]). John Dover Wilson maintains that flattery is seldom a problem in the sequence (*An Introduction to the Sonnets of Shakespeare for the Use of Historians and Others* [New York: Cambridge Univ. Press, 1964], pp. 39–41).

[78]Compare Grundy, pp. 48–49.

sequence, patterns of word usage are telling. "Flatter" and its cognates appear sixteen times altogether in the sequences of Daniel, Drayton, Shakespeare, Sidney, and Spenser, of which no fewer than eight appearances are in Shakespeare's sonnets.[79] And "praise" and its cognates are used exactly 100 times, with Shakespeare accounting for 36; his nearest rival is Drayton, who employs these words 20 times, while Sidney and Spenser each do so 18 times and Daniel only 8.[80] The length of Shakespeare's sequence can account for only a small fraction of these differences: they must be traced primarily to his preoccupation with the question of praise.

In examining that problem, Shakespeare characteristically adds moral ambiguity to what is hardly a simple issue to begin with: even if we see the uncritical adoration that some of the sonnets express for the Friend as questionable, he obviously does merit at least some of the compliments he receives. If nothing else, Shakespeare was writing in an age when many people (not unlike the editors of our own fashion magazines) saw physical beauty as an outward and visible sign of one's total worth. And Shakespeare's emphasis on time repeatedly reminds us that, even if praise may assume certain suspect functions, it can promise immortality.

Against this backdrop, however, is staged a demonstration of the pernicious effects of praise. Shakespeare encourages us to recognize those effects—to label the poisoned bottle of compliments with an unmistakable skull and crossbones—by reminding us of the multiple connotations and denotations of the word "flatter." In Sonnet 28, for instance, it is clearly linked to deception, although of a comparatively innocuous type:[81]

> I tell the day to please him thou art bright,
> And dost him grace when clouds do blot the heaven.
> So flatter I the swart-complexioned night,
> When sparkling stars twire not, thou gild'st the even.
>
> (9–12)

In Sonnet 33 the word is associated not only with delusion and gratification but also with caressing or stroking.[82] The *Oxford English Dic-*

---

[79]See Herbert S. Donow, *A Concordance to the Sonnet Sequences of Daniel, Drayton, Shakespeare, Sidney, and Spenser* (Carbondale and London: Southern Illinois Univ. Press and Feffer and Simons, 1969), s.v. "flatter," "flattered," "flatterer," "flattery."

[80]Donow, s.v. "praise," "praised," "praiseth," "praising."

[81]Ingram and Redpath gloss "flatter" here as "beguile by telling" (p. 70), but this reading need not preclude the other interpretations I am suggesting.

[82]Compare Booth, *Sonnets*, p. 186.

The Sonnets

tionary documents a few instances of this usage,[83] and in Sonnet 33 the conjunction of "Flatter" (2) and "Kissing" (3) also lends itself to such a reading:

> Full many a glorious morning have I seen
> Flatter the mountain tops with sovereign eye,
> Kissing with golden face the meadows green,
> Gilding pale streams with heav'nly alchemy.
>
> (1–4)

As we observed when analyzing *The Rape of Lucrece*, Shakespeare sometimes hints that flattery may almost be a type of sexual foreplay. Reading lines like those in Sonnet 33 invites us, too, to muse on the complexities of the word in question in modern English: we are, for example, pleased when an item of clothing is flattering but not when a remark is.

Sonnet 114 takes flattery for its principal subject, and it is here that Shakespeare most thoroughly rings the changes on the meanings of the word:

> Or whether doth my mind, being crowned with you,
> Drink up the monarch's plague, this flattery?
> Or whether shall I say mine eye saith true,
> And that your love taught it this alchemy—
> To make of monsters and things indigest
> Such cherubins as your sweet self resemble,
> Creating every bad a perfect best
> As fast as objects to his beams assemble?
> O 'tis the first, 'tis flatt'ry in my seeing,
> And my great mind most kingly drinks it up.
> Mine eye well knows what with his gust is greeing,
> And to his palate doth prepare the cup.
>   If it be poisoned, 'tis the lesser sin
>   That mine eye loves it and doth first begin.

One editor claims this poem is constantly in danger of being merely cute,[84] but in fact it rises above that level: the conflict between the self-consciously clever jokes and the darker implications enacts the tension between the speaker's desire to see the results of flattery as wholly positive, or at least not seriously threatening, and our—and his—

---

[83]*Oxford English Dictionary*, s.v. "flatter."
[84]Booth, *Sonnets*, p. 377.

recognition that they can indeed be poisonous. Thus, for example, "being crowned with you" (1) hints at the grandeur associated with kingship and the flattery a king receives,[85] while the second line reminds us of the dangers of praise. And if "shall I say" (3) suggests the gamelike element of the conceits in this sonnet, it also invokes the difficulties in perception that flattering and being flattered can cause. In line 9, "flatt'ry" can simply be glossed as "deception," but the word also serves to connect that deception with the process of admiring the Friend. In the next line, "most kingly" (10) underscores the ambivalent nature and effects of offering compliments: the adjective reminds us both of the genuine grandeur of a king and of the types of aggrandizement that this sonnet has traced. Throughout the poem, in other words, we witness a series of metamorphoses: the speaker turns into a king, monsters turn into the Friend, potentially threatening problems turn into a lighthearted version of themselves—and, finally, flattery keeps changing back and forth from a witty game to a devastating "plague" (2), a shift very like one we will find in the "ugly beauty" sonnets examined in Section VII.

The sonnets also comment explicitly at several points on transformations performed on and by flattery. In Sonnet 79, for instance, praise is described as a kind of robbery—"He lends thee virtue, and he stole that word / From thy behaviour" (9–10)—an image that gains resonance from the many other allusions to thieves in the sequence. And Shakespeare devalues praise by linking it to buying and selling.[86] A line like "I will not praise that purpose not to sell" (21.14) reminds us of comparable moments in the plays, such as Benedick's reply when asked what he thinks of Beatrice: "Would you buy her?" (I.i.159).

Above all, however, the sonnets demonstrate the perils of praise by bodying them forth in the speaker's behavior. We have already seen that the instability in his judgments of the Friend and Dark Lady are sometimes reflected in an unstable movement between compliments and rebukes; one danger of praise, clearly, is that pressures to bestow it, whether internal or external, can subvert one's true feelings, lead-

---

[85]The link between flattery and kingship is also discussed in Murray Krieger, *A Window to Criticism: Shakespeare's "Sonnets" and Modern Poetics* (Princeton: Princeton Univ. Press, 1964), esp. p. 135.

[86]For a different analysis of the relationship between praise and financial language, see Neal L. Goldstien, "Money and Love in Shakespeare's Sonnets," *Bucknell Review*, 17 (1969), 91–106. He notes that positive connotations of money are played against negative ones in the sequence.

ing to both a rhetorical imbalance within the sonnet in question and an emotional imbalance within its speaker.

Most critics have dismissed Sonnet 28 as an unoriginal version of the absence poem, but in the context of the rest of the sequence the lines we examined earlier—

> I tell the day to please him thou art bright,
> And dost him grace when clouds do blot the heaven.
> So flatter I the swart-complexioned night,
> When sparkling stars twire not, thou gild'st the even.
>
> (9–12)

—reflect not merely the conventions of this subgenre but also the idiosyncrasies of this particular speaker. For he is treating the day and night just as he treats the Friend, flattering them in several senses of the word (and in so doing, of course, further flattering the Friend, too). Again we suspect that the exigencies of courtly praise have become a cast of mind.

Sonnet 23 helps us further to understand that cast of mind:

> As an unperfect actor on the stage,
> Who with his fear is put besides his part,
> Or some fierce thing replete with too much rage,
> Whose strength's abundance weakens his own heart;
> So I for fear of trust forget to say
> The perfect ceremony of love's rite.
>
> (1–6)

Once again the metaphors undermine the discursive level of the poem; the allusion to acting hints at what is artificial about praise, while the simile of the "fierce thing" (3) introduces a tension between praise as a civilized ceremony—a "rite" (6) and a right—and praise as the product of uncontrolled "rage" (3).[87] "Fear of trust" (5) introduces another type of tension: while editors generally assume that it refers to the speaker's fear that the person he is complimenting will not trust him, it could in fact also suggest that he does not trust that person, a reading for which the other sonnets offer ample support. Thus here, as in several other poems in the sequence, the speaker is not merely referring to the difficulties of offering compliments but

---

[87]Stephen Booth suggests that "rage" can connote both bestial anger and lust (*Sonnets*, p. 171).

actually demonstrating those difficulties through the contradictions in his language.

"For I have *sworn* thee fair, and thought thee bright" (147.13; italics added). In the sonnets as in *Venus and Adonis*, praising is associated with naming—and with misnaming.[88] When the speaker calls the corrupted Friend and Dark Lady fair, as when Venus terms breath "heavenly moisture" (63), we are more conscious of the effects of this mislabeling on the person who does it than of the threat to the hearers or to language. For in both works to give something the wrong name is to slip into the habit of lying to others and also to oneself.[89] Though the speaker of the sonnets accuses others of falsehoods, he is frequently liable to the same charge. He regularly confesses to swearing false oaths. And his preoccupation with truth and falsehood is reflected in the fact that it recurs even in apparently casual or playful observations: "Or whether shall I say mine eye *saith true*" (114.3; italics added). Above all, of course, Sonnet 138 demonstrates both the pleasures and the perils of lying—and demonstrates, too, that those pleasures and perils, like deception and self-deception or verbal and sexual lying, are inextricably entwined. As Michael Cameron Andrews has observed, "The speaker . . . cannot bear very much sincerity; when we think we have found where truth resides, we probably have found only where it lies."[90]

If, then, the couplet is one of the most central problems posed by the form of a sonnet, praise is one of the most central ones raised by its content. Shakespeare meets these challenges in the same way he confronts the potential dangers of the Senecan set speech in *The Rape of Lucrece*: rather than ignoring them or attempting to solve them wholly through formal or intellectual strategies, he relates them to the ways people think and behave.

VII

Sonnet 130 is among the most frequently anthologized poems in the collection, which not only reflects how often we read it but also

[88]On naming and misnaming in the sequence, see David Toor's suggestion that Sonnet 20 puns on "addition" in the sense of "title" ("Shakespeare's Sonnet XX," *Expl.*, 32 [1974], Item 38).
[89]A number of critics have discussed lying in the sequence. See esp. Murray Krieger, "Truth and Troth, Fact and Faith: Accuracy to the World and Fidelity to Vision," *Journal of Comparative Literature and Aesthetics*, 1 (1978), 51–58, and *A Window to Criticism*, pt. 2, chap. 2; Christopher Ricks, "Lies," *Critical Inquiry*, 2 (1975), 121–142.
[90]Andrews, p. 327.

suggests how often we misread it. For scholars have been prone to interpret this work as though it actually appeared, as it were, in an anthology—that is, to separate it from the rest of the sequence and from the literary motif it exemplifies. When we examine Sonnet 130 and the related poems in the sequence in light of that motif, which has been termed the ugly beauty conceit, our understanding of how their author approaches the traditions of anti-Petrarchism deepens: we come to realize that he is far more critical of them than his readers have acknowledged.[91] The sonnets confront anti-Petrarchism in much the same way they respond to the other rhetorical issues and strategies that we have been anatomizing: they demonstrate that it is at once a symptom and a source of problems in their speaker's temperament. Characteristically choosing to invoke the conceits of anti-Petrarchism in order to escape the aesthetic and moral dangers of Petrarchism, he yet again finds himself a captive victor: freed from one set of dilemmas, he is entrapped by another.

For all its self-conscious originality, the ugly beauty motif, like so many other apparent rebellions in literary history, can claim a long and distinguished ancestry: both by precept and by example, many classical authors contributed to the tradition. Behind it lies the paradoxical encomium, which was not only composed by such figures as Gorgias, Isocrates, Lucian, and Plato himself but also frequently employed as a school exercise.[92] And a number of Latin writers anatomize and advocate the ironic compliment; in *Ars amatoria*, for instance, Ovid wryly suggests that rather than reproaching women for their faults, we should reinterpret those apparent deficiencies as virtues. Renaissance love poets proceeded to practice what Ovid and other classical writers had preached.[93] The members of the Pléiade in particular frequently praise women who do not conform to the conventional standards of beauty. Ronsard, for example, celebrates the

[91]Compare Anne Ferry's suggestion that the eternizing metaphors in the sequence are treated ironically (*All in War with Time*, chap. 1).

[92]See Henry Knight Miller, "The Paradoxical Encomium with Special Reference to Its Vogue in England, 1600–1800," *MP*, 53 (1956), 145. On the paradoxical encomium also see Theodore Burgess, *Epideictic Literature* (Chicago: Univ. of Chicago Press, 1902); Rosalie L. Colie, *Paradoxia Epidemica: The Renaissance Tradition of Paradox* (Princeton: Princeton Univ. Press, 1966); J. B. Leishman, *The Monarch of Wit* (London: Hutchinson, 1951), pp. 74–81; Arthur Stanley Pease, "Things without Honor," *CP*, 21 (1926), 27–42. I am indebted to these sources in my summary of the classical traditions.

[93]The best discussion of this tradition in English is the brief but suggestive introduction in Conrad Hilberry, ed., *The Poems of John Collop* (Madison: Univ. of Wisconsin Press, 1962), pp. 19–26. Also see T. W. Baldwin, *On the Literary Genetics of Shakspere's Poems and Sonnets*, pp. 321–339, and Albert-Marie Schmidt, ed., *L'Amour noir* (Monaco: Editions du Rochers, 1959), "Introduction."

dark eyes and hair of his Cassandre (*Amours de Cassandre*, 152). He delivers, too, a renowned prophecy about his mistress' old age, a poem that hints at the ways the carpe diem topos may contribute to the tradition we are examining (*Sonnets pour Hélène*, II, 42 ["Quand vous serez bien vieille, au soir, à la chandelle"]). But perhaps the most influential of the Continental models is a sonnet by the sixteenth-century Italian writer Francesco Berni, "Chiome d'argento fine, irte, ed attorte." Exemplifying the *capitoli*, paradoxical encomia that Berni and his friends were composing in prodigious numbers, the poem interchanges the attributes normally associated with particular features of the lady's face. In works of this type, we are informed that the lady has, say, red eyes and blue lips, or yellow teeth and white hair—visual antimetabole in poems that sometime include more conventional instances of that figure as well.

Poems like Berni's and Ronsard's inspired many imitations during the English Renaissance. Elizabethan examples include the poem on Mopsa in the third chapter of Sidney's *Arcadia*; the tribute to a singularly unappetizing beauty that Tophas delivers in Lyly's *Endymion*; Davies' Epigram 26; Barnabe Barnes' Sonnet 13, one of the more peculiar poems in that consistently peculiar sequence *Parthenophil and Parthenope*; and, if his principal editor's hypotheses about dating are to be trusted, three of Donne's elegies, "The Autumnall," "The Comparison," and "The Anagram."[94] As this list would suggest, much as the paradoxical encomium coexisted with the "straight" version of the form in classical literature, so many of the ostensibly anti-Petrarchan poems we are examining were composed at the same time Petrarchan sonnets were in vogue; these ironic texts may, indeed, in a sense be just another branch of Petrarchism. But the motif came to enjoy a considerable popularity in the seventeenth century as well, with such figures as Drayton, Carew, Herrick, Suckling, and Edward Herbert of Cherbury all contributing poems. The most prolific writer of ugly beauty poems, however, is also the most neglected, that little-known but intriguing seventeenth-century poet John Collop.

The primary link uniting all of these works is, of course, their preoccupation with Petrarchism. Attempting to balance the *mel* of the sonnet with *sal*, writers typically allude to the Petrarchan traditions with which—and, in general, within which—they are playing. Suckling, for example, labels three of his love poems, including the one that employs the motif we are examining, "Sonnets"; while that term

---

[94]On the dating of Donne's elegies, see Helen Gardner, ed., *John Donne: The Elegies and the Songs and Sonnets* (Oxford: Clarendon Press, 1965), pp. xxxii-xxxiii.

could be used loosely in his period,[95] it seems more than likely that he is inviting us to compare his sequence with Petrarch's. Other poets rely not on their prosody or their titles but rather on their imagery to refer to the form they are inverting. An especially interesting instance is Collop's praise of a woman with a twisted back:

> The enamell'd wardrobe of rich Nature view;
> All drooping imitate, and bow like you.
> The bashful Roses shrink into their beds;
> Lillies in emulation hang down heads.
> ("On a Crooked Lady, M.V.," 7–10)[96]

The perverse ways in which the flowers imitate the lady (they are miming what would seem her least attractive attribute) parallel the equally perverse ways Collop is himself imitating literary conventions; the Petrarchan flowers, roses and lilies, are twisted much as Petrarchan norms are twisted throughout the lyric.

But the deepest link between these poems—and the one most relevant to Shakespeare's sequence—is their confident assertion of many forms of freedom and power. Above all, their speakers flaunt their mastery of their own emotions. The poems on the theme of the "indifferent" lover establish this control explicitly, but it is also implicit in many other versions of the ugly beauty conceit: if, by what is presented as a deliberate act of choice, the poet-lover can decide to praise a woman with black teeth, then he is clearly not a slave to Cupid. Closely connected to this type of freedom is the fact that the speaker is not subservient to the lady; he is, indeed, not the creature but rather the creator of whatever beauty she might claim to have. Like the Petrarchan poet, these speakers are performing a morally suspect version of persuasive oratory, perhaps even trading praise for favors, but they are doing so voluntarily and doing so for a lady who, far from despising their devotion, desperately needs it. And, through many rhetorical devices, notably the imperious commands that are sometimes inserted in the poems, they are establishing yet another type of control, their sovereignty over the internal audience of the lyric, whether it be the lady or, as in Donne's "The Comparison," another and less discriminating lover. Collop's speaker announces and, indeed, glories in many of these kinds of power and freedom when he declares,

[95] *Oxford English Dictionary*, s.v. "sonnet."
[96] I quote *The Poems of John Collop*, ed. Conrad Hilberry.

> Scorn but my fancy, thou again art poor;
> Horses with Yellows shall be valued more.
> I'le say the Yellow Jaundies doth thee die;
> . . . . .
> I made thee gold, 'tis I can make thee brasse.
> (Collop, "To Aureola," 11–13, 21)

For the actual poets behind these imperious speakers, too, the motif offers types of freedom. We certainly sense antagonism in some of the more grotesque descriptions of ugly beauties—antagonism toward women in general, perhaps, and certainly toward the literary practice of praising them. Political tensions may also lie behind certain of these poems: if classical and Continental analogues sparked English experiments with the motif we are examining, a resentment of Elizabeth's demands for extravagant compliments may well have fueled some of these experiments, especially those written during her reign. In any event, the tradition allows writers to express all of these tensions in a format that is reassuringly labeled game. Like the jokes analyzed by Freud and others, the ugly beauty convention permits one to express the unconventional, say the unsayable.

Despite these similarities in their motivations, poets employing the motif describe different types of mistresses—and do so in very different tones. Some merely praise a characteristic that, though not generally celebrated in Petrarchan love poetry, does not seem intrinsically distasteful, such as dark eyes. We encounter no direct mockery of the literary tradition as we read these poems and certainly none of the lady herself; their tone is often as grave and stately as that of any traditional Petrarchan sonnet. Closely related to these declarations that black is beautiful are works that praise even more unconventional skin and hair color, such as the tribute Collop offers to a lady with yellow skin. The tone of poems like these is characteristically ambiguous: it is difficult to know to what extent, if at all, a line like Collop's "Thy arms are wax, nay honey too, / Colour and sweetnesse hath from you" ("The Praise of a Yellow Skin," 5–6) is intended ironically.[97] The problems in interpreting such works are, in fact, suggestively similar to those involved in reading metaphysical verse. Yet other lyrics praise qualities that seem even more unappealing. Both Carew and Edward Herbert of Cherbury write paeans to mistresses suffering from the green sickness (and in so doing cleverly twist the Petrarchan topos of the lady's illness), while Davies composes Epi-

---

[97]Compare Hilberry, pp. 21–23.

gram 26, a blazon to a prostitute so repulsive that she evidently could attract no clients save poets eager to write epigrams about her. Works like these are clearly deploying wit to make the foul seem fair: there is no possibility that the compliments are anything but ironic. All is indeed changed, changed utterly when this terrible beauty is born.

One implication of these differences among the poems in the tradition is that critics are prone to mislabel it. Allusions to "ugly beauty" or the "deformed mistress" are adequate for certain poems but inappropriate for those whose subject, while not a strong contender in a beauty contest judged by Petrarch and his followers, is evidently neither ugly nor deformed. "The unconventional mistress tradition" suggests itself as a more accurate, if perhaps more cumbersome, title. Another implication is that Shakespeare himself inherited a varied group of models, a wide range of potentialities. He was to explore and exploit that variety, as we will see.

When Shakespeare does participate in the tradition, he writes not only within it but also against it. Most of his counterparts focus primarily on criticizing conventional Petrarchism, while he also calls the values of this type of anti-Petrarchism into question, much as *The Rape of Lucrece* at once deploys and defuses the values of the complaint. And, characteristically enough, in so doing the sonnets also reexamine the values of their speaker.

Thus Sonnet 127 is on one level a witty though trifling example of the unconventional mistress motif and hence a critique of "straight" Petrarchism[98]—and yet on another level also a critique of that conceit and hence of anti-Petrarchism itself:

> In the old age black was not counted fair,
> Or if it were it bore not beauty's name.
> But now is black beauty's successive heir,

[98]For instances of this traditional reading of the poem, which has been adopted without qualification by most critics, see Winny, p. 92; Edward Hubler, *The Sense of Shakespeare's Sonnets* (New York: Hill and Wang, 1952), p. 39, and C. F. Williamson, "Themes and Patterns in Shakespeare's Sonnets," *EIC*, 26 (1976), 202–203. One of the few scholars discerning criticism of the Dark Lady in the poem is Richard Levin ("Shakespeare's Sonnet 127," *Expl.*, 38 [1979], 31–33); his argument is, however, based on the unlikely assertion that she is herself wearing cosmetics. Anne Ferry also suggests that the mistress in Sonnet 127 is being rebuked, though the grounds she cites are different from mine (*The "Inward Language": Sonnets of Wyatt, Sidney, Shakespeare, Donne* [Chicago: Univ. of Chicago Press, 1983], pp. 184–188). Also see Thomas P. Roche, Jr., "How Petrarchan Is Shakespeare?" *Proceedings of the Comparative Literature Symposium*, 12 (1981), 159–160, on the aesthetic attitudes in Sonnet 127.

And beauty slandered with a bastard shame;
For since each hand hath put on nature's pow'r,
Fairing the foul with art's false borrowed face,
Sweet beauty hath no name, no holy bow'r,
But is profaned, if not lives in disgrace.
Therefore my mistress' eyes are raven black,
Her eyes so suited, and they mourners seem
At such who, not born fair, no beauty lack,
Sland'ring creation with a false esteem.
   Yet so they mourn becoming of their woe,
   That every tongue says beauty should look so.

In lamenting his contemporaries' values, the speaker plays on two meaning of blackness, the moral imperfection of wearing cosmetics and the physical imperfection of having dark hair and a dark complexion.[99] From these issues, though, he moves to a graceful compliment: his mistress' dark eyes mourn the blackness around her with such charm that all admire her own blackness. In other words, her eyes, like those praised in Ronsard's poems on Hélène and Sidney's on Stella, threaten neither moral nor aesthetic norms: the poem is solidly rooted in the values and assumptions of conventional Petrarchism.

Though this straightforward reading encapsulates the primary meaning of the poem, some complexities remain. The apparent levity of the sestet jars with the gravity of the octet—a gravity signally absent from the poem that may well have been Shakespeare's model, *Astrophil and Stella* 7. Rather than viewing line 2 ("Or if it were it bore not beauty's name") as a mere restatement of line 1, as critics have been prone to do, we can find in the distinction between the first line and the second a reminder that what we call things is very important, an idea whose resonance is apparent to any reader of the nondramatic poems. Recognizing this undertone of seriousness in the octet encourages us to speculate further about the succeeding lines. In interpreting the poem merely as a compliment to the Dark Lady, we accepted without question the total difference between her own blackness and the types that she is lamenting. Now we may well find it odd that she should mourn blackness by displaying it herself. And we cannot completely dismiss the troubling thought that the mourning itself is a ruse

---

[99]In appearance she may be even darker than Booth's text suggests: many editors emend "eyes" in line 10 to "brows," hence suggesting that her hair is dark. See Ingram and Redpath, pp. 290–291.

("and they mourners *seem*" [10; italics added]), even an excuse to conceal the true reasons for her blackness. The possible identification between her behavior and that of the women described in the opening quatrain is mirrored syntactically, for the subject of line 12 ("Sland'ring creation with a false esteem") could conceivably be the poet's mistress as well as, or rather than, the other women.[100] Hence in this poem, as in so many of the ones addressed to the Friend, praise may be tinged with blame, and the rose the speaker proffers (like the rose to whom he proffers it) may have a canker at its center. This reading, then, relates the Dark Lady's blackness not to the poems by Sidney and Ronsard to which I referred but rather to more unsettling versions of the ugly beauty motif, such as those by Collop and Carew. In short, the tension between the two interpretations the poem invites enacts the tension between two ways the motif itself can be approached.

When we interpret Sonnet 127 in light of other poems in the sequence, our tentative reservations about it receive some support, for those other sonnets do establish her blackness as moral corruption. And the rest of the collection raises troubling questions about how the speaker is behaving in this particular sonnet: if he is employing the unconventional mistress conceit to reduce blackness that should be taken seriously to a courtly joke, then he has found yet another device for offering excuses. Hence from this perspective the poem casts doubt not only on conventional Petrarchism but also on the nonchalant form of anti-Petrarchism in poems that praise black hair and eyes: we are reminded that man's erected wit may be misused to make the foul seem fair (and his erected will may lead him to wish to do so). Sonnet 127, like Sonnet 138 and so many other poems in the sequence, enacts the tension betweeen the successful and graceful participation in courtly and rhetorical games and the discovery that the stakes may be higher than one had realized.

Our reactions to Sonnet 132, which in many ways resembles the poem we have just examined, are very similar.

> Thine eyes I love, and they as pitying me,
> Knowing thy heart torment me with disdain,
> Have put on black, and loving mourners be,
> Looking with pretty ruth upon my pain.
>
> (1–4)

---

[100]Compare Levin, p. 32.

On first reading, this is merely a clever conceit, combining an anti-Petrarchan praise of black beauty with a typically Petrarchan acknowledgment of the pain that women cause. And even on subsequent readings that remains the primary interpretation. Yet we cannot but be aware that the speaker is again manifesting his tendency to offer excuses and, in particular, to explain away potential or real faults by transforming them into virtues. As the poem progresses, we encounter a series of charming compliments that go a long way toward persuading us that our doubts are misplaced and that blackness is indeed a pleasing alternative to conventional Petrarchan beauty. The couplet confirms that impression, offering yet another graceful compliment: "Then will I swear beauty herself is black. / And all they foul that thy complexion lack" (13–14). At the same time, though, these lines lovingly promise a continuation of that predilection for offering excuses, a repeated invocation of the unconventional mistress motif in the service of a mistress who may be unconventional in her morality as well as in her appearance.

In the poems we have examined so far, anti-Petrarchism retains its status as a clever rhetorical game, one that allows a poet to buy his freedom from tyrannous literary clichés as well as a tyrannous mistress, even though we may wonder uneasily if he is in fact entrapped by that very game. Sonnet 131, however, discusses entrapment far more overtly and unmistakably. Its opening lines suggest that the poet cannot help but love the Dark Lady despite her failings, which, in light of the rest of the sequence, we associate with her darkness:

> Thou art as tyrannous, so as thou art,
> As those whose beauties proudly make them cruel;
> For well thou know'st to my dear doting heart
> Thou art the fairest and most precious jewel.
>
> (1–4)

Though she does not look like a Petrarchan mistress, she behaves like one. The poem proceeds to compare different forms of "saying":

> Yet in good faith some say that thee behold
> Thy face hath not the pow'r to make love groan;
> To say they err I dare not be so bold,
> Although I swear it to myself alone.
> And to be sure that is not false I swear
> A thousand groans but thinking on thy face

> One on another's neck do witness bear
> Thy black is fairest in my judgement's place.
>
> (5–12)

The judgments of others are juxtaposed with the poet's swearing his lady's fairness, a swearing that is reenacted in the poem itself. Until the couplet the tone of the sonnet is wry, even a little playful perhaps; in a sense by showing her power over the speaker, the poem is complimenting the Dark Lady. Hence the couplet—"In nothing art thou black save in thy deeds, / And thence this slander as I think proceeds" (131.13–14)—startles us. It forces us to view blackness more gravely than we did when we read the earlier lines.

Like Sonnets 127 and 132, then, this poem plays different interpretations of blackness against each other; but the bitterness and decisiveness of the couplet lend force to the most opprobrious of those interpretations. That couplet exemplifies a pattern familiar to readers of this sequence: latent doubts surface violently, leading us to wonder whether the speaker is reacting so strongly not only against the Dark Lady's own behavior but against his own characteristic tendency to compliment her despite it, to use rhetoric to make the foul fair.

The tones and the techniques of the poems we have just been studying recur in the subsequent sonnets on the Dark Lady's blackness. In both Sonnets 140 and 141 we find Petrarchan language so clichéd—"cruel" (140.1), "disdain" (140.2), "pity-wanting pain" (140.4), "serving thee" (141.10), "Thy proud heart's slave and vassal wretch" (141.12)—that we cannot help but be puzzled by it.[101] Even if we question Patrick Cruttwell's judgment that the Dark Lady sonnets contain "most of the greatness and most of the maturity in the whole sequence,"[102] they are sometimes polished enough and almost always powerful enough to make the presence of these trite expressions surprising. Responding to this dilemma, many readers dismiss Sonnets 140 and 141 as failures, perhaps juvenile efforts; and one critic even offers the unpersuasive suggestion that, like other poems in the sequence, they are parodic.[103] Instead, however, these two sonnets develop the pattern that was foreshadowed by the use of "tyrannous" (1) and "cruel" (2) in Sonnet 131. The highly conventionalized lan-

---

[101]For a reading different from mine, see Booth, *Sonnets*, pp. 488–491.

[102]*The Shakespearean Moment and Its Place in the Poetry of the Seventeenth Century* (London: Chatto and Windus, 1954), p. 11.

[103]Wilson, chap. 3.

guage in these sonnets is purposeful: they are loaded, indeed over-loaded, with clichés so that we will play them against anti-Petrarchan statements such as Sonnet 130 and in so doing realize that this speaker, like Astrophil, cannot wholly or finally escape Petrarchism despite all his efforts. Though the Dark Lady does not look or behave like a Petrarchan mistress in some of the more important ways, she indulges in certain forms of Petrarchan behavior, notably tyranny, and her lover is trapped into behaving like a Petrarchan sonneteer.

We are now in a position to return to the celebrated lines of Sonnet 130. In most regards the poem is an unusually clever adaptation of the unconventional mistress motif, a sonnet whose speaker in effect announces that he is rejecting the hyperboles and clichés of Petrarchism.

> My mistress' eyes are nothing like the sun—
> Coral is far more red than her lips' red—
> If snow be white, why then her breasts are dun—
> If hairs be wires, black wires grow on her head:
> I have seen roses damasked, red and white,
> But no such roses see I in her cheeks,
> And in some pérfumes is there more delight
> Than in the breath that from my mistress reeks.
> I love to hear her speak, yet well I know
> That music hath a far more pleasing sound.
> I grant I never saw a goddess go;
> My mistress when she walks treads on the ground.
>   And yet by heav'n I think my love as rare
>   As any she belied with false compare.

It is suggestive that even in the terms of this straightforward reading of the sonnet it is dramatic in the sense that we do witness some change in the speaker's reactions: the movement from "my mistress" (1, 8, 12) to "my love" (13) suggests a surge of emotion toward her, an intensified immediacy that is foreshadowed by the increasing use of first-person pronouns as the poem progresses. But we also encounter a more confusing surge of emotions in line 8, "Than in the breath that from my mistress reeks." It is hard to believe that Shakespeare is merely using "to reek" in the sense of "to emanate," having somehow purged from the word the negative connotations that it often carried in Elizabethan, as in modern, English.[104] Yet the absence of other

---

[104]See *Oxford English Dictionary*, s.v. "reeks," and cf. Booth, *Sonnets*, pp. 454–455.

criticisms of this sort makes it unlikely that the speaker is engaging in a deliberate and consistent strategy of mocking the Dark Lady. Rather, the abrupt interjection of a word with pejorative connotations like "reeks" (8) mirrors the way his doubts about her occasionally surface, even if he is not fully aware that they have done so.

The couplet at once discredits and intensifies the concerns raised by the curious verb we are examining. It is, of course, primarily a climactic compliment to the lady and as such stills any ripple of criticism we found earlier. We appreciate its role all the more if we read through the poem substituting another type of couplet Shakespeare could have composed, such as "When her mouth she opes, no pearls we spy, / Diamonds I have seen, but none in her eye." These lines differ neither in tone nor in content from the twelve that compose the quatrains. Yet they would radically alter the poem. For by ending on a compliment rather than on a continuation of anti-Petrarchism like my couplet, the speaker says straightforwardly what the sonnet has implied throughout: loving this lady—and writing poems to celebrate that love—is a joyous experience.

But, as is so often the case when we read these lyrics, our confidence that we have interpreted a passage correctly is soon succeeded by our consciousness of an alternative and often contradictory gloss: if, as J. B. Leishman says, the poet-lover oscillates between "doubt at the heart of assurance and assurance at the heart of doubt,"[105] the reader undergoes a similar process. For the couplet can also support our suspicion, stirred by "reeks" (8), that the speaker is blinding himself to the faults he only dimly suspects: it can be paraphrased not only as "Despite her deviations from Petrarchan standards, my mistress is beautiful" but also as "Despite those deviations, I cannot help but *think* her beautiful." With this gloss in mind, we may observe that the poem acquires different and more disturbing resonances when we read it in terms of our knowledge of the Dark Lady's faults. Its speaker is resolutely and resoundingly rejecting Petrarchan clichés; but he, no less than a typical Petrarchan lover, is caught in a relationship that is in many senses destructive.

Like other poets' tributes to unconventional mistresses, then, Sonnet 130 is using the sonnet form metaphorically to represent a whole series of values and attitudes associated with Petrarchism; but unlike those other poems this one offers two contradictory and very complicated statements about the sonnet form and the values it represents. In terms of the principal meaning of this lyric, its speaker is demon-

---

[105]*Themes and Variations in Shakespeare's Sonnets*, p. 230.

strating that he can liberate his genre and himself: as the poem itself testifies, he can and will continue to compose sonnets, but by refusing Petrarchan clichés he will avoid the aesthetic faults normally associated with that literary type. In terms of the cross-currents that conflict with the positive reading of the poem, however, his decision to cast his observations about Petrarchism in the form of a sonnet is a sign not of freedom but of entrapment. In other words, on the generic level the poem mirrors one meaning of its couplet: by writing a sonnet that criticizes sonnets, the poet is demonstrating that he cannot in fact escape sonneteering, perhaps because on some level he does not want to, much as he may be declaring in lines 13 and 14 that he cannot escape the feelings a sonnet mistress normally engenders even if his own lady is not worthy of them. Anti-Petrarchism offers the hope of a different vision, but this poem hints at what literary historians have long reminded us: new anti-Petrarchism is but old Petrarchism writ large.

Sonnet 130 exemplifies, then, the ways all the poems we have examined relate to the unconventional mistress tradition. In many respects they proffer themselves as textbook examples of that motif, celebrating a mistress who does not correspond to conventional Petrarchan notions of beauty and in so doing mocking such notions and those who adhere to them. But just as the complaint in *The Rape of Lucrece* draws attention to the moral problems inherent in its genre, issues that Daniel had touched on more briefly and others had completely ignored, so Shakespeare's versions of the ugly beauty motif remind us that the conceit itself is potentially ugly. The contrast in tone between his laments about those who steal hair from others, hence slandering beauty "with a bastard shame" (127.4) and Herrick's casual reference to those who "weare / Locks incurl'd of other haire" ("Love Dislikes Nothing," 10–11)[106] demonstrates the distinction: Shakespeare forces us to think about the moral implications behind the lady's physical blackness, while Herrick, like many other writers, downplays or ignores such questions.

But there is a deeper difference as well and one more germane to this study. Most other poets in the tradition direct their criticism only outward, toward the woman and the school of poetry being satirized. If they raise broader questions—what type of poet and what type of speaker would celebrate an unconventional mistress? when does wit degenerate into sheer nastiness?—these issues remain latent. Shakespeare's speaker, however, rubs the sal of the motif into his own

---

[106]*The Poetical Works of Robert Herrick*, ed. L. C. Martin (Oxford: Clarendon, 1956).

wounds, criticizing not only other poets but also his own sorties into conventional Petrarchan poetry and his own vain attempts to avoid its clichés through the unconventional mistress motif. Shakespeare's sequence, then, repeatedly draws our attention to the problems of invoking that motif. We are often delighted by its wit, but we are never allowed to forget that praising an unconventional mistress, like praising a conventional one, can threaten the poet-lover.

Other poems in the tradition emphasize their authors' and their speakers' freedom: freedom from traditional literary topoi, from traditional attitudes to love, and from the traditional behavior enjoined by an unfeeling mistress. Shakespeare's speaker sometimes achieves this liberation; the primary mood of Sonnet 130, despite all its undercurrents, is an energetic delight: *joie de vivre* and, so to speak, *joie d'écrire*. But for all the brightness of their praise of darkness, Shakespeare's sonnets never let us forget the dangerous potentialities of that paradoxical activity. In reading these poems we, like their speaker, learn how quickly "bright things come to confusion."

VIII

The imagery of Shakespeare's sonnets has hardly been neglected. Though the decline of the New Criticism has resulted in scholars devoting less time to the images of many other works than they would have done some twenty or thirty years ago, an interest in this subject continues to surface in many studies of the sonnets. Such analyses, however, generally focus on the most obvious points: the darkness of the mistress, the Friend as iconic rose, and so on. Hence we have given less attention than we should to a pattern of imagery that reveals quite as much about these poems as the configurations of imagery we more commonly chart—that is, the figures that express the breakdown of codes and rules, especially those of the legal system and of real estate.[107] This pattern recurs not only when the speaker is writing of the Friend and Dark Lady but also when he is describing the world they inhabit, much as synecdoche in *The Rape of Lucrece* not only expresses the nature of rape but also implies that the rest of society is infused with an analogous violence. And, again like the central rhetorical figures in Shakespeare's narrative poems, the image-

[107]For a different but not incompatible reading of these and other images, see Colie, *Shakespeare's Living Art*, pp. 133–134; she relates the presence of social values to epigrammatic elements in the sonnet.

ry of codes in the sonnets bodies forth the temperament of the main character in the work. Hence an analysis of these allusions will encapsulate what we have been observing about the speaker's sensibility and how the sonnets evoke it.

The sonnets portray a world dominated by legal, social, and verbal bonds.[108] Like other sonnet writers, many of whom had actually sojourned at the Inns of Court, Shakespeare frequently refers to the law. Sonnet 46 describes the "mortal war" (1) of the eye and heart in terms of legal, not military, battles—"the defendant doth that plea deny" (7) and so on. Not only is the relationship with the Friend seen legally ("The charter of thy worth gives thee releasing" [87.3]), but the rest of the world is also evoked in terms of legal metaphors ("And summer's lease hath all too short a date" [18.4]). Yet in this sequence, unlike many others, allusions to the law figure in a larger pattern of references to other codes as well. Thus the feudal images on which we have already commented also imply relationships determined by an elaborate series of bonds; however hyperbolic lines like "Lord of my love, to whom in vassalage / Thy merit hath my duty strongly knit" (26.1–2) may be, they do serve to suggest behavior governed not by freely offered "mutual render" (125.12) but rather by strictly observed codes. References to swearing, such as "Then will I swear beauty herself is black" (132.13), remind us of the codes of language itself. Certain poems juxtapose the invocation (and, as we will see, the destruction) of a number of different systems of rules:

> In loving thee thou know'st I am *forsworn*,
> But thou art twice *forsworn* to me love *swearing*,
> In act thy *bed-vow* broke and *new faith* torn
> In *vowing* new hate after new love bearing.
> (152.1–4; italics added)

Possession is nine-tenths of the law in Shakespeare's sonnets: many references to codes involve ownership, and the issue also surfaces even where legal systems are not in question.[109] Here, as in the narra-

---

[108]Vendler, "Jakobson, Richards, and Shakespeare's Sonnet CXXIX," p. 184, discusses the breakdown of social bonds in Sonnet 129.

[109]These and related metaphors have been analyzed from angles different from mine. Thus Klause (p. 307) relates the commercial and legal metaphors to the fact that supplies of time itself are running short; Goldstien notes that nearly one-quarter of the sonnets mention money (p. 91). Also see Melchiori, chap. 5, on the imagery of Sonnet 146.

tive poems, the beloved is repeatedly seen as a possession. "So am I as the rich whose blessèd key / Can bring him to his sweet up-lockèd treasure," observes the speaker in Sonnet 52 (1–2), while elsewhere he describes the mixed blessings of apparent ownership: "Now proud as an enjoyer, and anon / Doubting the filching age will steal his treasure" (75.5–6). Sonnet 129 suggests other negative consequences: "Mad in pursuit, and in possession so" (9) evidently links together love and demonic possession. But questions of ownership surface even in contexts ostensibly unconnected to the Friend and Dark Lady. The metaphor behind Sonnet 46 invokes a dispute about land titles. The dead are dispossessed when their tresses are shorn, Sonnet 68 reminds us, while the procreation sonnets suggest that "Nature's bequest" (4.3) is not an unencumbered gift but rather a loan. The reference to "the lords and owners of their faces" (94.7) acquires additional resonance when we read it in relation to the imagery we are tracing; implicitly linking the possession of property with self-possession and identity itself, the line hints at a contrast between aristocrats and those forced to make themselves "a motley to the view" (110.2). Finally, one striking figure connects possession and real estate: "Why should my heart think that a several plot, / Which my heart knows the wide world's common place" (137.9–10), the speaker demands, tying the tensions of his jealousy to those of the contemporary debates about enclosure.[110]

Yet codes exist in the sonnets in much the same way as in *King Lear*: the insistent allusions to them serve primarily to remind us how often they are broken. In particular, these lyrics are more concerned with dispossession than with possession: if titles like "fair" and "foul" lose their significance, so too do the titles that ostensibly determine who owns property. The legal system itself is, as the imagery of the sonnets repeatedly implies, corrupt and unreliable. In Daniel's *Delia* 8 that system holds out the hope of justice:

> And you my verse, the Aduocates of loue,
> Haue followed hard the processe of my case:
> And vrg'd that title which dooth plainely proue,
> My faith should win, if iustice might haue place.
>   Yet though I see, that nought we doe can moue her,
>   Tis not disdaine must make me leaue to loue her.
>
>   (9–14)

[110]Cruttwell, p. 12, also notes the allusion to enclosure.

Problems remain, but they lie not in the law but rather in Delia's unwillingness to play by its rules. In the sonnets, in contrast, the world of law is itself lawless, much as the Friend offers not a respite from but an intensification of the tensions of romantic love. Once again, we encounter a type of syneciosis. Thus the apparently light lines of Sonnet 46 include a reference to a packed jury: "To 'cide this title is impannelléd / A quest of thoughts, all tenants to the heart" (9–10).[111] Power corrupts, and the absolute power of a landlord, we suspect, corrupts absolutely. Both legal and literary codes break down when the speaker assumes the responsibility of "Authórizing thy trespass with compare" (35.6); as the poem proceeds to tell us, the roles of adversary, advocate, and accessary become conflated and confounded. The law characteristically protects not the weak but the strong: "To leave poor me thou hast the strength of laws" (49.13), he laments, and elsewhere acknowledges that "The charter of thy worth gives thee releasing" (87.3). The very weakness of the underdog, rather than affording him or her the protection of the law, virtually guarantees failure: "How with this rage shall beauty hold a plea, / Whose action is no stronger than a flower?" (65.3–4). In short, the sonnets remind us of one of the implications of the *Henry IV* plays: the court's leaders cannot protect us from crime because they themselves have stolen a crown.

Again as in *Henry IV*, the fault lines in the behavior of the lawmakers are juxtaposed and compared with the more overt threats from blatant robbers. Most obviously, the Friend steals the Dark Lady and vice versa, and the Rival Poet in turn steals the Friend. It is revealing, in fact, that Shakespeare's two principal additions to the action in other sequences, the introduction of the Friend and of the Rival Poet, both involve situations of robbery and betrayal: in Shakespeare's mental geometry, as in Hardy's, the triangle is the central figure, a fact that may well have contributed to his attraction to romantic comedy. And if the Rival Poet is wholly a fictive creation, as some readers have asserted,[112] it is telling that the aesthetic principles that Sidney, say, discusses more generally are here bodied forth in a figure who actually functions dramatically in the sequence—and particularly telling that he is seen as a thieving rival, while the poets whom Astrophil criticizes are not competing for Stella.

But the crime rate is high even in sonnets that do not allude specifi-

---

[111]On the legal background of this sonnet, see Paul S. Clarkson and Clyde T. Warren, "Pleading and Practice in Shakespeare's Sonnet XLVI," *MLN*, 62 (1947), 102–110.
[112]See, e.g., Colie, *Shakespeare's Living Art*, pp. 66–67.

cally to these rivalries and robberies. One sign that the procreation sonnets are more fully integrated into the sequence than some readers have acknowledged is that they too concern types of thievery. If the Friend does not reproduce, he will "eat the world's due" (1.14). And the sonnets are, of course, as concerned with succession as are the history plays: a child will "[prove] his beauty by succession thine" (2.12), a vision of lawful inheritance that is implicitly contrasted with thievery. Time is repeatedly described as a robber who threatens the Friend, "Stealing away the treasure of his spring" (63.8). The Friend may rob the speaker not only of the Dark Lady but also of himself: "But do thy worst to steal thyself away" (92.1). This preoccupation with robbery is, however, manifest above all in the fact that it appears even in lighthearted compliments and jokes: thus we learn in Sonnet 99 that flowers have stolen their beauty from the Friend, much as Sonnet 145 is a playful rendition of a very serious concern with how the future can alter the shape of what has come before.

If one's prized possessions are threatened by the prejudices of the legal system and the perfidies of robberies, they may also be wrested away through competition. At the end of *The Comedy of Errors*, the two Dromios compete about who will walk in first, then decide to go in hand in hand, a literal acting out and resolving of the concern for place present throughout the whole play. In the sonnets, however, there is no happy resolution. The very name that scholars have assigned to the Rival Poet reminds us that competitiveness is as central to these poems as it is to the Roman world of *The Rape of Lucrece*.

The imagery we have been charting reflects the very nature of the poems in which it appears. Just as the sonnets repeatedly allude to both the presence of legal and financial codes and their breakdown, so they draw attention to the existence of generic rules while also enacting their dissolution. The sonnet is, of course, among the most formally codified and even determined of genres. Shakespeare often reminds us of this by emphatically demarcating the divisions between the quatrains, as well as the octet-sestet division that remains latent even in the so-called Shakespearean sonnet; thus Sonnet 73 devotes each quatrain to a separate image, while Sonnet 15 opens the first two quatrains on "When" and, signaling the beginning of the sestet, begins the third on "Then." Yet this regular, even rigid, structure often cracks; in particular, as we have seen, the couplets may avoid their ostensible function of summarizing the quatrains. Unruly emotion cannot always be bent to the rules of the sonnet form. In a sense, then, Shakespeare is enacting through the formal structure of the sonnet the very experience that the form concerns, the very pattern that interests Freud himself so much: the attempt to civilize passion, to impose constraints on it—and the frequent failures of that exercise. Hence the imagery of broken codes that we have been exploring provide a kind of echo, a subplot, to the form itself.

But, as is virtually always the case in the poems this book examines, literary experience parallels and comments on human experience: the images in question serve above all to illuminate the nature of love and of the lover who is the central figure in this sequence. Yet again rhetorical patterns parallel psychological ones. The sonnets suggest that the affection of the beloved, or even our comprehension of how he or she really feels about us, is as slippery as a land title or a legal decision—or as slippery as the syntax of the poems and their attempts to achieve closure.

The imagery of codes reflects not only the speaker's approach to love but also the broader patterns that we have been observing in his behavior. It is no accident that a temperament that seeks the absolute truths, the orderly generalizations that form and deform so many of his couplets, should refer repeatedly to contracts and laws. Nor is it an accident that a speaker who so often desperately tries to avoid painful truths through quibbles should be attracted to the law, the field that many Elizabethans saw as the pinnacle of equivocation. And his frequent implications that the legal system protects the interests of the strong at the expense of the weak remind us of his own sense of being a helpless victim of power, whether it be the power of sexuality or of rank. Another flaw in the legal system, the indeterminacy of its judgments, in turn mirrors his difficulties in achieving closure. The images of broken legal and financial codes, in short, gloss the speaker's own experiences and his characteristic reactions to them even when they are ostensibly merely referring to someone or something else. Though potentially nothing more than a mechanical convention, these figures in fact serve to provide yet another reflection of the sensibility of Shakespeare's speaker.

Repeatedly witnessing the breakdown of a whole series of codes as we read the sonnets, Shakespeare's audience participates in a process similar to that which the speaker endures. We too put our trust in codes and rules of all types—the rules of genre, the patterns of closure, the assumptions of anti-Petrarchism—only to discover their limitations. What seemed written in stone proves to have been scribbled on sand.

In addition, however, the imagery of codes had special resonances for Elizabethan readers in particular, resonances that no doubt deepened their responses to this pattern and hence their identification with the speaker whose experiences it reflects. As we have already observed, the allusion to the Dark Lady as a "several plot" (137.9) must have struck a chord in readers preoccupied with enclosure. The other references to land titles and transfers were also charged with tension during the late sixteenth and seventeenth centuries, a period in which, however we determine the controversial issues about the status of the aristocracy, land was certainly changing hands rapidly.

Moreover, Shakespeare's sixteenth-century readers were no less aware of the instability of the law itself. Both the Elizabethan and Jacobean periods witnessed numerous complaints that honest men, far from being protected by the law, were likely to be its victims.[113] One of the most common charges was that procedures were unduly slow and cumbersome; another, that even the decision that was ultimately reached did not guarantee that the issue had been resolved, for cases were often passed from one court to the next. The insecurity that could result was intensified by a type of instability particularly relevant to land: the conditions of feudal tenure meant that it was all too easy to dispute even a seemingly clear title. Francis Bacon speaks for many of his countrymen when he enumerates the faults in question: "But certain it is, that our laws, as they now stand, are subject to great incertainties, and variety of opinion, delays, and evasions: whereof ensueth . . . that men's assurances of their lands and estates by patents, deeds, wills, are often subject to question, and hollow; and many the like inconveniencies" ("Proposition Touching the Amendment of the Laws").[114] Bacon, like Sir Edward Coke and Sir Thomas Egerton, attempted with comparatively little success to remedy the worst of these abuses.[115] In short, the tensions in Shakespeare's

---

[113]See Louis A. Knafla, *Law and Politics in Jacobean England: The Tracts of Lord Chancellor Ellesmere* (Cambridge: Cambridge Univ. Press, 1977), esp. chaps. 5, 6; James Spedding, Robert Leslie Ellis, and Douglas Denon Heath, *The Works of Francis Bacon*, 14 vols. (1857–1874; rpt. New York: Garrett Press, 1968), VII, 316; IX, 77–79; XII, 84–86; XIII, 61–71; White, esp. pp. 72–76.

[114]Spedding, XIII, 64.

[115]The references to usurpation present in the sonnets—and, of course, in so many of their authors' other works—may also have had a significance for contemporary readers that we have neglected. The political resonance of these allusions is obvious; but I would suggest that the threat of usurpation in the state echoed that of usurpation in the microcosm of the body politic, the family. The English Renaissance was, after all, a period in which many children lost at least one parent before adulthood and remarriages were common: in fact, over one-third of all first marriages contracted between 1558 and 1641 lasted fewer than fifteen years because of the death of one spouse or the other. (See Lawrence Stone, *The Crisis of the Aristocracy, 1558–1641* [Oxford: Clarendon, 1965], pp. 589–590.) Would such conditions not have bred in most children the

speaker resemble those in his milieu; rhetoric delineates not only the contours of an individual temperament but also those of the culture behind that temperament.

IX

We are now in a position to draw together our observations about the speaker in the sonnets. Many of the paradoxes we encounter in the sequence stem from his own temperament. He can manipulate language—and in so doing can manipulate his audience—as skillfully as Hamlet, and yet he is also prone to become carried away with his own words. Similarly, he delights in absolutes, in unchanging verities, whether they be represented by constancy in a relationship ("Then happy I that love and am belovèd / Where I may not remove, nor be removèd" [25.13–14]) or by hyperbole in rhetoric ("If this be error and upon me proved, / I never writ, nor no man ever loved" [116.13–14]); yet he is also haunted by the indeterminacy and mutability of love. Indeed, his sense of its fragility may well intensify that need for absolutes. In many of the poems he is defiant, especially toward time. Yet he is also prone to envision himself as a hapless and helpless victim, which may help to explain why his defiance does not always ring true. Demonstrating his own predilection for the passivity of the victim, he describes even his own death in terms of the Friend leaving him: "This thou perceiv'st, which makes thy love more strong, / To love that well which thou must leave ere long" (73.13–14). It is predictable, too, that the very character who sees himself as a victim repeatedly attempts to excuse the Friend by claiming he has been victimized.

Perhaps the most striking pattern we have noted, however, is his tendency toward indirection and deflection—in other words, his characteristic desire to give with one hand and take with the other, to offer blame but divert it onto an inappropriate object, at once to fulfill and to subvert demands. This style of action is closely related to his

---

recurrent fear—and perhaps in some cases the recurrent wish—that their mother's or father's place would be usurped by a stepparent? The preoccupation with political usurpation that dominates so much sixteenth-century literature may well have been intensified by this parallel between the state and the family (much as the concern in contemporary cinema about aliens who enter the home may reflect a fear of invasions by stepparents and stepchildren).

style of perception, especially his tendency toward fears and apprehensions rather than definite conclusions. A line from Sonnet 144 might gloss the way he sees many other situations as well: "Suspect I may, yet not directly tell" (10). Also related is his tendency to make nervous jokes, notably the puns on "will" in Sonnets 135 and 136. For this wordplay, like Sidney's puns on "rich," also allows him to have his cake and eat it: he insults the Dark Lady under the cover of a game, and he acknowledges the power of sexuality in a format playful enough to undermine that acknowledgment.

One consistent emotional pattern unites and helps to explain these and many of the other paradoxes we have observed in him: he wishes at once to express and deny his aggressions, to be victor and captive. Hence it is not at all surprising that he both uses language and is used by it: in this as in so many other ways, he actually becomes both aggressor and passive victim at once. This pattern may alert us to the similarities between his temperament and what has been termed passive-aggressive behavior.[116] The function of adducing such terminology is not to label syndromes in the interests of a reductive diagnosis but rather to recognize the underlying consistencies in what might otherwise seem wholly random details of characterization. In this case we can remember that passive-aggressive behavior is a response to power, to authority—in other words, to just the type of situation in which the speaker finds himself. It characteristically includes two of the mannerisms we repeatedly encountered in him, criticizing someone else for one's own fault and identifying with the aggressor. Also typical is precisely what this speaker so often does: a habit of resisting demands by delay and forgetfulness. The fault of which he accuses himself in lines like "Where art thou, muse, that thou forget'st so long / To speak of that which gives thee all thy might?" (100.1–2) may in fact be not a fortuitous mistake but rather yet another indirect response to the demands of the Friend. His passive-aggressive style is, in other words, an acting out of a rhetorical style: the use of occupatio, that trope in which we announce what we are not going to discuss and hence discuss it. If syneciosis is the central figure in *The Rape of Lucrece*, it is the rhetorical configurations of occupatio that best represent the emotional configurations of the speaker in the sonnets.

---

[116]On these psychological patterns, see Anna Freud, *The Ego and the Mechanisms of Defence*, trans. Cecil Baines (New York: International Universities Press, 1946), esp. chap. 9; George E. Vaillant, *Adaptation to Life* (Boston: Little, Brown, 1977), pp. 188, 190, 384.

X

Viewing a Winslow Homer seascape can be a profoundly upsetting experience. One reason is that, as Shakespeare himself puts it in another context, "And pérspective it is best painter's art" (24.4). That is, the perspective of the canvas is designed to generate the illusion that we have no footing on dry land or even on a rock, as we do when surveying, for example, one of the Cuyp paintings that include the sea: rather, we too are at the mercy of the waves. In reading Shakespeare's sonnets we often have a comparable sense that we have lost control, and the reason is similar: we ourselves are experiencing the same tumultuous emotions as the speaker. For, as we have already observed at several points, these poems evoke in their readers reactions very like the ones they are reporting.[117]

One of the speaker's most characteristic patterns is an obsessive rehearsal of his thoughts and feelings; over and over he reinterprets them without arriving at a definitive conclusion. Similarly, the structure of both individual poems and the sequence as a whole leads us into rereadings, literal and metaphorical, of what has come before.[118] This process is not uncommon in sonnet sequences—after all, our awareness of Laura's death encourages us, like her lover, to view the "in vita" sonnets from a different perspective[119]—but it is especially frequent and often especially troubling in Shakespeare's sonnets. Thus within a particular poem a given word or idea will cast what has come before in a new light. When we first encounter the images in Sonnet 12, we are primarily aware of the sense of loss inherent in the idea of "the brave day sunk in hideous night" (2) or "lofty trees . . . barren of leaves" (5); the allusion to "breed" (14) in the couplet, however qualified it may be, reminds us that the earlier figures may represent not the finality of death but rather the hopefulness of a cycle of rebirth. Another day follows night, no matter how hideous; and trees generally produce a new growth of leaves. And, of course, as we read Sonnet 94 our interpretations of earlier lines keep shifting: "They that have pow'r to hurt, and will do none" (1), to

---

[117]One of the best reader-response studies of the sonnets is Booth, *Essay.* For other interesting perspectives on these questions, see, e.g., Hammond; Arthur Mizener, "The Structure of Figurative Language in Shakespeare's Sonnets," *Southern Review,* 5 (1940), 746.

[118]On the ways we must revise our earlier interpretations of words, compare J. Bunselmeyer, "Appearance and Verbal Paradox: Sonnets 129 and 138," *SQ,* 25 (1974), esp. 106.

[119]On this process in the *Canzonière,* compare Durling, pp. 10–11.

choose one of many instances, may at first suggest positive qualities like concern for others, but "That do not do the thing they most do show" (2) immediately leads us to interpret "and will do none" (1) more negatively. A similar process of reinterpretation occurs when one sonnet is played against another: latent meanings are activated. We have observed how Sonnet 127 seems more menacing when read with the other poems on the Dark Lady. "O that you were yourself, but love you are / No longer yours than you yourself here live" (13.1–2) in its immediate context seems only to refer to the loss of self occasioned by death. Later sonnets, however, testify that the Friend may not be himself—or may not be the person the speaker wanted to believe he was—because he is corrupted. When we read the conclusion of Sonnet 33 ("Suns of the world may stain when heav'n's sun staineth" [14]) in light only of the previous lines of the poem, "stain" simply seems to mean "be corrupted," but other sonnets in effect remind us that the verb may also mean "corrupt others" and that such an interpretation is all too apt for the Friend.

Nor do our growing doubts about the behavior of the Friend and Dark Lady issue in clear-cut interpretations of their characters.[120] One reason is that negative visions of them continue to be interlaced with more positive ones. The lack of linearity in the sequence prevents us from merely dismissing the praise they receive as a symptom of a misguided earlier apprehension on the speaker's part: certainly we do not continue to believe that the Friend unquestionably merits the praise of Sonnet 53 or that the Dark Lady indubitably deserves compliments like, "And truly not the morning sun of heav'n / Better becomes the gray cheeks of the east" (132.5–6), but we are not completely sure exactly how evil they are. For, as we have observed, we come to distrust the speaker's own judgment and hence to doubt his objectivity. We are always highly conscious of his perspective but never sure it is wholly reliable, much as the speaker himself is very aware of the world's opinions but also dubious of them. For this and many other reasons, doubt is as central to our experience of reading the sonnets as it is to the experience of their speaker.

One result of that doubt is that in reading these lyrics, as in reading *The Rape of Lucrece* and *Venus and Adonis*, we seesaw between a sympathetic identification with the principal character and a more detached and dubious response. The sense of identification is in fact far deeper in the case of the sonnets than that of the narrative poems. The other

---

[120]Compare Cyrus Hoy, "Shakespeare and the Revenge of Art," *Rice University Studies*, 60 (1974), 76; Barbara Herrnstein Smith, "Introduction," pp. 18–19.

participants in the sequence are so shadowy that no sense of affinity with or sympathy for them dilutes our closeness to the speaker; in *Venus and Adonis*, in contrast, our identification with Venus dissolves in the moments when we see her actions from Adonis' perspective. Nor are we distanced from the speaker of the sonnets by mythological allegories, as we are in so many other sequences. Above all, however, the bond we feel with him is intensified simply because our reactions mime his so often and so closely.

On the other hand, in literary as in other encounters, self-pity can quickly generate distaste: to the extent that we see the speaker's humility—"And so should you, to love things nothing worth" (72.14) and so forth—as something more than a rhetorical ploy, we recoil from it. And when he includes a meaning that he does not intend or cannot fully acknowledge, as in the increasingly bitter metaphors of the opening quatrain of Sonnet 35, we feel more distance from him; indeed, those subterranean meanings function very much the way indirect discourse does in *Venus and Adonis*, demarcating the gap between the sense in which the character intends a statement and the sense in which we (and, in the case of Shakespeare's epyllion, the narrator) think it should be meant. Moreover, the repeated reminders that we cannot wholly rely on the speaker's judgments further distance us from him. And yet in a sense our very ambivalence about identifying with him breeds yet another form of identification: our responses to him are as shifting and uncertain as his own reactions to the Friend and Dark Lady.

We resemble the speaker not only in our preoccupation with doubt but also in our defenses against that preoccupation. Much as he reaches out for the simple answers expressed in his couplets, so we reach out for a reordering of the poems that would replace their ambiguities with definitive and reassuring answers. And if he has trouble facing his feelings fully and honestly, choosing instead to qualify and subvert praise with blame and vice versa, we too are prone to notice only what we want or expect to see, to peruse these poems much as Lucrece reads her tapestry. Thus it is telling that many of the reinterpretations to which I referred earlier involve acknowledging a negative significance that has been latent in the poem all along; frequently an overtly critical statement like "You to your beauteous blessings add a curse, / Being fond on praise, which makes your praises worse" (84.13–14) is preceded by hints of rebukes that we may not have noticed. This propensity for finding the meanings we wish to find helps to explain why even the repeated rereadings that these poems call for and receive do not necessarily prevent us from omitting certain valid interpretations each time. But this is only one side of the coin. As the critical history of the sonnets demonstrates, if some readers have been prone to stress their assured moments and underplay the turmoil, others have taken the opposite approach, finding in these poems only a sea of troubles and ignoring the islands of tranquillity. It is very difficult to respond to their speaker's unbalanced sensibility with balanced judgments, but our attempt to do so is not the least of the many experiences that educate us as we read these poems.

It is, then, through the formal resources of the sonnets—through their adoption of a mode that is undramatic in certain regards but intensely dramatic in others, through their approach to poetic problems like closure, through their reinterpretation and reinvigoration of the motifs of Petrarchism and anti-Petrarchism—that Shakespeare's speaker is bodied forth. The character thus created is often unable to achieve the courage of his convictions and hence unable to speak or to act in an unqualified and forthright manner. He is as immobilized by his own doubts as Hamlet, as betrayed by his own language as Othello. Yet at many points in the sequence we also respect and admire him, whether it be for the intensity of his devotion or the cleverness of his language. These and other paradoxes in the sequence may be traced in part to the central paradox suggested by my title: Shakespeare's speaker is enlivened and empowered by his wit, but he is also its victim. He becomes entangled in the very thread designed to lead him through and from the labyrinth of his emotions. And as readers we come not only to survey but also to share the experiences that produce both his extraordinary perceptions and his equally extraordinary self-deceptions. For just as form mirrors content to an unusual degree in the sonnets, so the experiences of the reader mirror those of the speaker to an extent unusual in even the greatest art.

[4]

Conclusion

I must lie down where all the ladders start,
In the foul rag-and-bone shop of the heart.
William Butler Yeats

Venus and Adonis culminates on a metamorphosis: Adonis turns into a short-lived but lovely flower. Metamorphoses are, of course, hardly uncommon in literature, but they assume an unusual prominence in not only *Venus and Adonis* but Shakespeare's other major poems as well. Works that themselves spring from fruitful changes in generic patterns and potentialities describe characters and entire cultures that are variously enervated and energized by an extraordinary degree of flux.

Some of these alterations are positive. In *The Rape of Lucrece*, however we respond to Brutus himself, we cannot but be cheered by the movement toward Rome and the changes that geographical shift represents: a evolution from helpless sorrow to political action, from tyranny to justice. Though subsequently cropped by Venus, the flower into which Adonis is transformed at first reassures and charms us. It is telling, however, that even these instances of change are hedged with qualifications: the behavior of Brutus and of Venus casts a shadow on the otherwise positive metamorphoses with which they are associated. And on the whole in Shakespeare's nondramatic poetry flux is in fact more often associated with loss than with gain.

Some of the most obvious changes are centrally located on the levels of plot and theme. Adonis loses his life; Lucrece first her chastity and then her life; the sonnets' speaker anticipates the pain that time will inflict and suffers abandonment by the Friend and Dark Lady when they turn to each other. These alterations are mirrored by other changes in the material world: physical possessions are as slippery as truth, robbers as common (and as dangerous) as lovers. Distinctions

Conclusion

and categories of all types break down; in *The Rape of Lucrece* the villain and his victim become troublingly similar, while in the sonnets linguistic differences repeatedly blur. As some of these instances hint, the most frequent and most frightening shifts in Shakespeare's non-dramatic poetry are internal ones: the very identity of the principal characters is threatened. Venus essentially tries to deny Adonis' autonomy by making him into a mirror image of herself; she refuses to acknowledge just how different their attitudes are. In the other two works, however, the alterations of identity are more pronounced. Over and over we are, so to speak, surprised by syneciosis. Not only does Lucrece come to resemble Tarquin, her husband and father mime her own helplessness and speechlessness. In the sonnets the speaker and his Friend, opposites in certain of the lyrics, are twinned in others.

Two of the principal changes that Shakespeare's nondramatic poems concern are effected by mysterious outsiders, agents who have not played a significant role earlier: the boar kills Adonis, and Brutus orchestrates the radical political change in Rome. Hence flux seems even harder to predict and to codify; change in these instances resembles not the orderly pattern of waves that Shakespeare describes in Sonnet 60 but rather the abrupt movement of a gust of wind or even a tornado.

All of the transformations we are observing help to explain why history is so important in *The Rape of Lucrece* and why its analogue in the personal sphere, the type of autobiographical storytelling exemplified by Venus' account of Mars, is so important in *Venus and Adonis*. History is an attempt to freeze eddying changes into a pattern that we can understand (and that we can use to our own ends). The task is not impossible. But it is often frustrated by the rapidity and ambiguity of the events in question or complicated by the duplicity of the historian: the Argument of *The Rape of Lucrece* leaves out important subtleties, as do the versions of history proffered by the characters themselves.

Indeed, as we have often noted in the course of this study, Shakespeare's primary interests in all three works are character and characters; when we read these poems we focus less on the changes they describe per se than on how the people in them variously respond to flux. One of the principal ways Shakespeare charts their distinctive personalities is by contrasting their reactions to problems like instability as well as to such issues as the nature of perception, of power, and of love itself; those reactions form part of very distinctive styles of behavior. Certain characters respond to change opportunistically;

[259]

much of the competition in these poems is a kind of social Darwinism, and Brutus in particular uses political ferment to elevate his own status. But *Venus and Adonis, The Rape of Lucrece,* and the sonnets all include characters who instead try to oppose change with some type of alternative ideal. The elegiac vision to which both the speaker in the sonnets and Lucrece subscribe is in a sense a refusal to accept how the world has changed and is changing, a cast of mind that one suspects tempted Shakespeare himself. Similarly, the speaker in the sonnets deifies constancy; that value is subverted in practice, but it remains an ideal against which failures are measured, whether it be represented by unswerving fidelity in love or by the seeming stability of the couplet.

Another symptom of these characters' difficulties in acknowledging flux and its attending uncertainties is their predilection for repetition. Delighting in the rhetorical forms of repetition, these poems body forth people who depend on the psychological forms of it. Each of the characters, however, tends toward a distinctive type of repetition that defines the contours of his or her personality, much as the differences between, say, epizeuxis and anaphora may define differences in rhetorical styles. Thus Venus' comic reliance on the very strategies of seduction that have been found wanting shortly before reflects her blind self-centeredness: she simply cannot face the idea that she cannot have what she wants or, indeed, that Adonis does not want the same things. When Lucrece repeats the attitudes and judgments that had characterized her behavior before the rape, continuing, for instance, to assume that a face is a reliable index of character, we witness the belief in absolutes that is so central to her. And the repetitions by the speaker in the sonnets reflect the same kind of obsessiveness and its attending indecisiveness. At times he can offer ringing pronouncements, but elsewhere he is more likely to hesitate and to hedge than to deliver a statement decisively.

The connection between love (or lust) and mutability is, of course, a commonplace of Renaissance literature, with writers variously contrasting the instable sublunary world and the higher domains of love or citing love itself as the prime source of change. Shakespeare's nondramatic poems evidently raise these issues: Adonis' death testifies to the brevity of earthly love, Tarquin's lust is quickly sated, though its consequences last a long time ("This momentary joy breeds months of pain" [690]), while in the sonnets Shakespeare's speaker lives "all in war with time" (15.13). But the main role love assumes in all three works is not to introduce abstract questions about mutability but rather to provide yet another coordinate against which human behavior and human personality can be charted. The characters who populate these poems are by love possessed—and dispossessed.

Sometimes its effects on them are positive, at least in part. Venus responds to passion with energy and determination that, for all our reservations, are often appealing. At times love in its many forms inspires in the speaker of the sonnets the wit of Rosalind, the tenderness of Viola, the gusto of Cleopatra. On the whole, however, what each of the three poems maps are the different ways various temperaments are victimized by Cupid. It is a cliché that love breeds not only deception of others but also self-deception; yet Shakespeare renders that familiar observation more trenchant by charting the forms such self-deception assumes. Thus Venus characteristically believes her power is greater than it in fact is. Tarquin appropriates military metaphors to justify his attack, a strategy that shows the dangers of such language both for his sensibility and for his society as a whole. And, though the sonnets are an anthology of types of self-deception, certain common characteristics unite them and reveal the temperament of their speaker. He is, for example, peculiarly prone to deceive himself in the course of deceiving others. And his propensity to excuse the Friend and Dark Lady mirrors his tendency to excuse his own actions; thus one result of lacing praise with blame is to deny that one is really complimenting someone who does not deserve it or, alternatively, that one is really criticizing someone whom one hesitates to rebuke.

Love is connected with entrapment in all three works—a link manifest in the images of Adonis caught in Venus' arms and Lucrece penned in by the bedclothes—but again the personages respond in characteristic ways. In the sonnets, both the speaker's verbal and intellectual resourcefulness and, more disturbingly, his appetite for having his cake and eating it, undoing what he does, are apparent in his attempt to transform the notion of imprisonment into an attractive vision of stasis; he is, he boasts, "to constancy confined" (105.7). The tension between these two views of enclosure is also mirrored by one of the most intriguing images in the procreation sonnets, "A liquid pris'ner pent in walls of glass" (5.10). The entrapment of Lucrece by her attacker is the culmination of the passivity that has marked her role all along. Both the feeble excuses ("I am . . . expected of my friends" [718]) and the sententiae with which Adonis attempts to extricate himself reflect the callowness that at certain key points diverts sympathy from him and toward the goddess of love.

It is a measure of the perspective common to all three poems that one cannot discuss how their characters approach love for very long without finding oneself talking about power. Both what is admirably energetic about Venus' temperament and, more to the point, what is merely comic are manifest in her tendency to translate mastery into physical action, tucking her prey under her arm. Tarquin, as we just noted, asserts power in ways that testify to the dangers of a military ethic. And it is significant that in *The Rape of Lucrece* lust generates not only rape but also the form of it that stresses domination, which modern theorists have called the power rape. In the sonnets the speaker attempts to assert control over the beloved through language. The urge toward power is, then, entwined with the urge toward love in all three works. Shakespeare's preoccupation with this connection probably stems in part from his exploration of two stock metaphors: love as war and as a hunt. But those metaphors are themselves rooted in the ways lovers act, and Shakespeare's own concern with them no doubt reflects his observations of actual behavior—facts that remind us that formal roots of literature and its roots in actual experience are inextricably knotted.

Power is, of course, relevant in many situations aside from love throughout all three poems. One distinction we observed between *Venus and Adonis* and other epyllia is that the world Shakespeare evokes is postlapsarian, with its animals hunting each other quite as determinedly and far more destructively than Venus pursues Adonis. Though Lucrece is unable to speak at several key points in the poem, elsewhere she acquires power through language. For her, like Venus (and, for that matter, like such characters as Petruchio and Prince Hal), the act of naming is a crucial assertion of control over others. But when she names her attacker she tells the truth, while the false-hoods involved in Venus' calling breath "heavenly moisture" (63) are a microcosm of the ways she misuses power throughout the poem.

Venus and Adonis, *The Rape of Lucrece*, and the sonnets are also very much involved with powerlessness. *Titus Andronicus* suggests that this issue may have been of especial concern to Shakespeare at the time he was writing his narrative poems. Certainly these works, as well as the sonnets, trace the ways different temperaments respond to helpless-ness. Adonis' reactions we have already seen. Venus attempts to flat-ter and cajole death; like the sonnets' speaker, who flatters even the "swart-complexioned night" (28.11), she applies a long-standing habit to a situation where it is palpably inappropriate. Against her behavior and that of Adonis is played that of Wat, the victim who, despite the acuity of his senses, has no recourse save flight. In *The Rape of Lucrece*, powerlessness is above all symbolized by silence, a fact that reminds us yet again of the potentialities of words. In the sonnets the speaker also

Conclusion

sometimes describes his helplessness by invoking a convention, the inability to write. But this inability is part of a broader and more characteristic pattern in him: yet another symptom of his ambivalence is his predilection for passive-aggressive responses. He often fights back even while announcing that he cannot and will not do so: on the other hand, a poem like Sonnet 35 opens on a magisterial assertion and closes on an acknowledgment of impotence ("That I an áccessary *needs must be*" [13; italics added]).

As the instance of this speaker suggests, in all three poems we encounter yet another form of syneciosis: power sometimes leads to powerlessness (witness Tarquin and the underlying metaphor of detumescence when he departs from Lucrece), and powerlessness generates a reassertion of power, whether or not successful (witness the shifts in the ways the protagonist in the sonnets refers to time). In fact, it is neither one state nor the other but rather the ambiguous threshold between them that interests Shakespeare most throughout these three poems and hence that is most significant in the several modes of response of his characters. One finds indications that he is interested in the oxymoron of powerful powerlessness elsewhere in the canon as well. Though he inherited the tricky servant figure from Latin comedy, the prominence accorded to such characters in plays as early as *The Two Gentlemen of Verona* and as late as *The Tempest* suggests that this type—like the Fools, which are closely related—was of especial concern to Shakespeare. Contemporary studies of power in Renaissance literature and culture often stress its self-perpetuating invincibility, its capacity for controlling and containing the forms of opposition that it permits to exist, but Shakespeare himself is intrigued as well with the ways power may undermine and destroy itself.

In any event, both *The Rape of Lucrece* and the sonnets involve a whole series of marginal states, yet another form of ambiguity in poems already so full of it: Lucrece is at once chaste and defiled, alive and dead, while the speaker in the sonnets is himself an oxymoron. Though *Venus and Adonis* is less concerned with such situations, we do find a hint of them in the ways that Venus is very much an earthly woman in most regards but very much a goddess in others. To all of these marginal and shifting modes of being, then, is added another: the characters in the three poems seesaw between exerting power and enduring powerlessness. The pattern is perhaps most obvious in Shakespeare's epyllion, but we encounter many instances of it in the other two works as well. Thus Lucrece's suicide is, as Rembrandt's contrasting depictions of it would suggest, at once an establishment of potency and its final and most extreme loss. In lavishing praise on the Friend, the speaker asserts his own power, whether it be over time or, more ominously, over the young man who is "fond on praise" (84.13). But the very fact that he offers these compliments also testifies to his weakness in the face of the social superiority of his Friend, the demands of the patronage system, and the ambivalence of his own temperament.

Shakespeare explores the sensibilities of his characters in relationship to another and broader issue as well: how they perceive and order experience. We observed that our own responses as readers draw attention to these problems, and they are even more in evidence in the responses of the characters. These poems trace the sources and the consequences of various forms of distorted perception. Living in a world in which "knowledge is historical, flowing and flown," as Elizabeth Bishop puts it ("At the Fishhouses," 83),[1] both Adonis and Lucrece nonetheless attempt to arrest that flow and that flight with sententiae. In the case of Adonis, such saws are symptomatic of a certainty that at its best offers a moral anchor to counter Venus' stormy demands but at its worst descends to a callow smugness. In the instance of Lucrece, sententiae signal the reliance on absolutes and antitheses that is so at odds with a world shaped by syneciosis. All three poems are also concerned with the characteristic ways their personages read and misread others. Thus Lucrece assumes against all the evidence not only that she can interpret faces correctly, but also that her own is equally legible. In this as so many other regards, she attempts to transform the opaque into the transparent, the symbol into the icon or index. The speaker in the sonnets, in contrast, is obsessed with the difficulty of reading accurately.

But two problems in particular raise these questions about perception: how the characters use language and how they attempt to bring about closure in its many manifestations. Rhetoric, as we have seen throughout this study, reveals the temperament of the rhetorician in many ways. A particular rhetorical or syntactical pattern may distinguish a character as clearly and unforgettably as a type of smile or a walk identifies the people we encounter daily: Shakespeare repeatedly reminds us that verbal habits are as revealing as physical ones. It is a sign of his achievement in *Venus and Adonis*—and of the concern for character and characterization in which that achievement is rooted—that no one but Venus could have spoken the deer park passage with which this book opened.

[1]*The Complete Poems, 1927—1979* (New York: Farrar, Straus and Giroux, 1979).

Conclusion

Their attitudes and approaches toward language further mark the characters in these poems. The significance of naming and misnaming we have already noted. Different styles of persuasion offer another important touchstone to different styles of personality. In certain regards Venus seems to be an effective orator, offering textbook examples of techniques that might have been culled from the many Renaissance handbooks on the subject: her peroration includes a chain of graceful compliments, she appeals repeatedly to pathos, and so on. She even enlivens her rhetoric with a series of dramatic gestures, culminating in that ambiguous faint. And yet she makes a series of rhetorical mistakes that manifest her self-centeredness and concern for mastery: she loses touch with Adonis' attitudes and responses, and her story of Mars is more likely to antagonize than to entice him. The procreation sonnets, tactful yet insistent, testify that their speaker can be an orator more skilled than the goddess of love ever is. And to the extent that the ambivalences and ambiguities that emerge when he mingles praise with blame result from a systematic strategy, he is far more acute about his listener than any of the other characters we have examined, save perhaps Brutus. Yet even this speaker deceives himself in the course of attempting to persuade others and at certain points becomes so overwhelmed with confusion and bitterness that they subvert his attempts to please and instruct.

But the question of flattery best illuminates how each of the temperaments we scrutinized approaches language. All three works in fact open on the bestowal of compliments, a type of speech that reveals much about the relationship between the participants, whatever the substantive content of what is being said. And it reveals even more about the person who delivers the praise: as the poems continue, their characters flatter each other in ways as distinctive and revealing as their various responses to power. Tarquin's praise of Collatine is, characteristically, unashamedly self-serving. The speaker in the sonnets, in contrast, is internally divided about praise as about many other issues. Like Sir Calidore, "he loathd leasing, and base flattery" (*FQ* VI.i.3); unlike Sir Calidore, he attempts in vain to avoid them. Empowered by his ability to craft graceful praise, he is also entrapped by it.

Closure, one of Shakespeare's principal concerns in all three poems, is another index to character. We have already seen some indications that he is interested in closure throughout his career, and one can cite other evidence of this preoccupation as well. The ending of *As You Like It*, for instance, foregrounds and lightly guys the urge for closure; Rosalind is a deft and undaunted stage manager in this as in so many other regards. *Hamlet*, like other revenge tragedies, is about the desire—aesthetic, moral, and legal—to create closure. Whatever Shakespeare himself believed or did not believe about purgatory, that state functions as an apt symbol for all the unfinished business with which the play is so concerned. Given the frequency and the constancy of Shakespeare's concern for closure, one suspects the sonnet form interested him in part because it poses that problem in such interesting ways; and he may well have been drawn to the plots of his two narrative poems partially because they too raise it.

But whatever the creative biographies of these works, they certainly study the varying forms an impulse toward closure assumes in different personalities; Shakespeare recognizes that styles of termination are as distinctive as styles of repetition and that in both may be traced the configurations of a particular temperament. Picking the flower and disappearing into thin air are characteristic of Venus: the first action once again reminds us of both her maternality and her self-centeredness, while the second relates to her propensity for avoiding unpleasant facts. Lucrece's suicide, the most dramatic and most problematic instance of closure in the three poems, is at once the ultimate demonstration of her characteristic passivity and a decisive gesture that galvanizes others. Her deed contrasts with the very different type of conclusion Brutus effects; he asserts the need for action, institutes a major political change, and in so doing reminds us that the motivations behind such changes may remain ambiguous even when the results are clear. The speaker in the sonnets is as ambivalent on this issue as on many others: he is attracted to the neat finality represented by the couplet, yet at many points he is either unable to achieve it or unwilling to sacrifice the complexities and indeterminacies of experience in the name of closure. He repeatedly questions, and forces the reader to question, whether all's well that ends well. Different though their responses may be, all of these characters support Melville's observation in *Billy Budd*, a novella that is itself concerned with issues about closure like those raised by Shakespeare's nondramatic poetry: "The symmetry of form attainable in pure fiction cannot so readily be achieved in a narration essentially having less to do with fable than with fact. Truth uncompromisingly told will always have its ragged edges; hence the conclusion of such a narration is apt to be less finished than an architectural finial."[2]

²*Billy Budd and Other Prose Pieces*, ed. Raymond W. Weaver (London: Constable, 1924), p. 109.

Conclusion

The characters in the three works we have examined are, then, captive victors in several senses. Their successes are Pyrrhic; they become entangled in the very nets they use to trap others. When the speaker in the sonnets praises someone who does not deserve it, he himself is harmed. Moral compromises are, Shakespeare reminds us, morally compromising. When Venus attempts to seduce Adonis through her enchanting language, she falls under its spell herself. And when Tarquin invokes the persona of a military hero to justify the rape, he soon retreats in disgrace, "A captive victor that hath lost in gain" (730). In short, Shakespeare enacts on the level of characterization the same paradox that informs his generic decisions: the irony of sonnets that criticize and hence reinvigorate the sonnet, of a complaint targeted against its own genre.

The same type of misunderstanding that has distorted our responses to the characters in Shakespeare's narrative poems has also misshaped our interpretations of a closely related issue, the larger ethical problems raised by those characters. Though accustomed to delicately untangling the knotty questions posed by the sonnets, many critics have found in *Venus and Adonis* and *The Rape of Lucrece* only the most straightforward and conventional expositions of subjects like the relationship between Love and Beauty or between the parts of the soul.[3] In point of fact, however, what these poems teach us about ethical dilemmas through their characters is quite as complex as what they teach us about those characters per se. Here, as in life itself, much of what we learn is couched in negative terms: implying rather than asserting moral norms, all three works warn us not to make the same mistakes as their protagonists. At the same time, however, we come to appreciate not only what makes those mistakes tempting but also what makes them ambiguous: errors are not without their redeeming features, and working out the balances can be difficult. Thus we primarily regard Adonis' sententiae as a simplistic response to a situation he cannot handle any better, and yet those axioms serve certain important ends. Another type of moral complexity resides in the fact that even apparent solutions to problems themselves prove problematical: the "unconventional mistress" motif does not in fact avoid the moral or aesthetic dilemmas of conventional Petrarchism. And even seemingly virtuous states of mind do not guarantee pro-

---

[3]See, e.g., T. W. Baldwin, *On the Literary Genetics of Shakspere's Poems*, chap. 3; David N. Beauregard, "*Venus and Adonis*: Shakespeare's Representation of the Passions," *Shakespeare Studies*, 8 (1975), 83–98.

bity; Lucrece's guilt, unlike that of her counterparts in other complaints, is a symptom not of a pure heart but rather of a troubled spirit.

If what these works teach us is complex, the way they teach it is equally so. Ethical issues, like aesthetic ones, are bodied forth in nuanced portraits; we learn by wrestling with our own divided reactions to the characters. Thus we judge Lucrece's suicide by recognizing it as a characteristic, even predictable, reaction from one of her temperament, and in weighing how the speaker in the sonnets responds to his patron we evaluate the problems of praise. Dilemmas like these seldom admit of simple answers; sententiae and couplets more often serve to represent the dangerous process of clinging to pat answers than to present eternal verities, and the ambiguities that run throughout all three poems warn us against our own proclivity for those pat answers. Resisting and repudiating closure on so many other levels, these works demonstrate the danger of intellectual and moral certainty.

It is above all by experimenting with a range of literary strategies, especially tropes and the patterns of genres and modes, that Shakespeare explores human character and human behavior. In all three works, as in their author's plays, the motifs and moods of certain genres are dramatized, enacted by the personages of the poems. Thus in Venus and in Adonis respectively we encounter the eroticism of Ovidianism and the morality of Ovide moralisé. Lucrece represents the vision of the complaint, Brutus and Aeneas that of the epic. The character of the speaker of the sonnets reflects the character of the sonnet itself; its propensity for praise, for instance, is linked throughout to patterns in his own temperament, and the issue to which we keep returning, closure, is a psychological problem for him no less than an aesthetic one for his genre.

Literary types relate to character in another way as well: Shakespeare weaves the warp of genre and the woof of mode together in different ways in each of the works, but in all three the result is the same: nuances of personality, details of behavior, become far more prominent in the texture of these poems than in other works in the same genres. It is primarily Shakespeare's careful and complex approach to the dramatic mode that accomplishes this. To be sure, *Venus and Adonis* is dramatic in certain ways his other major poems are not. Whereas that epyllion dramatizes its episodes, the sonnets are far less concerned with specific incidents than most critics have asserted. And whereas *Venus and Adonis* is structured around a group of dialogues, *The Rape of Lucrece* and the sonnets depend more heavily on monologues. Nonetheless, all three works are intensely dramatic in many other senses. Language may be primarily the instrument of meditation in *The Rape of Lucrece* and the sonnets, but in these poems, as in *Venus and Adonis*, it is also the vehicle for action and interaction. Shakespeare is no less concerned than J. L. Austin with the ways a statement is also an act: Venus offers promises, Brutus and the knights in *The Rape of Lucrece* make vows, the speaker in the sonnets alternately praises and threatens, and so on. Though the Friend and Dark Lady generally are not present as an immediate audience, much of the speaker's behavior stems from his strategies for influencing them.

Venus and Adonis, *The Rape of Lucrece*, and the sonnets are, however, dramatic in a sense more central to those poems and to this study: they focus intensively and extensively on character. J. B. Leishman has written of their author's attitude toward the Friend, "It is as though Shakespeare could only apprehend the meaningfulness of life when it was, for him, incarnated in a person."[4] Originally intended as a comment on the sonnets, this observation aptly glosses all of the nondramatic poetry. In Shakespeare's nondramatic poems a whole range of aesthetic and moral problems is embodied in and examined through human behavior, whether it is that of the characters or that of the reader. Thus Venus herself is a study in self-deception. And in the same poem we learn about both the temptations and the limitations of a Neo-Platonic paradigm through our own attraction to it. In *The Rape of Lucrece* we explore the problems of reading and writing history by watching a series of people struggle with them. And, having recognized that Lucrece's temperament predisposes her to partial readings of the tapestry, we also come to realize that our own interpretations of historical events may be dangerously synecdochic. The sonnets are, so to speak, a map of misreading: they are as concerned as contemporary criticism with how and why we misinterpret experience, whether it is the experience of serving a patron, loving a woman, or thinking about a sonnet. Though some of the lyrics refer explicitly to these issues, more often we become familiar with them because they are bodied forth in the speaker's responses—or in our own.

If, then, the dramatic mode of the poems deepens our understanding of human behavior, so too do many of their other formal devices. Shakespeare invokes a whole range of rhetorical strategies to mime in the texture of the works themselves and in the reactions of their

---

[4]*Themes and Variations in Shakespeare's Sonnets*, p. 51.

readers the very experiences their characters are undergoing. The shifts in mood and tense in the opening of *Venus and Adonis* mirror the way the goddess of love unseats and unsettles her victim. Our sense of unease about the end of that narrative echoes Venus' own problems in achieving closure. But it is above all through linguistic patterns, particularly tropes, that Shakespeare reveals subtleties of temperaments and behavior. At some points a single figure may encapsulate a culture and the individuals within it; syneciosis and, to a lesser extent, synecdoche do so in *The Rape of Lucrece*, while in the sonnets occupatio is the rhetorical equivalent of the speaker's habit of saying and unsaying at once. Both syntactical patterns and rhetorical figures reflect the idiosyncrasies of particular temperaments; Venus' predilection for conditionals reveals her sensibility, as does Lucrece's use of predication. The most conventional rhetorical devices may reveal the most idiosyncratic forms of behavior; Senecan set speeches normally include various types of copia, but the content of Lucrece's repetitious passages, as well as her tendency to return to the same point repeatedly, illuminates her character. If the formal features of literature—its genres, topoi, rhetorical formulas—are a type of *langue*, Shakespeare's ear is attuned to the idiolect within it.

Writers, of course, have never respected the neat divisions between "intrinsic" and "extrinsic" criticism that many critics have propounded and maintained: it is hardly uncommon for an author to employ the formal devices of his craft in order to explore issues about human nature. But the frequency and the depth with which Shakespeare does so in the three works we have examined are unusual, especially when one juxtaposes these poems with others in their genres. One explanation relates to the fact that both of the narrative poems are early works, while at least a few of the sonnets may well also have been written in the early and mid 1590s.[5] During those years of his career Shakespeare was indulging—but also evaluating—his appetite for the "great feast of languages" that *Love's Labour's Lost* both mentions (V.i.35–36) and exemplifies. Attracted to sententiae, he also began to recognize their dangers. Delighting in a brocade of tropes and schemes, he also felt the countervailing pull of Berowne's "russet yeas and honest kersey noes" (V.ii.414). Interested in the Petrarchan storehouse he inherited, he also realized that it could lead to Romeo's unthinking worship of Rosaline. And similar tensions charged his responses to other aesthetic problems; *A Midsummer Night's Dream*

[5]On the dating of the sonnets, see Booth, *Sonnets*, p. 545, and Rollins, *Sonnets*, II, 53–73.

Conclusion

bears witness to his delight in a neat denouement, while *As You Like It* testifies to his ambivalence about that form of closure. One reason his nondramatic poetry (like his dramatic) embodies so many aesthetic issues in the behavior of its characters, I would suggest, is to enable its author to externalize and hence more readily evaluate his own proclivities as an artist. Often the motivation behind these projections is critical; when Lucrece delivers an overly long lament, Shakespeare is at once admitting and distancing himself from that potential mistake. At other points, however, the ambiguities in the characters' actions reflect their creator's divided responses to his own art; in Venus' storytelling, for instance, we see both the dangers and the delights of getting carried away with words.

But the main reason Shakespeare marries the formal and the psychological, rhetoric and character, throughout *Venus and Adonis*, *The Rape of Lucrece*, and the sonnets is that he believes such unions to be as inevitable as they are fruitful. *Verba* matter above all because of their connection to *res*; the "forms" of literature in Rosalie Colie's broad and useful sense of the word are significant primarily because of their relationship to the forms of human behavior and human character. Not the least of the dichotomies that are redefined and ultimately transcended in Shakespeare's nondramatic poetry is the Yeatsian one on which we began. It is in the very act of putting his version of the circus animals through their paces that Shakespeare leaves their insistently noisy arena and descends to "the foul rag-and-bone shop of the heart" (40).[6] And it is from the dark and musty confines of that shop that he achieves and shares with us what Thoreau, another explorer, terms "insight and . . . far sight."[7]

[6]*The Collected Poems of W. B. Yeats*, 2d ed. (New York: Macmillan, 1951).
[7]*Walden*, ed. J. Lyndon Shanley (Princeton: Princeton Univ. Press, 1971), p. 288.

Index

Index

Library of Congress Cataloging-in-Publication Data

Dubrow, Heather
  Captive victors.

  Includes index.
  1. Shakespeare, William, 1564–1916—Poetic works. I. Title.
PR2984.D77   1987   821'.3   86-19627
ISBN 0-8014-1975-1 (alk. paper)